One of the surprise pleasures of busting myths is encountering those that I always thought were true, and so Great Myths of Child Development provided me with a number of such surprises. Identical twins are not genetically identical? A woman can get pregnant during a pregnancy? Not all girls have XX sex chromosomes and not all boys have XY chromosomes? Fathers don't use more corporal punishment than mothers? These, and many more myths, are considered with the best available science, instead of how most of us parents do it by intuition, rumor, and word-of-mouth. This book should be on every parent's nightstand and referenced every time you worry that you might be doing something wrong.

Michael Shermer, Publisher *Skeptic* magazine, monthly columnist *Scientific American*, author of *Why People Believe Weird Things*, *The Believing Brain*, and *The Moral Arc*

What everyone claims to "know" about child development can be shown to simply not be so. To the rescue comes this book, which can easily be consulted when we are confronted by claims about child development that are accompanied by "authoritative" pronouncements and scientifically weak foundations. I suspect my copy will be well thumbed very soon.

Patrick C. Friman, Ph.D., ABPP, Vice President of Behavioral Health, Boys Town and Clinical Professor of Pediatrics, UNMC

It's great to see this new addition to the sparse but growing literature on popular misunderstandings of child development. From the entertaining riff on Dr. Spock's advice to the references to entertainment media, *Great Myths of Child Development* is engaging, informative, and much needed. Instructors will be pleased with the "speed busting" sections, which can easily be used as assignments to be modeled on the longer critiques.

Jean Mercer, Professor Emerita, Richard Stockton College, Galloway NJ, Author of *Child Development: Myths & Misunderstandings*

Authors Hupp and Jewell systematically dissect and destroy 50 myths of child development that are too-often propagated in the popular media and by well-intentioned child-rearing experts. Most importantly, the authors don't just shoot down common misconceptions, they offer concise recommendations and resources to help readers make scientifically-informed child-rearing decisions. As a research-based child psychologist, I hope this book makes it into the hands of all parents, teachers, coaches, and pediatricians.

Brett R. Kuhn, PhD., pediatric psychologist and co-author of *The Toddler Owner's Manual: Operating Instructions, Trouble-shooting Tips, and Advice on System Maintenance*

Great Myths of Psychology

Series Editors

Scott O. Lilienfeld
Steven Jay Lynn

This superb series of books tackles a host of fascinating myths and misconceptions regarding specific domains of psychology, including child development, aging, marriage, brain science, and mental illness, among many others. Each book not only dispels multiple erroneous but widespread psychological beliefs, but provides readers with accurate and up-to-date scientific information to counter them. Written in engaging, upbeat, and user-friendly language, the books in the myths series are replete with scores of intriguing examples drawn from everyday psychology. As a result, readers will emerge from each book entertained and enlightened. These unique volumes will be invaluable additions to the bookshelves of educated laypersons interested in human nature, as well as of students, instructors, researchers, journalists, and mental health professionals of all stripes.

www.wiley.com/go/psychmyths

Published

50 Great Myths of Popular Psychology
Scott O. Lilienfeld, Steven Jay Lynn, John Ruscio, and Barry L. Beyerstein

Great Myths of Aging
Joan T. Erber and Lenore T. Szuchman

Great Myths of the Brain
Christian Jarrett

Forthcoming

Great Myths of Child Development
Stephen Hupp and Jeremy Jewell

Great Myths of Intimate Relations
Matthew D. Johnson

Great Myths of Personality
M. Brent Donnellan and Richard E. Lucas

Great Myths of Autism
James D. Herbert

Great Myths of Education and Learning
Jeffrey D. Holmes and Aaron S. Richmond

50 Great Myths of Popular Psychology, Second Edition
Scott O. Lilienfeld, Steven Jay Lynn, John Ruscio, and Barry L. Beyerstein

GREAT MYTHS OF CHILD DEVELOPMENT

Stephen Hupp
and
Jeremy Jewell

WILEY Blackwell

This edition first published 2015
© 2015 John Wiley & Sons, Inc.

Registered Office
John Wiley & Sons, Ltd, The Atrium, Southern Gate, Chichester,
West Sussex, PO19 8SQ, UK

Editorial Offices
350 Main Street, Malden, MA 02148-5020, USA
9600 Garsington Road, Oxford, OX4 2DQ, UK
The Atrium, Southern Gate, Chichester, West Sussex, PO19 8SQ, UK

For details of our global editorial offices, for customer services, and for information about how to apply for permission to reuse the copyright material in this book please see our website at www.wiley.com/wiley-blackwell.

The right of Stephen Hupp and Jeremy Jewell to be identified as the authors of this work has been asserted in accordance with the UK Copyright, Designs and Patents Act 1988.

Wiley also publishes its books in a variety of electronic formats. Some content that appears in print may not be available in electronic books.

Designations used by companies to distinguish their products are often claimed as trademarks. All brand names and product names used in this book are trade names, service marks, trademarks or registered trademarks of their respective owners. The publisher is not associated with any product or vendor mentioned in this book.

Limit of Liability/Disclaimer of Warranty: While the publisher and authors have used their best efforts in preparing this book, they make no representations or warranties with respect to the accuracy or completeness of the contents of this book and specifically disclaim any implied warranties of merchantability or fitness for a particular purpose. It is sold on the understanding that the publisher is not engaged in rendering professional services and neither the publisher nor the author shall be liable for damages arising herefrom. If professional advice or other expert assistance is required, the services of a competent professional should be sought.

Library of Congress Cataloging-in-Publication Data

Hupp, Stephen.
    Great myths of child development / Stephen Hupp and Jeremy Jewell.
        pages   cm
    Includes bibliographical references and index.
    ISBN 978-1-118-52122-9 (cloth) – ISBN 978-1-118-52123-6 (pbk.)
    1. Child development.   2. Child psychology.   I. Jewell, Jeremy.   II. Title.
    HQ767.9.H87 2015
    305.231–dc23
                                                2014033017

A catalogue record for this book is available from the British Library.

Cover image: Silhouettes © rangepuppies / istock and © YAY Media AS / Alamy

Set in 10/12pt Sabon by SPi Publisher Services, Pondicherry, India

Printed and bound in Malaysia by Vivar Printing Sdn Bhd

1   2015

To my folks, who taught me more than I knew they did, and my kids, who taught me I know less than I thought I did (S.H.)

To my wife, Kelly, and my daughters, Brea and Chaney. I'm the luckiest guy in the world to have such a great family (J.J.)

CONTENTS

2 Growth, Body, & Mind 47

3 Emotions & Behavior 92

PREFACE

An entire book focused on myths related to children might not seem like a critically important topic, until you realize that some of the myths influence lives in profound ways, affecting both physical and psychological health. Many of the myths, for example, get in the way of people receiving effective psychological treatments. Other myths cause people to feel guilty, judge others, or waste money. When we become more aware of what research has to say about important topics in child development, we are more likely to make decisions that promote a healthier lifestyle in children and the adults in their lives. Our book follows in the tradition of *Great Myths of Popular Psychology* [1] by: (i) debunking commonly believed myths; (ii) uncovering *why* people believe these myths; and (iii) discussing research-supported practices.

Our book was written with two primary target audiences in mind. First, we wrote this book for parents that often get conflicting advice from family, friends, professionals, and celebrities. Both of us are parents, and like a lot of people we believed many of these myths throughout much of our lives. We considered having this subtitle to the book: "What Every Parent Needs to NOT Know." Second, this book is also intended to be a text in a college classroom. For example, it could be used as a supplemental book in an undergraduate child development course, or in upper level undergraduate and graduate courses related to child psychology. We also considered this subtitle: "What Every Student Needs to NOT Study." Others that might find this book useful include teachers, policy makers, and other people with inquisitive minds.

With the college classroom in mind, we organized this book in a manner consistent with typical child development courses. Although some college courses cover the material chronologically (e.g., first conception, then infancy, then early childhood, then older children), many other courses cover their material topically (e.g., beginnings, physical growth, cognitive development, emotional development, etc.). We developed our book with a topically organized classroom as a guide.

Specifically, all of the Child Psychology courses at our university use Robert Kail's textbook [2], and our chapters follow a complementary order. In fact, most topically organized textbooks follow a very similar order as Kail's book, so our book should work pretty well with most topical child development texts. For example, our opening myth focuses on twin telepathy that originates in the womb, and child development textbooks often include the topic of twin research in the first chapter. Similarly, all of our early chapters focus on conception, pregnancy, or newborns, which are also usually covered in the first chapters of textbooks.

The second section, "Growth, Body, & Mind" corresponds with textbook chapters covering growth, motor development, cognitive development, and language. The third section "Emotions & Behavior" corresponds with textbook chapters that cover emotional development and behavioral issues. Finally, the fourth section, "Social Environment," corresponds with chapters related to the family and influences outside of the family.

Like many universities, our university has separate Child Development and Adolescent Development courses. Because of this, the topics in our book are derived from topics in a Child Development course, rather than an Adolescent Development course. Although there are many great myths of adolescent development, we tended to veer away from those topics (e.g., sex, drugs, and rock 'n' roll). Thus, there is still a great need for a book entitled something like *Great Myths of Adolescent Development*.

We have a lot of people that we'd like to thank for helping make this book happen. First, we are very appreciative of Scott O. Lilienfeld and Steven Jay Lynn (the series editors) for creating this series and for giving us the opportunity to contribute to it. With great enthusiasm we read *50 Great Myths of Popular Psychology* [1] soon after its publication, and we are very proud to be a part of its tradition. Over the past two years, Scott and Steve have also provided immensely valuable advice and feedback covering big issues (e.g., which myths to include) to small issues (e.g., where to place punctuation marks) and everything in between (e.g., how to effectively communicate our message). We'd also like to thank our editors at Wiley-Blackwell. Specifically, Matthew Bennett worked with us to get the project started, and Danielle Descoteaux has enthusiastically supported the project through its completion. We are also grateful to several colleagues, friends, family members, and students who contributed ideas and gave us feedback on many of the chapters. One especially notable research assistant is Catrina Salama who conducted a great deal of research for this book.

References

[1] Lilienfeld, S. O., Lynn, S. J., Ruscio, J., & Beyerstein, B. L. (2010). *50 Great Myths of Popular Psychology: Shattering Widespread Misconceptions about Human Behavior*. Malden, MA: Wiley-Blackwell.

[2] Kail, R. V. (2012). *Children and their Development*. Upper Saddle River, NJ: Pearson Education.

INTRODUCTION

For several decades, Dr. Benjamin Spock [1], a pediatrician and author, calmed parents with his mantra, "You know more than you think you do" (p. 3), and we agree that this is a good message to send to parents. Parents get a lot of advice from family, friends, the media, and, of course, parenting experts. Dr. Spock warned that advice from others can be contradictory when he wrote, "You hear that a baby must be handled as little as possible, and that a baby must be cuddled plenty; that spinach is the most valuable vegetable, that spinach is a worthless vegetable; that fairy tales make children nervous, and that fairy tales are a wholesome outlet" (p. 3). And now, decades later, parents continue to hear mixed messages like these and more.

With contradictory advice from different sources in mind, Spock's reassurance that parents already know a lot on their own is helpful because parents can usually figure parenting out without any specialized training, baby workshops, or parenting courses. In fact, sometimes "expert advice" can actually steer parents in the wrong direction, and at times parents would be better off making decisions for themselves instead of listening to others. Parents are exposed to countless claims about what is best for a fetus, infant, or child. Some of these claims have research support; some of the claims have never been researched; and some of the claims have research that shows they're wrong.

When professionals make confident claims that are not supported by research, we call these claims "myths." In addition to Spock, some of the advice-givers that have propagated myths of child development include Sigmund Freud, William Sears, James Dobson, and Laura Schlessinger. We'll address some of their advice, and the advice of many

Great Myths of Child Development, First Edition. Stephen Hupp and Jeremy Jewell.
© 2015 John Wiley & Sons, Inc. Published 2015 by John Wiley & Sons, Inc.

other parenting gurus. But to be fair, everyone, including us, has believed in some myths at some time. In fact, we believed many of the Great Myths uncovered in this book until we started delving into the research. Some of our favorite myths are the myths that we believed until recently. Thus, while we agree with Spock's reassuring words at the beginning of this Introduction, there is another (slightly modified) mantra that will be the focus of our book: You know more *myths* than you think you do.

Our book will do more than just explore claims from the experts, like Dr. Spock. We're also interested in the other Spock, the one from the Starship Enterprise, who lives a few centuries in the future. In one episode of the original *Star Trek* series [2], Mr. Spock hears the doctor from his ship using "baby talk" with an infant on another planet. He's baffled, as this is clearly not the normative way for adult Vulcans to interact with little baby Vulcans. Does baby talk hurt or help language development? This is an important question, but it's also important to ask how television shows, like this example from *Star Trek*, might help shape our beliefs.

Some other examples from television shows that we'll relate to the myths in this book include: *Modern Family, The Office, Seinfeld, Cake Boss, The Simpsons, Beavis and Butthead, America's Got Talent, Mad Men, Glee, Moonshiners, Game of Thrones*, and *Duck Dynasty*. If you prefer movies, we have examples from: *Frozen, Meet the Fockers, Little Fockers, American Psycho, The Sixth Sense, Sex and the City*, and *Cheech and Chong's The Corsican Brothers*. We'll also share examples from celebrities such as: Kourtney Kardashian, John Travolta, Salma Hayek, Neil Patrick Harris, Jenny McCarthy, Bill Engvall, and Rembrandt (yes, the artist). If you're more of a reader, we have examples from *The Dark Tower* Series and *Care Bears*. Okay, we admit it, we don't reference a lot of literary fiction, but hopefully you were excited about our amazing listing of television shows, movies, and celebrities!

Beyond parenting experts and the media shaping our beliefs, we often come to our own conclusions based on what seems like common sense. Unfortunately, common sense is often misdirected. In the Introduction of their book, Lilienfeld and colleagues [3] indicate that one of their goals "is to encourage you to mistrust your common sense when evaluating psychological claims" (p. 6). Why is common sense often wrong? Lilienfeld et al. offer "The 10 Sources of Psychological Myths" (p. 9) which can help explain common errors that contribute to believing in myths. Luckily, once you have a firm grasp of the sources of myths, your immunity to myths will be strengthened.

We're all prone to making the errors in thinking that are represented by the different sources of myths. We will cover each of the Lilienfeld et al. sources of psychological myths briefly [3].

1. *Word-of-Mouth.* We tend to believe information that we have heard repeatedly or that sounds catchy. For example, we have all heard the catchy description of the "terrible twos," but the age of 2 years old doesn't have to be so terrible.

2. *Desire for Easy Answers and Quick Fixes.* It's human nature to seek the greatest rewards for the least amount of effort, and this leads us to want to believe that many problems have easy solutions. For example, it would sure be nice if we could sit our infants in front of videos that would make them smarter, but videos have no such effect on intelligence.

3. *Selective Perception and Memory.* Once we hear a claim, we often begin to see (and then remember) all of the times the claim is supported, while we also ignore (or forget) all of the times the claim is not supported. For example, we tend to remember the times when identical twins had a mysterious pain at the same time, but we don't tend to notice the thousands of times when one twin gets hurt and the other is just fine.

4. *Inferring Causation from Correlation.* We often believe that one variable causes another variable just because the two variables tend to occur together. For example, over the past few decades, children have been receiving an increasing number of vaccines. At the same time, children are being diagnosed with an Autism Spectrum Disorder at increasing rates. Additionally, over the last decade Miley Cyrus has been getting more popular. That is, Miley Cyrus's popularity is correlated with increased rates of autism. Why do vaccines get blamed for autism but Miley Cyrus gets away scot-free?

5. *Post Hoc, Ergo Propter Hoc Reasoning.* This is Latin for "after this, therefore because of this," and it means that when one event happens before the other event, we tend to believe that the first event caused the second event. For example, couples sometimes get pregnant soon after adopting a child; however, this doesn't mean that the adoption *caused* the pregnancy.

6. *Exposure to a Biased Sample.* We have a tendency to believe that the few people we see from one group represent all of the people from that group. For example, when daycare teachers are featured in the news, it's usually because of something negative that happened. This might lead one to believe that a large number of daycare teachers are

problematic, when in fact the far majority of daycare teachers do countless great things for children that rarely make the news.

7. *Reasoning by Representativeness*. When we see that two things are similar in some way, we tend to think that the similarity gives the two things a meaningful connection. For example, boys like sports such as basketball, and girls are sweet like watermelons; thus, some people incorrectly assume that a pregnant belly shaped like one of these objects could represent the sex of the fetus (we agree that this is a sexist comparison, and we didn't make it up).

8. *Misleading Film and Media Portrayals*. When the media portrays psychological phenomena, they tend to sensationalize the phenomena, which we then assume to be accurate depictions. For example, television shows and movies love to show how hyperactive children can become after they've consumed some sugar. Calm children rarely make great television!

9. *Exaggeration of a Kernel of Truth*. We tend to accept little facts as evidence for broader, more complicated, claims. For example, there are several benefits to breastfeeding an infant for about a year, but some have claimed that there are benefits to breastfeeding for five, six, or seven years, even though there's no research to support this claim.

10. *Terminological Confusion*. We often accept terms at face value even though the terms themselves may be misrepresentative. For example, the term "identical twins" suggests that they have exactly the same (i.e., "identical") genes. However, if you read ahead to one of the Speed Busting myths, you'll see that this term can be deceptive.

Definition of a "Great Myth"

This book includes 50 "Great Myths," and we had to choose these myths from hundreds of possibilities. As part of this decision-making process we felt the need to define what it means to be one of the Great Myths of child development. Here are our seven criteria for the definition of a Great Myth:

1 A lot of people have already *heard of* the myth.
2. A lot of people currently *believe* the myth.
3. When the myth is heard for the first time, it "rings true" and is believable.
4. The myth is espoused by many professionals (or pseudo-professionals).
5. There is compelling contradictory evidence against the myth.
6. Belief in the myth can, in at least some cases, be harmful.
7. The myth discourages use of an available evidence-based practice.

Other factors that influenced myth selection were based on the desire to cover myths that are: (i) on a wide range of topics (e.g., walking, talking, and balking); (ii) across different age groups (e.g., fetuses, babies, and children); (iii) focused primarily on children (as opposed to adolescents or adults); and (iv) unique to this book (as opposed to myths covered in Lilienfeld et al.'s original book).

In our book, we focus the greatest attention on the 22 myths that were the most reflective of the Great Myth definition described above. In addition to these myths, we also review another 28 myths during a few sections dedicated to "speed busting," for a grand total of 50 myths. Myths were placed in the Speed Busting sections because they ranked lower based on our definition of Great Myths; however, we still felt these myths were important enough to warrant some discussion herein.

Park [4] describes another valuable way of thinking about myths with his categories of questionable claims in his book, *Voodoo Science: The Road from Foolishness to Fraud*. First, *pathological science* occurs when well-meaning scientists conduct research and actually fool themselves because of inherent problems with their research design. Second, *junk science* occurs when theorists deliberately make arguments without research. Third, *pseudoscience* occurs when practitioners purposefully make their unsupported claims sound scientific because they believe them to be true. Finally, *fraudulent science* occurs when poorly done research is purposefully exploited in order to make a quick buck. As you can see, Park's categorizations of voodoo science all focus on different ways that professionals (or people acting like professionals) spread misinformation, whether it's accidental or intentional. In a similar vein, one could also consider different categories of myths to be: pathological myths, junk myths, pseudoscientific myths, or fraudulent myths.

Admittedly, we believe that we need to be careful about using words like "pseudoscience" or "myth." For example, a claim of space aliens visiting earth is a myth inasmuch as there is currently no credible evidence that it has happened, but it's very hard to "prove" a negative. Little green men could potentially visit us one day; thus, something that is a myth now could become a reality at some point in the future (don't get your hopes up for space aliens, though). It's also important to be careful about using terms like "proof" or "truth" because our state of knowledge is continually growing and evolving.

What you need to know: Evidence-based practice and resources

There are a lot of myths that we'd all be better off not believing. By its very nature, then, our book is mostly focused on what you need *not* know (although, we think it's important for you to know what you shouldn't know).

Nevertheless, we wanted to spend some time writing about what many parents and students actually may want to know about child development. The last criterion in our operational definition of a Great Myth was that "The myth discourages use of an available evidence-based practice." This raises the question: Are there evidence-based practices in child development?

Psychologist and best-selling author, John Rosemond [5], wrote recently that "the efficacy of no form of child therapy – not one! – has ever been demonstrated in controlled studies" (p. 47). He wrote this statement in a book, like ours, in which he was debunking several myths of child psychology. A lot of his book is pretty good, but Rosemond helps us illustrate the difference between skepticism and cynicism. Rosemond takes a cynical outlook regarding his (and our) profession of clinical child psychology. Skepticism requires evidence. Cynicism accepts no evidence. Indeed, there is plenty of evidence to suggest that there are many different types of evidence-based practices in clinical child psychology.

One common thread across most of the chapters in our book will be that of evidence-based practice. For example, a task force from the American Psychological Association has developed criteria for different therapeutic approaches to be classified as "well-established" or "probably efficacious" based on the quantity and quality of research studies examining their efficacy [6]. This task force summarized hundreds (if not thousands) of well-controlled studies involving psychosocial treatments for children. We point interested readers to www.effectivechildtherapy.com, a website sponsored by the Society of Clinical Child and Adolescent Psychology. This website provides useful links to information about research-supported treatments for common challenges of childhood.

We can understand some level of discouragement about the current practice of child therapy. A lot of myths are out there. Luckily, there are plenty of truths to be discovered, too. Many people have worked hard to be able to distinguish between the Great Myths of psychology and the science of psychology. As Carl Sagan [7] wrote, "Each field of science has its own complement of pseudoscience" (p. 43). Indeed, myths are not unique to psychology. Sagan, though, was a skeptic, not a cynic. The title of his book, *The Demon-Haunted World: Science as a Candle in the Dark* (1996), evokes the optimistic view that the best answer for the darkness of pseudoscience is the light of science.

Throughout our book, in addition to sharing research that debunks the Great Myths of child development, we will also share information regarding evidence-based practices in child development. At the end of most of the chapters, we include a brief section called "What You Need to Know," in which we share research, websites, and books that may be helpful to parents and students of child development. We selected resources based on evidence-based practices, and many times the same clinicians who conducted the research also wrote the books.

We view our book as a way for parents and students to develop a critical eye for finding valuable information. That is, our book is a resource for finding self-help books and other resources that are based on research. In this way, we hope parents (and future parents) will be able to use our book as a *meta-self-help* book. That is, traditional self-help books go into great detail on one topic, whereas our meta-self-help book surveys a very broad range of topics and refers readers to traditional (research-based) self-help books. Hopefully, in this way, our book can help illuminate many of the existing candles in the dark.

Our research

Although we sometimes easily found opinion polls related to the myths in our book, other times the polls were elusive. Because of this challenge we decided to conduct our own research to survey beliefs about the myths of child development. In each chapter we refer to "our research" [8], and we will describe our research here so that we don't need to provide the details in each chapter. We first developed a questionnaire called the *Opinions About Kids Scale (OAKS)*. This survey includes 26 statements that we consider to be myths (e.g., "Baby walkers help young children learn to walk"). The myths are interspersed with 26 statements considered to be supported by research (e.g., "The vision of most babies is worse than the vision of most adults"). Respondents had four options in their rating of each statement. They could "agree," "somewhat agree," "somewhat disagree," or "disagree." For ease in interpretation, "agree" responses and "somewhat agree" responses were combined to represent people that agreed (at least to some degree) with the statement.

We then gave the survey to two groups of people. First, we administered the survey to 163 undergraduate students on the first day of their course in Child Psychology at a mid-sized university in the Midwest. Their participation in the research was voluntary, confidential, and not tied to their course grade. Second, we administered the survey to 205 parents across America by using a survey via the Internet.

Our results revealed that undergraduate students and parents responded in very similar ways. For example, 78% of college students reported that they agreed with the myth that "Baby walkers help young children learn to walk." Similarly, 76% of parents agreed with this myth. By comparison, we'll also share the results of the beliefs about one of the evidence-based statements. Specifically, 52% of students and 66% of parents agreed with the evidence-based statement that "The vision of most babies is worse than the vision of most adults." Thus, the participants actually believed in the myth more than the evidence-based statement! We'll continue to share similar results about the myths throughout the book.

A final word before you continue

We're going to spend a lot of time disagreeing with a lot of smart people, and we worked hard to avoid making statements that other skeptics could debunk in the future. We realize, however, that a few errors on our part seem inevitable. Because we hope to encourage your skeptical thinking about child development, it's only fair that you read our work with a healthy degree of skepticism (but not cynicism). Feel free to look for errors in our arguments or research, and send us tweets with other myths, pop culture examples, or research studies that we should have added. Your input could help shape any future editions of this book. We look forward to hearing from you via Twitter: @StephenHupp and @DoctorJewell. Also, you can find other related information on our websites: www.stephenhupp.com and www.doctorjewell.com.

References

[1] Spock, B. (1946). *The Common Sense Book of Baby and Child Care.* New York, NY: Duell, Sloan and Pearce.
[2] Roddenberry, G., Fontana, D. C. (Writers), & Pevney, J. (Director) (1967). Friday's Child [Television series episode]. In G. Roddenberry (Executive producer), *Star Trek.* Desilu Productions.
[3] Lilienfeld, S. O., Lynn, S. J., Ruscio, J., & Beyerstein, B. L. (2010). *50 Great Myths of Popular Psychology: Shattering Widespread Misconceptions about Human Behavior.* Malden, MA: Wiley-Blackwell.
[4] Park, R. L. (2000). *Voodoo Science: The Road from Foolishness to Fraud.* New York, NY: Oxford University Press.
[5] Rosemond, J. K. (2012). *Parent-Babble: How Parents can Recover from Fifty Years of Bad Expert Advice.* Kansas City, MO: Andrews McMeel Pub.
[6] Silverman, W. K. & Hinshaw, S. P. (2008). The second special issue on evidence-based psychosocial treatments for children and adolescents: A 10-year update. *Journal of Clinical Child and Adolescent Psychology, 37,* 1–7.
[7] Sagan, C. (1996). *The Demon-Haunted World: Science as a Candle in the Dark.* New York, NY: Random House.
[8] Hupp, S., Stary, A., & Jewell, J. (submitted). Beliefs about myths related to child psychology, development, and parenting: Which myths need the most debunking?

1 BEGINNINGS

Great Myths of Child Development, First Edition. Stephen Hupp and Jeremy Jewell.
© 2015 John Wiley & Sons, Inc. Published 2015 by John Wiley & Sons, Inc.

Myth #1 Identical twins have a telepathic connection that originates in the womb

Perhaps you've heard a story like that of Silvia and Marta Landa; these 4-year-old twins made news when Marta burned her hand on an iron, and Silvia, who was miles away, felt a sharp pain and developed an identical blister [1]. During subsequent investigation, even when separated in different rooms, when Marta's knee was tapped, Silvia's leg started swinging; when Marta smelled perfume, Silvia covered her nose; when light was shined in Marta's eye, Silvia's eyes blinked. They seemed to have a special telepathic connection.

In 2011, the television news program *Nightline* began a spinoff called *Primetime Nightline: Beyond Belief*. The first episode in the series, "Twin-Tuition: A Telepathic Connection?," examined special relationships between identical twins. The show's reporter, Juju Chang, claimed "There are certain unexplained phenomena that occur between twins that even modern science simply can't explain" [2]. Chang went on to explain the potential cause of the telepathic connection, suggesting that "In the womb identical twins actually start out as one physical being, one embryo that splits in two during gestation, but perhaps their souls are still entangled, even when their bodies are separate." Jensen and Parker [3] referred to this connection that begins in the womb as "quantum entanglement" and suggested that the longer it takes the fertilized egg to split in two, the greater the special connection.

The *Primetime Nightline* episode includes the story of newborn twins, in which one twin frequently awakened from a deep sleep in another room at the exact same moment his identical twin brother was undergoing a medical procedure [2]. In another example, a 5-year-old started developing a black eye after her identical twin sister sustained an injury to the same eye in a playground. Chang asks, "Did one sister telepathically transfer her injury to her twin, or was it just a coincidence?"

The book *Twin Telepathy, 3rd Edition* [4] reports many similar anecdotal stories:

A 3-day-old twin "screams in terror for no obvious reason," helping his mother realize that his brother is "suffocating silently on the couch" (p. 2).

A 5-month-old twin "yells his head off" while his brother calmly receives a vaccination (p. 2).

A 6-year-old twin breaks his collar bone "within half an hour" of his brother breaking the same bone in a different manner (p. 59).

A 7-year-old twin tells her mother about a dream, and her sister (who had not heard about the dream) later describes having "exactly the same dream" (p. 42).

An 8-year-old twin starts searching for her sister upon inexplicably feeling "panic stricken," and she discovers her sister has broken a tooth (p. 46).

These examples all focus on children, and Playfair [4] uses an unpublished doctoral dissertation (Spinelli [5] as cited in Playfair) to suggest that telepathy peaks at 3 years old and by 8 years old the connection is lost. Similarly, others have suggested that it's best to study telepathy in twins before they reach adulthood because they will gradually become increasingly different due to life circumstances [6, 7]. Well-known and self-professed psychic Sylvia Browne suggests that psychic children are a window into "the spirit world of the Other Side ..." [8].

Other anecdotes from Playfair [4], however, involve adult twins choosing the same gifts for each other (as in the case of Gloria Vanderbilt and her twin), simultaneous deaths (on the same day and in the same manner), and corresponding murders (in which the second twin didn't know why he suddenly felt compelled to murder someone). Moreover, Elvis Presley was reported in the book to miss the companionship of his stillborn twin brother.

A telepathic twin connection is commonly represented in pop culture as well, and Playfair [1] indicated that *The Corsican Brothers*, a novel by Alexandre Dumas [9], is the first literary reference to this special connection. In this novel two identical twins could feel each other's pain. The first example presented in the novel occurs when one twin says "I have experienced terrible pains in the region of the heart, and palpitations, so it's evident to me that my brother is suffering some great grief" (p. 32).

Although there have been many stage and screen adaptations, perhaps the most notable is *Cheech and Chong's The Corsican Brothers* [10] in which, as stated in the official movie trailer, "when one brother was being hurt, the other felt the pain." Interestingly, the characters played by Cheech and Chong are not identical twins as in the novel by Dumas, but are in fact fraternal twins with different fathers (see the "Truth is More Surprising than Fiction" section in the Postscript of our book for more on this topic). In this movie adaptation, each twin intentionally and humorously hurts himself in order to cause pain to the other twin.

In the movie *Twins* [11], Arnold Schwarzenegger and Danny DeVito play genetically engineered "identical" twins that unevenly split from the same fertilized egg, and Schwarzenegger's character reveals, "We're twins:

I can feel your pain." A more recent movie, *Seconds Apart* [12], tells the story of a police detective (played by Orlando Jones) investigating deaths perpetrated by adolescent twins with a sinister telepathic connection. The telepathic twin connection is also depicted in recent literary fiction. For example, in Stephen King's *The Dark Tower* [13] series a villain attempts to take from the brains of children an "enzyme or secretion not produced by singleton children ... that created the supposed phenomenon of 'twin telepathy'" (p. 580).

Sir Francis Galton, who helped popularize the nature-versus-nurture debate, has been described as the first scientist to give twin telepathy serious attention [1]. Galton [14] indicates that about one third of twins have a "similarity in the association of their ideas" (p. 231), adding that they say the same thing at the same time, finish each other's sentences, and surprisingly buy each other the same gifts. Although Playfair [1] calls this similarity telepathy, it's probably unfair to Galton to suggest that he meant anything beyond the likelihood that it's the identical genes shared between the twins that influence similar behaviors.

In the book *Twins and Super-Twins* [15], Dr. Horatio Newman describes twin telepathy as a commonly held belief, and this myth continues to be believed today. According to a Gallop poll, 31% of Americans believe in telepathy and another 27% report being uncertain [16]. In our own research, 56% of college students and 76% of parents agreed that "Some identical twins can feel each other's physical pain" [17]. In another study published in *Behavior Genetics*, 40% of identical twins themselves (and 12% of fraternal twins) reported believing they had a telepathic connection [18]. In short, the belief in twin telepathy is widely held.

Because this belief is so popular, researchers have attempted to examine the possibility of a special connection between twins. For example, Nash and Buzby [19] investigated differences between identical twins and fraternal twins (who ranged in age from 5 to 13 years) using a test of extrasensory perception (ESP) to see if clairvoyance had a genetic basis. Over several trials the participants were asked to guess which of five symbols was on a card. Although the scores of the identical twins were positively correlated (meaning they were making similar guesses to each other) and reported to be significant, the fraternal twins' scores were non-significant, spurring the researchers to conclude that ESP does have a genetic basis. However, in a following commentary, Thiessen [20] high-lighted the fact that the scores for the identical twins were actually lower than chance. That is, each participant was tested across 150 trials and with only 5 possible symbol options they would be expected to get 30 of the 150 trials correct by chance alone. Nevertheless, their performance was, in fact, worse than chance, averaging less than 30 correct, providing no support for the hypothesis that the twins possessed ESP. Still, Nash and Buzby, unable to accept the conclusion that twins do not possess ESP, attributed their poor performance to a competition in which the twins telepathically tried to lower the score of each other.

Over decades of investigation, other researchers have failed to find a telepathic connection between twins. For example, one study published in the *Journal of the American Society for Psychical Research* [6] included nine pairs of adolescent-aged identical twins in which one twin viewed an exciting movie, while the other twin (in a different room) was monitored for signs of physiological arousal. This study failed to show any meaningful telepathic connection between the twins, although the researchers devoted substantial speculation to why "the experimental situation itself would be unfavorable to extrasensory communication" (p. 78). As can be seen across many studies, failure to find significant results is rarely accepted as meaning that twins are not telepathic after all. Rather, some investigators go to great lengths to find morsels of evidence supporting the telepathy hypothesis in their research with non-significant findings.

Researchers have continued to develop laboratory procedures for identifying a unique twin connection. Jensen and Parker [3] studied three pairs of identical twins, ranging in age from 9 to 21 years old. Like the previous study, the twins were separated in different rooms, and while one twin was exposed to exciting stimuli (e.g., a balloon popping behind their head) the other twin's physiological arousal was monitored. Overall, the researchers failed to find a significant connection between the twins' responses. A follow-up study yielded similar unimpressive results [21].

We would like to share one final piece of information to help debunk the notion that twins possess telepathy or that anyone possesses telepathic talents of any kind. In 1964, the famous skeptic James "The Amazing" Randi introduced an open challenge to the public for any person to come forward to provide evidence of any paranormal talent. That challenge continues today but is now called "The Million Dollar Challenge" and is offered by the James Randi Educational Foundation (www.randi.org). Despite hundreds of attempts to provide scientifically credible evidence of paranormal abilities, including several specifically related to telepathy, no individual has succeeded in passing even the preliminary round of tests.

Despite evidence to the contrary, many people, including twins themselves, believe that identical twins have a special telepathic connection, as our surveys indicated. Why is this? First, there is a long history across many cultures of giving special powers to twins. Newman [15] describes some cultural beliefs that twins are a good omen and a positive sign from fertility gods. Furthermore, twins have been thought to be endowed with supernatural powers, such as immunity from serpent poison, the talent of stopping water from boiling, and even the ability to predict a baby's sex (see Myth 3 for other misperceptions related to predicting a baby's sex). Thus, modern beliefs about twins may have evolved from earlier beliefs about twins and their supernatural powers.

Also contributing to the twin telepathy myth is the fact that identical twins do share important connections. They're very similar genetically, and because genes have a considerable impact on behavior, twins are more likely to respond similarly in a given situation. Furthermore, identical twins typically spend a lot of time together and are usually exposed to very similar environments. Thus, it's not at all surprising that they act in similar ways and are adept at anticipating and forecasting each other's reactions to events.

Some of the "Sources of Psychological Myths" also help explain the popularity of belief in twin telepathy. Specifically, the bias of selective perception and memory can cloud a person's judgment. Sometimes two people feel the same pain, think the same thought, wear the same clothes, buy the same gift, or call each other simultaneously. For people who are not twins, it's easy to assume that these situations are coincidences, but with twins these coincidences are more memorable. People, including the twins themselves, remember and tell stories about the coincidences, but they quickly forget (and don't tell stories about) all of the other times they don't feel the same pain, don't think the same thought, don't wear the same clothes, don't buy the same gift, or don't call each other at the same time.

A belief in twin telepathy has been particularly harmful in cultures in which twins (with their purported supernatural powers) are a sign of evil. Newman [15] reports that in the Benin territory in West Africa, twins were once "regarded as visitations of a devil" (p. 15), leading to human sacrifice. Another reason that belief in twin telepathy can be harmful is because it feeds into the broader belief that some humans have special psychic abilities. Many so-called "psychics" swindle people out of large sums of money and mislead police officers and parents when it comes to child abductions. Psychic Sylvia Browne, for example, appeared on *The Montel Williams Show* [22] and told the mother of Amanda Berry (kidnapped in 2002) that Amanda was dead. But a decade later, in 2013, Amanda shocked the world when she escaped from her abductor and heroically helped others escape. Despite Browne's terrible record of making psychic predictions, one chapter of her book serves as an "instruction manual" for raising children with psychic abilities such as telepathy [8]. Unfortunately, a manual such as Browne's serves only to promote uncritical thinking in parents and their children.

What you need to know

Raising two children of the same age can be more difficult at times than raising two children of different ages. Furthermore, parents of twins try to strike the balance between keeping a strong bond between the twins while also encouraging each twin to be independent. The book *Raising Twins: From Pregnancy to Preschool* [23], published by the American Academy of Pediatrics, includes tips related to pregnancy, premature births, breastfeeding, sleeping, sharing toys, socialization, fairness, one-on-one time, and preschool issues. However, it doesn't include tips for promoting telepathy between twins – and we think that is a good thing.

References

[1] Playfair, G. L. (1999). Identical twins and telepathy. *Journal of the Society for Psychical Research*, 63, 86–98.

[2] Chang, Juju (News Correspondent). (2011, June 29). Twin-tuition [Television Series Episode] in *Primetime Nightline: Beyond Belief*. New York, NY: ABC Broadcasting. Retrieved from: http://abcnews.go.com/Nightline/video/twin-tuition-telepathic-connection-13962998 [accessed August 2014].

[3] Jensen, C. G. & Parker, A. (2012). Entangled in the womb? A pilot study on the possible physiological connectedness between identical twins with different embryonic backgrounds. *Explore*, 8, 339–347. doi: 10.1016/j.explore.2012.08.001.

[4] Playfair, G. L. (2012). *Twin Telepathy* (3rd edn). United Kingdom: White Crow Books.

[5] Spinelli, E. (1983). Human development and paranormal cognition, Unpublished doctoral dissertation, University of Surrey, United Kingdom.

[6] Barron, F. & Mordkoff, A. M. (1968). An attempt to relate creativity to possible extrasensory empathy as measured by physiological arousal in identical twins. *Journal of the American Society for Psychical Research*, 62, 73–79.

[7] Sommer, R., Osmond, H., & Pancyr, L. (1961). Selection of twins for ESP experimentation. *International Journal of Parapsychology*, 3, 55–69.

[8] Browne, S. & Harrison, L. (2007). *Psychic Children: Revealing the Intuitive Gifts and Hidden Abilities of Boys and Girls*. New York, NY: Dutton.

[9] Dumas, A. (1844). *The Corsican Brothers*. Chicago, IL: M.A. Donohue & Co.

[10] Macgregor-Scott, P. (Producer) & Chong, T. (Director). *Cheech & Chong's The Corsican Brothers* [Motion picture]. United States: Orion Pictures.

[11] Reitman, I. (Producer & Director) (1988). *Twins* [Motion picture]. United States: Universal Pictures.

[12] Shannon, D., Swift, M., Walker, G. M., et al. (Producers) & Negret, A. (Director) (2011). *Seconds Apart* [Motion picture]. United States: Lions Gate.

[13] King, S. (2003). *The Dark Tower V*. New York, NY: Simon & Schuster.

[14] Galton, F. (1883). *Enquiries into Human Faculty*. London: Macmillan.

[15] Newman, H. H. (1942). *Twins and Super-twins: A Study of Twins, Triplets, Quadruplets and Quintuplets*. New York, NY: Hutchinson's Scientific and Technical Publications.

[16] Moore (2005, June 16). Three in four Americans believe in paranormal. Retrieved from http://www.gallup.com [accessed August 2014].

[17] Hupp, S., Stary, A., & Jewell, J. (submitted). Beliefs about myths related to child psychology, development, and parenting: Which myths need the most debunking?

[18] Lichtenstein, P. & Baker, M. R. (1999). Telepathy in twins. *Behavior Genetics*, 29, 362.

[19] Nash, C. B. & Buzby, D. E. (1965). Extrasensory perception of identical and fraternal twins: Comparison of clairvoyance-test scores. *Journal of Heredity*, 56, 52–54.

[20] Thiessen, D. D. (1965). Comments on the genetics of extrasensory perception. *Journal of Heredity*, 56, 180.

[21] Parker, A. & Jensen, C. (2013). Further possible physiological connectedness between identical twins: The London Study. *Explore*, 9, 26–31. doi: 10.1016/j.explore.2012.10.001.

[22] *The Montel Williams Show* (2003, February 26). Retrieved from http://www.youtube.com/watch?v=67nnkxSzSYg [accessed August 2014].

[23] Flais, S. V. (2010). *Raising Twins: From Pregnancy to Preschool*. Elk Grove Village, IL: American Academy of Pediatrics.

Myth #2 Couples dealing with infertility are more likely to get pregnant if they adopt

Humans have long worried about their fertility, as evidenced by the hundreds of fertility gods people have created across many cultures. In Roman mythology, for example, Venus (mother of Cupid) inspired many superstitious behaviors related to fertility. In fact, many superstitions around fertility persist to this day, with perhaps the most prominent being the act of throwing rice, a symbol of fertility, at newly married couples.

Unlike people in ancient Rome, however, we now know a lot more about how to help couples deal with infertility. Even so, many couples still continue to have a difficult time getting pregnant in the 21st century. Estimates of prevalence rates vary widely depending on the definition of "infertility." Studies use "time of trying" cutoffs for infertility that range from one to seven years [1]. These studies reveal that many people who struggle with fertility for some time do eventually conceive a baby. Thus, most definitions of infertility capture the notion that a couple is having difficulty conceiving but not that it's impossible for them to ever conceive. About 10% of couples worldwide have to deal with either primary infertility, in which they have never been able to conceive a child, or secondary infertility, in which they haven't been able to conceive another child [2].

Because fertility has continued to be a challenge for many couples in the modern era, new superstitions have developed long after belief in Venus's power over fertility was viewed as mythical. For example, parenting experts Ilg and Ames [3] describe what often seems to happen when couples become discouraged with infertility and make the decision to adopt a child: "Before the adoption has even waited out its legal year's waiting period ... along comes a baby of their own" (p. 342). In these situations it's common for people to make a connection between the adoption and the subsequent pregnancy. In fact, the connection between these two events was also made earlier in a 1936 article published in *Eugenical News*. Perkins [4] declared that "there does appear to be a basis in fact for the popular belief that the adoption of a child by a childless couple does sometimes, and not infrequently, help to overcome infertility" (p. 95), leading Perkins to recommend adoption to couples to increase their odds of natural conception.

The quote from Perkins [4] indicates that the belief that adoption increases fertility has a long history, and it's still commonly believed today. In our research, 30% of students and 36% of parents agreed with the statement that "Couples that are struggling with fertility have an increased chance of getting pregnant after they adopt a child" [5]. This belief is also commonly represented in modern media. Surprise pregnancies also make for great television. In the show *King of Queens*, Carrie and Doug Heffernan struggle with fertility, and in the series finale they fly to China to adopt a daughter [6]. While Doug is holding this new baby in the hotel room, Carrie tells him she is pregnant and that "It happens all the time: when couples don't think they can get pregnant, they stop trying, and then they adopt a baby ..." and then they get pregnant. The television show *Sex and the City* [7] uses a similar storyline. In the fourth season, Charlotte's marriage ends partly due to the couple's struggle with fertility, and in the final season she gets remarried and unsuccessfully tries fertility treatments. By the last episode, they decide to adopt a child from China. The first *Sex and the City* movie [8] picks up on the couple after they have adopted a daughter. Then, upon visiting her doctor, Charlotte says, "people always say that when you stop trying it can happen, and my doctor says that she knows other couples who've adopted and then they get pregnant ... Carrie, I'm pregnant!"

Many writers have attempted to provide an explanation for why adoption might increase fertility. Some suggest that the adoption itself represents "giving up" and thus purges the couple of the stress associated with their unsuccessful attempts to conceive [9]. Thus, for some couples, psychological problems are thought to cause infertility. Psychoanalytic psychologists in particular have postulated numerous psychological mechanisms that cause infertility, such as the woman's unconscious opposition to motherhood or her unconscious choice of a man who is infertile [10]. In a description of three cases, Christie [11] indicated that infertility could be overcome following the "woman's increasing capacity to retrieve her negative feelings and achieve a more balanced awareness of having strong feelings both for and against allowing the baby to arrive" (p. 232) and goes on to link infertility to "the legendary Oedipus himself, whose parents tried to kill him in infancy" (p. 234).

Other suggested causes of infertility include: (i) hostility toward the couple's own mothers; (ii) fear of hostility from their future child; (iii) the unconscious wish to avoid having children; and (iv) failure to cope with a previous trauma [11]. Christie argues that psychoanalysis is the key to treating "psychologically-caused" infertility, whereas other psychodynamic therapists suggest that adopting a child may help one cope with this intra-psychic conflict [12]. These arguments all include the psychodynamic paradox of "If I want a child I must stop wanting a child" (as summarized by Wischmann [13]). It's the adoption of a child that signifies the couple has given up on conceiving a child, and this opens the door for a successful pregnancy, or so the theory goes.

Recent research on the potential connection between adoption and pregnancy is scarce; however, over two decades ago Thomas Gilovich was already able to debunk the adoption-causes-pregnancy myth in his book, *How We Know What Isn't So* [14]. There was a time when researchers were quite interested in the relation between adoption and conception. A 1965 study [15] examined 362 couples contending with infertility and showed that 23% of adopting couples became pregnant after the adoption. That might seem like a high percentage until you learn that the control group (couples dealing with infertility who didn't adopt) became pregnant *more* often (i.e., 35% of the time). A similar study followed 533 couples, and 20% of the couples who adopted later became pregnant, whereas 66% of couples of non-adopting couples later became pregnant [16]. An even larger study [17] with 895 couples found a 32% pregnancy rate in the adoption group and a 42% pregnancy rate in the no-adoption group. Taken together, it seems clear that adoption does not increase fertility.

Looking at these results, in fact, might lead you to the opposite hypothesis: that the adoption actually makes pregnancy less likely. Nevertheless, we would caution against this interpretation. The shortcoming of all of these studies is that the research cannot control which couples adopt or not. That is, the researchers weren't able to use random assignment in these studies, so it's problematic to make an interpretation regarding the cause of the differences between the groups. Very possibly, there is some difference in the type of couples who choose to adopt versus those who choose not to adopt. For example, some couples that choose to adopt might decrease their time spent trying to get pregnant, thus lowering their likelihood of conception.

This belief might be popular due to several of the "Sources of Psychological Myths," such as word-of-mouth, selective perception, misleading media, and post hoc, ergo propter hoc reasoning. Most of us have heard a story about someone who became pregnant after adopting a child. Indeed, research shows that some couples do get pregnant after having considered themselves to be infertile. The problem is that many couples also never get pregnant no matter how many babies they adopt. We're also less likely to hear stories about couples that never get pregnant than we are about couples that do get pregnant because surprise pregnancies are a lot more fun to talk about. Regarding the media examples provided earlier, the problem with these shows is not that couples get pregnant after they have adopted a child, because that really does happen. The problem is that these shows suggest that a direct connection exists between the adoption and the pregnancy when research clearly shows that adoption does not increase the likelihood of natural conception.

Adoption itself can also be a wonderful solution for helping families grow. Nevertheless, believing that the adoption will somehow cause the couple to naturally conceive a child can be problematic. It's possible that a couple might adopt a child due to this mistaken notion, which could ultimately result in rushing this important decision or even create resentment if the couple does not subsequently become pregnant as they had hoped. Adoption should be an option for all couples to consider, but there are many better reasons to adopt a child than a myth about fertility.

What you need to know

Pregnancy is a complicated, some might say miraculous, process in which many potential obstacles can get in the way. The American Society for Reproductive Medicine (ASRM) published a free resource called *Infertility: An Overview* [18] which outlines the complications that can occur and many options for facing the challenges of infertility. As described in this resource, one of the first steps is to get an infertility evaluation. For the male partner, a semen analysis provides information about sperm quality. For the female partner, the evaluation includes consideration of factors such as ovulation (e.g., are mature eggs being released?), tubal function (e.g., are the fallopian tubes open?), and peritoneal conditions (e.g., is scar tissue affecting internal organs?). Furthermore, age also influences the interpretation of the evaluation, because fertility tends to decline around the mid-30s. Finally, about 10% of the time the cause of the infertility is unknown [18]. Once a complicating factor has been identified, or even when the cause is unknown, there are many possible solutions. Specifically, medications and surgical procedures are available for both men and women. Also, assisted reproductive technologies offer other possibilities such as in vitro fertilization (i.e., combining egg and sperm in a laboratory dish), donations (i.e., eggs, sperm, or embryos can be donated), or surrogacy (i.e., when the pregnancy is carried out by another woman).

Several helpful books also describe the best ways to emotionally cope with the challenge of infertility. The book *When You're Not Expecting: An Infertility Survival Guide* [19] provides a woman's perspective, and *How to Make Love to a Plastic Cup: A Guy's Guide to the World of Infertility* [20] offers one male's perspective. To be clear, these emotional coping strategies by themselves are not designed to make natural conception more likely, as some psychodynamic psychologists would suggest. Also, because some cases of infertility have been caused by preventable sexually transmitted infections (STIs), many forms of STI prevention can help prevent fertility problems.

References

[1] Gurunath, S., Pandian, Z., Anderson, R. A., & Bhattacharya, S. (2011). Defining infertility – a systematic review of prevalence studies. *Human Reproduction Update*, 17, 575–588. doi:10.1093/humupd/dmr015.

[2] Mascarenhas, M. N., Flaxman, S. R., Boerma, T., et al. (2012). National, regional, and global trends in infertility prevalence since 1990: A systematic analysis of 277 health surveys. *PLoS Medicine*, 9, e1001356, 1–12. doi:10.1371/journal.pmed.1001356.

[3] Ilg, F. L. & Ames, L. B. (1955). *Child Behavior: A Realistic Parents' Guide to Children's Behavior from Birth to Ten*. New York, NY: Dell Publishing Company, Inc.

[4] Perkins, H. F. (1936). Adoption and fertility. *Eugenical News*, 21, 95–101.

[5] Hupp, S., Stary, A., & Jewell, J. (submitted). Beliefs about myths related to child psychology, development, and parenting: Which myths need the most debunking?

[6] Weithorn, M. J., Litt, D. (Writers), & Schiller, R. (Director) (2007). China Syndrome [Television series episode]. In M. J. Weithorn, T. Sheehan, & J. Sussman (Executive producers), *King of Queens*. Culver City, CA: Sony Pictures Television and CBS Productions.

[7] Star, D. (Creator) (1998–2003). *Sex and the City* [Television series]. United States: HBO Original Programming.

[8] Dubiecki, D., Clifford, J., King, M. P., et al. (Producers), & King, M. P. (Director) (2008). *Sex and the City* [Motion picture]. United States: Warner Home Video.

[9] Katz, R. K., Marshall, D. B., Romanowski, S. B., & Stewart, N. (1985). Is the adoption process an aid to achieving pregnancy? *Social Work*, 30, 63–68. doi: 10.1093/sw/30.1.63.

[10] Apfel, R. J. & Keylor, R. G. (2002). Psychoanalysis and infertility: Myths and realities. *International Journal of Psychoanalysis*, 83, 85–104. doi:10.1516/ 4089-JBCW-YNT8-QTCM.

[11] Christie, G. L. (1998). Some socio-cultural and psychological aspects of infertility. *Human Reproduction*, 13, 232–241. doi:10.1093/humrep/13.1.232.

[12] Orr, D. W. (1941). Pregnancy following the decision to adopt. *Psychosomatic Medicine*, 3, 441–446.

[13] Wischmann, T. H. (2003). Psychogenic infertility – Myths and facts. *Journal of Reproduction and Genetics*, 20, 485–494. doi:10.1023/B:JARG.0000013648. 74404.9d.

[14] Gilovich, T. (1991). *How We Know What Isn't So: The Fallibility of Human Reason in Everyday Life*. New York, NY: The Free Press.

[15] Rock, J., Tietze, C., & McLaughlin, H. B. (1965). Effect of adoption on infertility. *Fertility & Sterility*, 16, 305–312.

[16] Arronet, G. H., Bergquist, C. A., & Parekh, M. C. (1974). The influence of adoption on subsequent pregnancy in infertile marriage. *International Journal of Fertility*, 19, 159–162. doi:10.1097/00006254-197601000-00014.

[17] Lamb, J. L. & Leurgans, S. (1979). Does adoption affect subsequent fertility? *Transactions of the Pacific Coast Obstetrical and Gynecological Society*, 46, 37–43.

[18] American Society for Reproductive Medicine (2012). *Infertility: An Overview*. Birmingham, AL: American Society for Reproductive Medicine.

[19] Shapiro, C. H. (2010). *When You're Not Expecting: An Infertility Guide*. Mississauga, Ontario: John Wiley & Sons Canada, Ltd.

[20] Wolfe, G. (2010). *How to Make Love to a Plastic Cup: A Guy's Guide to the World of Infertility*. New York, NY: Harper.

Parents can predict the sex of a fetus by examining the shape of the mother's body

Pregnancy is an exciting time for prospective parents, regardless of whether they're anticipating their first child or adding to an already established family. During this special time, numerous decisions often become a priority, one of which is this: What color should the nursery be painted? This decision, however, requires some thought as many parents decorate the nursery according to the anticipated sex of the baby. Friends and family often join in the fun, using a variety of methods to try to predict the baby's sex.

Research by Goldfarb [1] uncovered 32 different methods believed to determine the sex of the fetus. For example, some of the methods suggest that the shape of the mother's face and body is useful in predicting sex. Specifically, "If a pregnant woman's face becomes prettier or more radiant, the child will be a boy; the same or uglier and swollen, a girl; if the mother is carrying high or to the front, it's a boy; low or to the back, a girl" (p. 896). The book *Boy or Girl: 50 Fun Ways to Find Out* [2] also suggests that the baby is more likely to be a girl if the pregnant mother has a more ample face, a bulging waistline, or more weight gain on her rear end (a good friend might be wise to say "it looks to me like you're having a boy"). Furthermore, a belly shaped like a watermelon is said to predict a girl, whereas a basketball shape predicts a boy; and carrying high predicts a girl, whereas carrying low predicts a boy. Both of the above sources also include the "pendulum test" in which an object (often a wedding ring) is tied to a thread (or the mother's hair) and held over the pregnant belly with the direction of its movement indicating a girl (i.e., in a circle) or a boy (i.e., side to side).

These prediction methods can be amusing, but do people really believe they accurately predict the sex of the child? One study surveyed 104 pregnant women who didn't know the sex of their unborn child and found that 30% used the shape of their belly to predict the baby's sex [3]. Of these women, 79% were at least "somewhat sure" about their prediction. Interestingly, 14% of the participants used a dream to make a prediction about gender, and their confidence in their prediction was fairly high with about half being at least "somewhat sure." In our research, 31% of students and 20% of parents agreed with the statement that "The shape of the mother's belly is one factor that can help doctors predict the sex of a fetus" [4].

There are many examples of this belief in modern media. For example, in the show *Cake Boss* [5], Buddy Valastro's sisters employ two of the above-mentioned methods for predicting his baby's sex. When chatting with Buddy's wife, one sister mentions she can predict the baby's sex "from your face – because they say the girls take away the mom's beauty – you're still pretty Lisa, so I think you're having a boy." Another sister then applies the pendulum test that also predicts she will have a girl. Similarly, in a recent interview with Matt Lauer from the *Today Show* [6], actress Kate Hudson described several ways that she had ascertained that her baby-on-the-way was to be a girl. These methods included the way she was carrying the baby and the pendulum test. More recently, in the summer of 2013, the fate of the British monarchy was about to be shaped for the first time in decades. Would Prince William and Kate Middleton have a little prince or a princess? Would their baby be the future King of England? In a CNN news report [7], Dr. Fiona Mathews, a reproductive biologist, predicted that the royal couple was more likely to have a girl, partly based on the shape of Kate's waist.

In all three of the above media examples, the prediction was a baby *girl*, and in all three examples the parents welcomed baby *boys* into the world. Specifically, Lisa Valastro gave birth to Carlo (named after the original owner of the bakery) on Valentine's Day; Kate Hudson gave birth to Bingham; and Kate Middleton gave birth to George Alexander Lewis, the future King of England!

We don't have to rely on these anecdotal case examples, though, because researchers have examined the effectiveness of popular methods for predicting a baby's sex. For example, Perry and colleagues [3] found that pregnant women using these types of methods were no more accurate in their prediction of the baby's sex than a flip of a coin. Furthermore, the ability to place belly shapes into different categories was fairly unreliable, with considerable disagreements between the mothers and another belly shape judge. Most interesting, however, was that participants' understanding of the meaning of the belly shape was often contradictory. That is, many participants believed that carrying the child high was a sign of a boy, whereas several other participants believed this was a sign of a girl. Finally, there was no relation between the mother's confidence in her sex prediction and the actual sex of the baby. Indeed, using belly shape turned out to be one of the worst predictors of all. Regarding general weight gain, another study followed 304 pregnant women and found that mothers put on the same amount of weight whether they carried a boy or a girl [8]. Other sex prediction folklore has similarly been no more accurate than chance considering the fact that every method statistically has about a 50% chance of being correct [9, 10].

The sex prediction myth proliferates due to many of the "Sources of Psychological Myths." As evidenced by the pop culture examples, word-of-mouth and misleading media are two ways this myth is spread. Additionally, people remember the times the prediction was right and forget about the times it was wrong (i.e., selective perception and memory). Finally, some of these myths seem plausible due to reasoning by representativeness in which people seek meaning when two things are similar in some way. For example, a watermelon is sweet, so a watermelon shape represents a girl; whereas, the basketball shape may make some people think of a bouncing baby boy [2]. Please don't blame us if this seems sexist, as we are just reporting about this mistaken connection that has been around for quite some time.

Is there really any harm in people believing the myths about sex prediction? It depends. If family members use these methods for fun at a baby shower, and everyone realizes that no important decisions should be made based on the belly shape (or based on which direction a pendulum swings), then these myths are not really harmful. On the other hand, throughout history, and even in some cultures today, sex prediction in general has been associated with serious issues such as sex-selective abortion.

Folklore methods predate modern technology by several hundred years, and they were widely used at a time when couples were even more desperate to know the sex of their baby. Many cultures throughout history have held preferences for boys for both economic and religious reasons. For example, in many agrarian societies, sons were believed to be more able to engage in the physical work required in the home, and sons have been relied on to care for their parents as they become elderly [11]. Both China and India also have cultural and/or religious beliefs regarding the sacred place of the son, which daughters are not allowed to fulfill [11, 12].

Even in today's Western societies some people tend to prefer sons, especially firstborn sons. For example, Goldfarb [1] asked American college students about their preference for the sex of their hypothetical first- and secondborn child. In this study, 64% preferred their firstborn to be a boy, although this preference was significantly stronger for men. Goldfarb also reviewed research showing that Americans' preference for a firstborn son has been relatively stable for several decades. A 2011 Gallup poll of Americans found similar results. When asked whether they would prefer to have a boy or a girl if they could have only one child, 40% preferred a boy, 28% a girl, and 26% expressed no preference [13]. Nevertheless, similar to the results of Goldfarb [1], men's preference for a son was strong (49% preferring a boy compared with 22% a girl), whereas women were equally split between wanting a boy or a girl. An examination of previous Gallup polls indicates that these recent results are virtually identical to those obtained some 70 years ago [13].

The preference for a boy is particularly troublesome as it relates to abortion due to sex selection. In *Contraception and Abortion from the Ancient World to the Renaissance* [14], John Riddle provides detailed evidence that effective practices to cause an abortion were known and used at least as early as the time of the ancient Egyptians and throughout history. Further evidence of sex-selective abortions comes from the better documented cases of killing female infants after they're born, which has also been practiced in several cultures. In their exhaustive analysis, Coale and Bannister [15] present research findings from several Chinese demographic databases that they contend help explain tens of millions of "missing" Chinese females from the 1930s through the 1980s. From the earliest available data, they believe that 15% of females born in the late 1930s were likely victims of infanticide. In fact, the practice of infanticide with unwanted female infants was likely commonplace [15].

Although infanticide declined during the 1960s, the 1970s and 1980s brought a new trend in China, as parents opted to use birth control after they had achieved their first son during a time when their government was employing sanctions against families with more than one or two children [11, 15]. But it seems that the advent of ultrasound technology, which was available in the 1980s in China, only exacerbated the problem of sex-selective abortions, as the ratio of males to females has become even more lopsided in that country [15]. To further illustrate this problem, researchers estimate that by the year 2020 there will be about 30 million males in China who are not able to find women to marry as a result of the sex-selective abortion and contraception practices that occurred between 1985 and 1995 [16].

China is not the only country to struggle with this issue. Similar problems with higher rates of male births have been found in both South Korea [15] as well as India [12]. The problem in India has become so widespread that in 1994 the Indian government passed the Prenatal Diagnostic Techniques Act, which prevents the use of modern technology, such as ultrasounds, for the mere purpose of sex identification of the fetus due to the fear that this will lead to sex-selective abortion [17].

Clearly, even accurate modern technologies, like the inaccurate sex prediction myths, can be misapplied. Still, more often than not, when sex prediction myths are used in most modern societies, they probably don't cause great harm. The sex of Prince William's baby has less meaning today than it would have had in the past history of England; however, even the sex of that baby was not insignificant to the future of the royal throne.

What you need to know

If the low-tech folklore about predicting the child's sex is not accurate, what is? With regard to this question research is much more certain. That is, ultrasound technology performed in the second or third trimester is very accurate in determining the sex of the fetus. Ultrasound is able to provide conclusive predictions in about 90% of cases, and these predictions were accurate 97% of the time [18]. Another very accurate high-tech method of fetal sex determination is DNA analysis of the mother's plasma [19]. Nevertheless, it should be clear from the statistics that even the high-tech methods get it wrong sometimes; in fact, sex prediction is made even more complicated by the next myth.

References

[1] Goldfarb, C. S. (1988). The folklore of pregnancy. *Psychological Reports*, 62, 891–900.doi:10.2466/pr0.1988.62.3.891.

[2] Lavigne, S. (1992). *Boy or Girl? 50 Fun Ways to Find Out.* New York, NY: Dell Pub.

[3] Perry, D. F., DiPietro, J., & Costigan K. (1999). Are women carrying "basketballs" really having boys? Testing pregnancy folklore. *Birth*, 26, 172–177. doi:10.1046/j.1523-536x.1999.00172.x.

[4] Hupp, S., Stary, A., & Jewell, J. (submitted). Beliefs about myths related to child psychology, development, and parenting: Which myths need the most debunking?

[5] Young, T. (Writer) (February 7, 2011). Hot air balloon cake and happy little bakers. *Cake Boss*. Hoboken, NJ. High Noon Entertainment.

[6] Lauer, M. (2011, April 27). *The Today Show*. New York, NY: NBC.

[7] Landau, E. (2013, July 3). Royal baby slightly more likely to be female, scientist says. Retrieved from http://www.cnn.com [accessed August 2014].

[8] Tamimi, R. M., Lagiou, P., Mucci, L. A., et al. (2003). Average energy intake among pregnant women carrying a boy compared with a girl. *British Medical Journal*, 326(7401), 1245–1246.

[9] Ostler, S. & Sun, A. (1999). Fetal sex determination: The predictive value of 3 common myths. *Journal of Applied Mathematics and Computing*, 161, 1525–1526.

[10] Villamor, E., Dekker, L., Svensson, T., & Cnattingius, S. (2010). Accuracy of the Chinese lunar calendar method to predict a baby's sex: A population-based study. *Pediatric and Perinatal Epidemiology*, 24, 398–400. doi:10.1111/ j.1365-3016.2010.01129.x.

[11] Chan, C. L. W., Blyth, E., & Chan, C. H. Y. (2006). Attitudes to and practices regarding sex selection in China. *Prenatal Diagnosis*, 26, 610–613. doi:10.1002/pd.1477.

[12] Balen, F. V. & Inhorn, M. C. (2003). Son preference, sex selection, and the "new" new reproductive technologies. *International Journal of Health Services, 33*, 235–252. doi:10.2190/PP5X-V039-3QGK-YQJB.

[13] Newport, F. [Survey conducted June 9–12, 2011]. *Americans prefer boys to girls, just as they did in 1941; Men tend to want boys; Women are divided in gender preferences.* Gallup Poll. Retrieved from: http://www.gallup.com/poll/148187/Americans-Prefer-Boys-Girls-1941.aspx [accessed August 2014].

[14] Riddle, J. *Contraception and Abortion from the Ancient World to the Renaissance.* Cambridge, MA: Harvard University Press.

[15] Coale, A. & Banister, J. (1994). Five decades of missing females in China. *Demography, 31*, 459–479. doi:10.2307/2061752.

[16] Hudson, V. M. & Den Boer, A. M. (2004). *Bare Branches: The Security Implications of Asia's Surplus Male Population.* Cambridge, MA: MIT Press.

[17] Nehra, K. S. (2009). *Sex Selection & Abortion: India.* Library of Congress. Retrieved from: http://www.loc.gov/law/help/sex-selection/india.php [accessed July 15, 2013].

[18] Harrington, K., Armstrong, V., Freeman, J., Aquilina, J., & Campbell, S. (1996). Fetal sexing by ultrasound in the second trimester: Maternal preference and professional ability. *Ultrasound Obstetrics and Gynaecology, 8*, 318–321.

[19] Devaney, S. A., Palomaki, G. E., Scott, J. A., & Bianchi, D. W. (2011). Noninvasive fetal sex determination using cell-free fetal DNA: A systematic review and meta-analysis. *Journal of the American Medical Association, 306*(6), 627–636.

Myth #4   All boys have one Y chromosome (and all girls don't)

"Are you having a boy or a girl?" is one of the first questions we ask someone upon finding out they're pregnant. Although some parents choose to learn the baby's sex about mid-way into the pregnancy, other parents would rather be surprised on the actual day of birth. When people wonder about the baby's sex, they're assuming that the baby is either clearly a boy or clearly a girl. Doctors and nurses are usually quick to let the parents see the evidence of the baby's sex for themselves. A quick declaration of sex is then indicated on the birth certificate and used for choosing the correct celebratory cigars, helium balloons, and lawn signs.

New parents are not too concerned about the genes behind the gender, but any child development book informs students that girls have two X chromosomes (i.e., girls are XX), and boys have one Y chromosome and one X chromosome (i.e., boys are XY). One X is provided by the mother's egg, and the father's sperm provides either an X or a Y. These two chromosomes are called the sex chromosomes, and together they're one pair, out of the total 23 pairs, of chromosomes that make humans what we are (the other 22 pairs are called the autosomes).

The sex chromosomes influence several of a person's traits (including many traits unrelated to sex), but one of their primary responsibilities is to help determine if the baby is a boy or a girl. Gonads start off as undifferentiated sex glands, and the sex-determining region of the Y chromosome (SRY) causes the gonads to turn into testes during the embryonic stage. Without the SRY, the gonads become ovaries. Then, during the fetal stage (around the third month) the testes secrete hormones that cause a penis to grow. A vagina forms without these hormones from the testes.

This process is described in every child development textbook, but even before a college student takes a course in human development they already have a sense of the chromosomes behind a baby's sex. In our research, 82% of students and 79% of parents agreed with the statement that "The sex chromosomes of all girls are XX and all boys are XY" [1]. If things were that simple, however, this topic would not be a myth in this book.

The true story is considerably more complicated. Sometimes doctors are not quite sure at first if the baby is a boy or a girl. At first glance, there is only one good place on a baby's body to look for an answer, and some-times that place does not yield a clear verdict. Other times doctors may think they know the child's sex but are wrong. And yet still other times, after all the genetic tests are conducted, the answer still does not easily fit into the two choices of "boy" or "girl," at least not the way that most people understand these two categories. These are all examples of sexual ambiguity, and some research suggests that sexual ambiguity occurs in about up to 1% (or more) of live births [2]. Although this may seem like a small percentage, 1% of the current world population is about 70 million people.

In the book *Between XX and XY: Intersexuality and the Myth of the Two Sexes* [3], the author, Gerald N. Callahan, thoroughly debunks the notion that girls never have a Y chromosome and boys always have one Y chromosome. While it's true that all humans have at least one X chromosome, there are a wide range of possibilities when it comes to their other sex chromosome(s). Some of these possibilities were once referred to as "hermaphroditism," coming from Greek mythology when Hermaphroditus (the male son of Hermes and Aphrodite) became entangled with a female water nymph. This term, however, is now outdated and considered by some to be offensive.

In the 1990s, the term "intersex" was advocated over hermaphroditism, though many people find the term intersex to be misleading because it suggests that there is a third group of people that fall directly between male and female. More recently, a consensus statement emerged from a gathering of international experts which offered the term *Disorders of Sexual Development* (DSDs), and this term has since been widely used by the medical community [4]. The consensus statement also provides a classification system with three categories: (i) sex chromosome DSDs; (ii) 46,XX DSDs; and (iii) 46,XY DSDs.

To their credit, most child development textbooks provide a few examples of the first of these categories (i.e., sex chromosome DSDs). To understand sex chromosome DSDs, it's valuable to know that a typical female's two X chromosomes are depicted as "46,XX," with the "46" representing the fact that most humans have 23 pairs of chromosomes and the "XX" representing the two sex chromosomes specifically. Females with Turner syndrome, however, have one sex chromosome instead of the typical two X chromosomes; thus they're depicted as 45,XO, with the "O" and the "45" both representing the fact that these girls do not have a second sex chromosome. Young girls with Turner syndrome develop much in the same way as any other girl; however, instead of ovaries they have "streak gonads" that do not produce hormones in the way that ovaries would. This becomes most noticeable during puberty when secondary sexual characteristics do not emerge as expected. In a literary depiction of this chromosome DSD, the main character in the novel *The Condition* [5] has Turner syndrome.

In Turner syndrome there is one sex chromosome missing, and by contrast, in Klinefelter's syndrome there is at least one *extra* sex chromosome. When first discovered, Klinefelter's syndrome described males with an extra X chromosome and was depicted as 47,XXY. Since the initial discovery, other variations have been discovered including 48,XXXY and 48,XXYY. In all of these variations, the person has at least one Y chromosome and at least two X chromosomes. Commonly, Klinefelter's syndrome is not noticed until the adult man goes in for fertility testing after failing to have children. Men with Klinefelter's tend to be taller and infertile. In fact, characteristics such as these have led some to speculate that President George Washington may have had Klinefelter's syndrome (see Amory [6] for the debate).

Up to this point, we've started to chip away at beliefs related to sex chromosomes, and you've now seen one condition in which boys can have more than one Y chromosome. But if we left things here you would end your day believing that girls *never* have a Y chromosome. In fact, child development textbooks rarely depict this part of the myth. One way to debunk this myth requires some understanding of the possibility of double fertilization.

Astonishingly, sometimes one egg can have two nuclei. This one egg can then be fertilized by two different sperm. This scenario creates one zygote that has two different sets of genetic material. Thus, some cells in the body (those that make the left eye, for example) have one set of genes, while other cells in the body (those that make the right eye, for example) have a different set of genes. These people have two sets of genetic material in their body. Now here's what you really need to know: in double fertilization, it's possible for one sperm to carry an X chromosome while the other sperm carries a Y chromosome. Thus, some of the person's cells are XX while some of their other cells are XY, and this one person would be depicted as 46,XX/46,XY (with the slash representing the fact that some of their body's cells differ in regards to the sex chromosomes). Other variations of this "mosaicism" might include one person that is 45,XO/46,XX or another person that is 45,XO/47,XXY, to name just a few (rare) possibilities.

A person with this mixed genetic makeup might be a typical looking male or a typical looking female, but there is also a good chance that they could have both male and female characteristics such as one testis and one ovary. Or perhaps they might have two *ovotestes*, which contain both types of tissue. Similarly, they might have a penis in addition to a vagina and breasts. There are many different possible outcomes.

A similar type of sex chromosome DSD can also be created when two fertilized eggs become one. That is, typically when two different eggs are fertilized by two different sperm, the result is fraternal twins (also known as non-identical twins), but sometimes those two fertilized eggs merge together and develop into one person with two different sets of genetic material. Similar to the mosaicism described earlier, it's possible for one of the fertilized eggs to be 46,XX while the other is 46,XY; thus this one person would be depicted as 46,XX/46XY. There are a lot of other possibilities, too. This type of mosaicism is sometimes referred to as chimerism, although the term chimerism (from chimera) has the same drawbacks as the term hermaphroditism in that they both conjure up images of strange mythical creatures.

So far we have only uncovered *one* of the *three* broad categories of DSDs. The second category includes the 46,XX DSDs. In this category, the person has two X chromosomes, and you might expect the individual to appear female. However, sometimes during sperm development one of the X chromosomes can actually have the SRY (sex-determining region of the Y chromosome) even though the person does not have a Y chromosome. If this sperm fertilizes an egg, the result will be a person with a DSD who has two X chromosomes, and one of the X chromosomes will include the SRY. The SRY begins the process of turning this fertilized egg into an XX male (without the Y chromosome).

At this point, you might think that it's just the SRY that determines the sex characteristics of a person. However, in the case of congenital adrenal hyperplasia, the person does not have the SRY as part of the genetic makeup. Congenital adrenal hyperplasia, a type of 46,XX DSD, is the result of a mutation in one gene that, during early fetal development, causes masculinization of the genitalia which can range from an enlarged clitoris to an actual penis, making sex assignment on the birth certificate challenging.

The third category in the classification system includes the 46,XY DSDs. A person in this category has a Y chromosome, so you might expect them to be male; however, sometimes they're clearly female. If during sperm development a sperm carrying the Y chromosome somehow drops the SRY, the person would typically develop as an XY female with underdeveloped ovaries.

In another example of a 46,XY DSD, a person with complete androgen insensitivity syndrome has a gene on the X chromosome that blocks the body's ability to use androgens, and the person develops as a female. In fact, due to the inability to use androgens, as well as the conversion of testosterone into estrogen, such individuals are often very feminine. On the other hand, someone with partial androgen insensitivity syndrome would be a female with a more masculine body (e.g., more muscular). The documentary *Orchids: My Intersex Adventure* [7] describes Phoebe Hart's experience in discovering she has androgen insensitivity syndrome.

The last 46,XY DSD to be discussed here is called 5-alpha reductase deficiency. It's similar to androgen insensitivity syndrome in that the baby is born with the same external appearance of any baby girl. While the girl would have testes, the testes do not descend so they stay in the position where the ovaries would typically be. Also, what looks like a vagina is actually a nonfunctional pouch. Typically, people with this DSD live their entire childhood as girls. Then comes puberty when a new wave of hormones causes (what was once thought to be) the clitoris to grow into a penis. Other changes at puberty include muscle growth and a deeper voice. Put simply, this previously apparent girl becomes a man. The main character in the novel *Middlesex* [8] has 5-alpha reductase deficiency, and this novel won the Pulitzer Prize.

It's worth noting that many aspects of sex development are actually influenced by genes on the autosomes (these are the other 22 pairs of chromosomes). That is to say, the sex chromosomes are not the only chromosome to influence sex development. Thus, there are a lot of other ways sex development can vary in addition to what we could describe in this chapter. We also didn't have the space to discuss how brain development is influenced by hormones. Accordingly, while there is a lot of variation in the genitalia of a person, there is also a lot of variation that occurs in the sex characteristics of the brain.

Believing the Y chromosome myth is a common error in thinking that can be described as an overreliance on representative heuristics (see Lilienfeld, Ammirati, and David [9] for a description of representative heuristics). Heuristics are rules of thumb that usually hold true and help us make sense of the complex world by putting things in categories. Oftentimes this categorization is quite helpful, but we become so accustomed to thinking about things in distinct categories that it's easy to forget that not everything in the world fits into the categories.

Physicians and parents have to make some difficult decisions if the sex of the child is not clear. For example, assigning a sex to the baby (i.e., announcing if the baby is a boy or girl) can be very challenging in some of the cases described. Also, decisions need to be made about performing surgery on the baby's genitalia to look more like a typical male or female. This decision can be difficult, partly because many adults with DSDs indicates that physicians are too quick to recommend irreversible surgeries that have the potential to inhibit sexual function and satisfaction later in life.

One final issue regarding categories of sex involves rules, regulations, and laws. Most sports are divided by sex, but this can cause complications when the person has a DSD. For example, Caster Semenya, South African runner and silver medal winner in the 2012 Olympics, has been surrounded in controversy leading to sex testing. Although the results have not been publicly released, some writers have suggested that she has a DSD complicating her ability to compete as a female, and others have even speculated that she purposefully avoided the gold medal in 2012 in order to escape more controversy [10]. Similarly, governments often require their citizens to be categorized as male or female for record-keeping purposes. In 2013, Germany became the first European country to allow parents to legally choose "undetermined" or "unspecified" on their baby's birth certificate [11]. Thus, while there are still many challenges associated with traditional notions of sex, increased knowledge about this myth can lead to real-world changes in the available choices for parents, their children, and adults with DSDs.

What you need to know

In response to concerns about problems associated with early gender assignment, the *Consensus Statement on Management of Intersex Disorders* [4] provides the follow guidelines:

(1) gender assignment must be avoided before expert evaluation in newborns; (2) evaluation and long-term management must be performed at a center with an experienced multidisciplinary team; (3) all individuals should receive a gender assignment; (4) open communication with patients and families is essential, and participation in decision-making is encouraged; and (5) patient and family concerns should be respected and addressed in strict confidence (p.490).

These guidelines were written with open communication as a central goal. Previously, many physicians didn't explain the DSD to parents, and they even conducted surgery without fully explaining the decision. Similarly, parents often do not explain the DSD to their child or otherwise provide an inadequate explanation. Although some adults may never discover they have a DSD, often DSDs do not get identified until adulthood. Nevertheless, the average age that a doctor is able to identify a DSD is about 6.5 years old, and over 60% of DSDs are identified by a doctor before the child reaches puberty [12]. Parents and their children often report distress about being kept in the dark about the DSD, making open communication a priority.

References

[1] Hupp, S., Stary, A., & Jewell, J. (submitted). Beliefs about myths related to child psychology, development, and parenting: Which myths need the most debunking?

[2] Blackless, M., Charuvastra, A., Derryck, A., et al. (2000). How sexually dimorphic are we? Review and synthesis. *American Journal of Human Biology*, 12, 151–166. doi:10.1002/(SICI)1520–6300(200003/04)12:2<151::AID-AJHB1>3.0.CO;2-F.

[3] Callahan, G. N. (2009). *Between XX and XY: Intersexuality and the Myth of Two Sexes*. Chicago, IL: Chicago Review Pr.

[4] Lee, P. A., Houk, C. P., Ahmed, F., & Hughes, I. A. (2006). Consensus statement on management of intersex disorders. *Pediatrics*, 118, e488–e500. doi:10.1542/peds.2006–0738.

[5] Haigh, J. (2008). *The Condition*. New York, NY: HarperCollins Publishers.

[6] Amory, J. K. (2004). George Washington's infertility: Why was the father of our country never a father? *Fertility & Sterility*, 81, 495–499. doi:10.1016/j.fertnstert.2003.08.035.

[7] Hart, P. (Producer & Director) (2010). *Orchids: My Intersex Adventure* [Documentary]. Worldwide: First Hand Films.

[8] Eugenides, J. (2002). *Middlesex*. New York, NY: Picador USA.

[9] Lilienfeld, S. O., Ammirati, R., & David, M. (2012). Distinguishing science from pseudoscience in school psychology: Science and scientific thinking as safeguards against human error. *Journal of School Psychology*, 50, 7–36. doi:10.1016/j.jsp.2011.09.006.

[10] Thomas, J. (2012, August 11). Did Caster Semenya lose the women's 800 meters on purpose? [Web log post]. Retrieved from http://www.slate.com/blogs/five_ring_circus/2012/08/11/caster_semenya_2012_olympics_did_the_south_african_runner_lose_the_women_s_800_meters_on_purpose_.html [accessed August 2014].

[11] James, S. D. (2013, August 22). Is baby male or female? Germans offer third gender. *ABC News*. Retrieved from http://www.abcnews.go.com [accessed August 2014].

[12] Erdoğan, S., Kara, C., Uçaktürk, A., & Aydin, M. (2011). Etiological classification and clinical assessment of children and adolescents with disorders of sex development. *Journal of Clinical Research in Pediatric Endocrinology*, 3, 77–83. doi:10.4274/jcrpe.v3i2.16.

Myth #5   The attachment parenting approach strengthens the mother–infant bond

You may not have heard of "attachment parenting" per se, but most parents have been exposed to it in some way. For example, *The Baby Book* [1] written by Dr. William Sears and his co-authors (who happen to be family members) introduces attachment parenting, and in the foreword *The Baby Book* proclaims that it "has been dubbed the 'baby bible' by millions of parents" (p. xiii). This seems to be a fair description, as it's one of the best-selling books for parents of all time, with considerably over one million copies sold. Attachment parenting has also been championed by celebrities such as actress Mayim Bialik (known for sitcoms like *Blossom* and *The Big Bang Theory*) who wrote a book about her experience with attachment parenting [2]. In the book's introduction, Dr. Jay Gordan indicates that Bialik's attachment parenting style "will show you how to excel at parenting" (p. ix).

Dr. Sears and his co-authors claim that attachment parenting is "the best way to achieve the proper fit between parents and child" (p. 3). Attachment parenting is a broad approach with several notable components that make it stand out. In particular, a few of the major ideas promoted by attachment parenting include the importance of immediate birth-bonding, extended breastfeeding, and bed-sharing. Because this is such a big topic, we're going to break the discussion of each of these components into subsections, meaning that you're going to get three myths here for the price of only one (that's two free myths!).

Importance of immediately bonding within the first two hours after birth

The attachment parenting emphasis on immediate birth-bonding [1] has origins in the work of zoologist Konrad Lorenz, who is well-known for his research on imprinting in geese. During imprinting, newborn chicks begin to follow the first moving object they see, and this is usually their mother. However, Lorenz was the first moving object that some chicks saw, and they followed him around instead. Lorenz also studied the time period within which imprinting could occur and discovered that chicks only imprinted within the first day or so of hatching. That is, they failed to imprint if they didn't see a "mother" within that critical period. Given this discovery, other researchers began looking for similar critical periods in humans.

Klaus and Kennell [3] believed that they found something like a critical period in human newborns, although they favored the term "sensitive period." Klaus and Kennell suggested "there is strong evidence that at least 30 to 60 minutes of early contact in privacy should be provided for every parent and infant to enhance the bonding experience" (p. 56). Kennell [4] even went so far as to suggest failure to bond immediately after birth would ultimately lead to child abuse or other "mothering disorders"(p. 294). The authors based their theory on preliminary research they conducted, although their study had serious methodological flaws, including a very small sample size [5, 6].

Soon after Klaus and Kennell published their original research, other research failed to find any benefit to attachment following from immediate birth-bonding [7, 8]. For example, Svejda et al. [8] compared mothers that received extra early contact with a control group of mothers without extra early contact and found no differences in any of 28 attachment behaviors between groups. Despite weak evidence, the idea contained in this myth appears to be widely held. We found that 83% of students and 82% of parents agreed with the statement that "Within about one hour after birth, babies need to bond with their mothers so that attachment is stronger over time" [9].

Goldberg [10] penned an excellent summary and critique of the impact of Klaus and Kennell's work by suggesting that many hospitals changed their practices as a result of their findings, and we do agree that this was a good change. Previously, childbirth was viewed as the end of an illness, and due partly to Klaus and Kennell's work childbirth came to be recognized as a healthy, rewarding experience. However, Goldberg adds that "the popularization of the ideas and work behind these changes has often led to the distorted view that the first hours after birth are critical for the establishment of parent-infant bonding ..." (p. 1379) and that bonding is impaired if parents are not able to have immediate contact with their newborns.

While Sears et al. [1] acknowledge that "Catch-up bonding is certainly possible" (p. 44), they also "believe that bonding during this biologically sensitive period does give the parent-infant relationship a head start" (p. 44). Furthermore, Sears et al. also suggest that "The way baby and parents get started with one another often sets the tone of how this early attachment unfolds" (p. 5). Although early contact seems like a reasonable goal, parents should not be made to feel distraught about the future of their relationship with their child if they need to be separated from their babies in the hours after birth, which may be necessary for medical and other reasons.

Value of extended breastfeeding for up to seven years

Evidence suggests that breastfeeding is good for babies and should be encouraged whenever possible. The American Academy of Pediatrics [11] recommends exclusive breastfeeding for the first six months of life and continued breastfeeding for at least a year because of several associated benefits. The World Health Organization [12], which also considers babies in third world countries, recommends breastfeeding for two years or more. Nevertheless, attachment parenting often goes well beyond that time period with the notion of child-led weaning.

Child-led weaning can result in weaning that lasts many years. For example, Sears et al. [1] suggest that some children have the need to suckle for up to three-and-a-half years. In another book about attachment parenting, Granju and Kennedy [13] suggest that breastfeeding should continue for a minimum of two-and-a-half years, but they also suggest that it would be natural to let it go on up to *seven* years based on the weaning practices of children in other cultures as well as the weaning practices of other primates [14]. Recently, the May 2012 *Time* magazine cover stirred up controversy with a picture of a mom breastfeeding her 3-year-old son.

Actress Mayim Bialik breastfed her son for about four years, and she reportedly used breastfeeding as a way to calm down tantrums [15]. Another attachment parenting celebrity advocate, singer-songwriter Alanis Morissette, told ABC News that she was prepared to breastfeed for up to six years [16]. These celebrity examples may represent attachment parenting taken to the extreme; however, it's easy to see how mothers are afraid of ending breastfeeding too early when Sears et al. [1] suggest that "securely attached babies (those who are not weaned before their time) eventually grow to be more independent, separate more easily from their mothers, move into new relationships with more security, and are, in fact, easier to discipline" (p. 203). Moreover, they warn that ending breastfeeding too early can increase "the risks of what we call *diseases of premature weaning*: anger, aggression, habitual tantrumlike behavior, anxious attachment to caregivers, and less ability to form deeper and more intimate relationships" (p. 206).

The advice of William Sears has apparently been quite influential. We found that 39% of students and 52% of parents agree with the statement that "Breastfeeding a baby for more than two years helps strengthen the attachment between the mother and child" [9].

It's worth noting that there are no documented harms in breastfeeding for several years, and Dr. Sears has likely done some good in the world by promoting breastfeeding in general. Nevertheless, he has also possibly done some harm by making exaggerated statements that go well beyond research findings and beyond timelines developed by professional organizations [11]. Research supports the notion that breastfeeding for a year or so is good for the baby [17]; however, there is no research to suggest there is any harm in ending the breastfeeding when the child is around 1 year old. In fact, most babies that are never breastfed likely still have a healthy attachment style.

Encouragement of nightly bed-sharing between babies and parents

Attachment parenting encourages bed-sharing with the baby sleeping between the mother and an added guardrail. One attachment parenting expert [13] discourages crib use altogether by referring to a crib as an "expensive, space-wasting 'babycage'"(p. 36). On her video blog, Reality TV star Kourtney Kardashian [18] posted her tips for how to bed-share safely. Bed-sharing is actually fairly common, with about 45% of infants sleeping at least part of the night in the adult bed. But the rate of parents who have their infants routinely sleep in their bed is quite a bit lower at about 13% [19]. In our research, 63% of students and 62% of parents agreed with the statement that "Having a baby sleep in the mother's bed promotes the baby's secure attachment" [9].

Bed-sharing, however, contradicts recommendations of the American Academy of Pediatrics [20]. In addition to there being no research that bed-sharing is important for parent–child attachment, there is also evidence that bed-sharing is a risk factor for sudden unexpected infant deaths such as Sudden Infant Death Syndrome (SIDS) [21, 22]. The American Academy of Pediatrics, report has several recommendations to prevent sudden unexpected infant deaths, with the most prominent being to have infants sleep on their back. Another important recommendation, however, is to have infants sleep in a crib (including a safe portable crib) in the same room as parents but not the same bed (i.e., room-sharing but not bed-sharing). The report cites research indicative of the suffocation dangers associated with bed-sharing, and it specifically warns against bed railings (as suggested by Sears et al. [1]) and devices on the market that purport to make bed-sharing safe (as suggested by Kardashian [18]).

The report acknowledges there is no research on additional sleepers (i.e., cribs) that attach to the side of the adult bed but suggests that even these side sleepers pose potential risks if improperly secured to the bed. Overall, the greatest risks associated with bed-sharing include entrapment, suffocation from bedding, and suffocation from an adult's body. Furthermore, alcohol or other drug use substantially increases the risk for accidental suffocation during bed-sharing because parents become less sensitive to their surroundings.

Although attachment parenting leaves room for parents to choose other sleep strategies, the promotion of bed-sharing is risky. It's unfortunate that Sudden Infant Death Syndrome has the nickname "crib death" because that nickname may give parents the false sense that cribs are more dangerous than the parental bed. Proponents of attachment parenting often suggest that bed-sharing has been around as long as the human species [1], and that cribs are a relatively new development. In fact, this is all true; however, it's also true that infant mortality rates (i.e., rates of infants that die in the first year of life) have been on a steady decline, partially due to safer sleeping practices.

It's worth mentioning that the report for the American Academy of Pediatrics [20] also cites research suggesting that bed-sharing can be supportive of breastfeeding; however, the risks outweigh this potential benefit. A safer option for mothers is to bring the infant into the bed for feeding and then put the baby back in the crib for sleep.

Attachment parenting in general

Despite the problems associated with these major components of attachment parenting, we found that 88% of students and 83% of parents agreed with the statement that "The Attachment Parenting approach strengthens the mother–infant bond" [9]. Sears et al. [1] give attachment parenting the hard sell by saying "In our experience of caring for families over the past forty years in pediatric practice and in our review of scientific studies, we have found that attachment-parented children are likely to be: smarter, healthier, more sensitive, more empathetic, easier to discipline, more bonded to people than to things" (p. 17 in a list form of a box), and they also list 26 other specific benefits that they claim are associated with attachment parenting (p. 14). Furthermore, they add that because of *The Baby Book* [1] "many children and parents are happier, healthier, and more connected" (p. xiii). Unfortunately, they do not cite any of the research that they supposedly reviewed to support most of these claims, they have not conducted their own research regarding these claims, and there is no research comparing attachment parenting with other parenting styles.

Attachment parenting has become popular due to many fallacies. One of the "Sources of Psychological Myths" is the exaggerated kernel of truth. That is, each of the above components has some kernel of truth in the sense that they're all aimed at promoting breastfeeding, and breastfeeding is a great option whenever possible. Moreover, the argument that something works because it has been used for a long time is called the appeal to tradition fallacy. Another fallacy at work here is the appeal to authority fallacy. William Sears has an M.D. and has sold millions of books. Similarly, Mayim Bialik has a Ph.D. in neuroscience. Having a doctoral degree does not mean you are automatically correct about everything you say. (However, if you are prone to be influenced by the appeal to authority fallacy, we'd like to take this moment to point out that both authors of this book also have doctoral degrees.)

In this chapter we have taken a critical look at three of the core aspects of attachment parenting. Another major aspect is immediately responding to the baby's cries during bedtime. Although most parents respond to most baby cries, there are times when parents should feel okay about letting a baby cry, even though this would be contrary to attachment parenting. In particular, Sears et al. [1] suggest that parents should "beware of sleep trainers" (p. 328) and that they should avoid the "cry-it-out" method. In fact, we have decided to dedicate Myth 13 to the belief that letting babies cry it out is harmful to their development.

What you need to know

Parents can find useful information regarding infants in the book *What to Expect in the First Year* [23], which provides a balanced approach to making decisions about breastfeeding, sleeping arrangements, and many other topics related to babies. While *The Baby Book* [1] pushes the attachment parenting approach, *What to Expect in the First Year* describes pros and cons associated with different and often challenging decisions that parents make in the first year.

References

[1] Sears, W., Sears, M., Sears, R., & Sears, J. M. (2013). *The Baby Book: Everything you Need to Know About Your Baby From Birth to Age Two*. New York, NY: Little, Brown, and Company.

[2] Bialik, M. (2012). *Beyond the Sling: A Real-Life Guide to Raising Confident, Loving Children the Attachment Parenting Way*. New York, NY: Simon & Schuster.

[3] Klaus, M. H. & Kennell, J. H. (1982). *Parent-Infant Bonding*. St. Louis, MO: Mosby.

[4] Lampe, J., Trause, M. A., & Kennell, J. (1977). Parental visiting of sick infants: The effect of living at home prior to hospitalization. *Pediatrics*, 59, 294–296.

[5] Klaus, M. H., Jerauld, R., Kreger, N. C., et al. (1972). Maternal attachment. Importance of the first post-partum days. *New England Journal of Medicine*, 286, 460–463. doi:10.1056/NEJM197203022860904.

[6] Ringler, N., Trause, M. A., Klaus, M., & Kennell, J. (1978). The effects of extra postpartum contact and maternal speech patterns on children's IQs, speech, and language comprehension at five. *Child Development*, 49, 862–865. doi: 10.2307/1128257.

[7] Rode, S. S., Chang, P. N., Fisch, R. O., & Sroufe, L. A. (1981). Attachment patterns of infants separated at birth. *Developmental Psychology*, 17, 188–191. doi:10.1037/0012-1649.17.2.188.

[8] Svejda, M. J., Campos, J. J., & Emde, R. N. (1980). Mother-infant "bonding": Failure to generalize. *Child Development*, 51, 775–779. doi:10.2307/1129464.

[9] Hupp, S., Stary, A., & Jewell, J. (submitted). Beliefs about myths related to child psychology, development, and parenting: Which myths need the most debunking?

[10] Goldberg, S. (1983). Parent-infant bonding: Another look. *Child Development*, 54, 1355–1382. doi:10.2307/1129800.

[11] Eidelman, A. I., Schanler, R. J., Johnston, M., et al. (2012). Breastfeeding and the use of human milk. *Pediatrics*, 129, e827–e841. doi:10.1542/peds.2011-3552.

[12] World Health Organization (n.d.). *Breastfeeding*. Retrieved from http://www.who.int/topics/breastfeeding/en/ [accessed August 2014].

[13] Granju, K. A. & Kennedy, B. (1999). *Attachment Parenting: Instinctive Care for your Baby and Young Child*. New York, NY: Pocket Books.

[14] Dettwyler, K. A. (1995). A time to wean: The hominid blueprint for the natural age of weaning in modern human populations. In P. Stuart-Macadam & K. A. Dettwyler (Eds), *Breastfeeding: Biocultural Perspectives*. Hawthorne, NY: Aldine de Gruyter.

[15] Malveaux, S. (2012, May 11). Mayin Bialik: I breast-feed my three year-old because he's not through breast-feeding. *CNN News*. Retrieved from http://cnnpressroom.blogs.cnn.com/2012/05/11/mayim-bialik-i-breast-feed-my-three-year-old-because-hes-not-through-breast-feeding/ [accessed August 2013].

[16] Dolak, K. (2012, May 31). Alanis Morissette, now a mother, dives into 'attachment parenting' and breastfeeding controversy. *ABC News*. Retrieved from http://abcnews.go.com/ [accessed August 2013].

[17] Chung, M., Raman, G., Chew, P., et al. (2007). Breastfeeding and maternal and infant health outcomes in developed countries. *Evidence Report and Technology Assessment (Full Report)*, 153, 1–186.

[18] Kardashian, K. (2012, September 2). Kourtney's mommy blog: Sleeping tips. Retrieved from http://www.youtube.com/watch?v=7MLUoJ4QPY0.

[19] Willinger, M., Ko, C. W., Hoffman, H. J., et al. (2003). Trends in infant bed sharing in the United States, 1993–2000: The National Infant Sleep Position Study. *Archives of Pediatrics & Adolescent Medicine*, 157, 43–49. doi:10.1001/archpedi.157.1.43.

[20] Moon, R. Y. (2011). SIDS and other sleep-related infant deaths: Expansion of recommendations for a safe infant sleeping environment. *Pediatrics*, 128, e1341–e1367. doi:10.1542/peds.2011-2285.

[21] Carpenter, R. G., Irgens, L. M., Blair, P. S., et al. (2004). Sudden unexplained infant death in 20 regions in Europe: Case control study. *The Lancet*, 363, 185–191. doi:10.1016/S0140-6736(03)15323-8.

[22] Tappin, D., Ecob, R., & Brooke, H. (2005). Bedsharing, roomsharing, and sudden infant death syndrome in Scotland: A case-control study. *Journal of Pediatrics*, 147, 32–37. doi:10.1016/j.jpeds.2005.01.035.

[23] Murkoff, H. E. & Mazel, S. (2010). *What to Expect the First Year*. New York, NY: Workman Publishing.

Speed busting for beginnings

Myth #6

Identical twins have identical genes

Do you remember in the Introduction when we said that we believed a lot of these myths until recently? Well, this myth might be the most recent one to be debunked for us, and it's a good example of how science continues to change the way we think about child development. Just about every child development textbook teaches that *fraternal twins* occur when two different sperm fertilize two different eggs, creating two different siblings with two different sets of genes. Alternatively, *identical twins* occur when one sperm fertilizes one egg, and then that zygote completely divides into two separate zygotes with identical genes. It turns out that the term "identical" is being used a little too loosely because research shows that identical twins commonly have very slight differences in their genetic make-up [1].

There are actually several different causes of variability in the genes of identical twins, and we'll focus on one of the most recent discoveries. After the original zygote divides into two different "identical" zygotes, those zygotes grow by making copies of themselves (and the DNA that they contain). By the end of the first week, each of the zygotes has over 100 cells (each containing the same DNA). Now, imagine making one photocopy of a sheet of paper; you now have two sheets of identical paper. Then, copy each of those papers one time so you have four sheets, and keep copying each sheet until you have over 100 sheets. Would all of the sheets be identical? Yes, pretty much, but there might be very slight differences between the sheets due to a speck of dust on the copy machine or due to the position of the paper when it was copied. This metaphor is designed to help make two points. First, due to "copy-number variations" (CNVs) any two cells in your own body can contain slightly different genetic information. Secondly, and because of this, many identical twins really don't have identical DNA. Do any twins have 100% identical DNA? It seems plausible, but the important point here is to recognize that a lot of identical twins really don't have identical DNA. We suggest that from now on, these monozygotic siblings should be referred to as *very-nearly identical twins*.

Myth #7 A woman who is already pregnant can't get pregnant again

Most of us assume that once a woman is pregnant she can't get pregnant a second time until after she has the first baby. Indeed, pregnancy does cause changes to a woman's body that make this assumption true most of the time. However, there are a few documented cases of what is called *superfetation*, defined as [2] "the fertilization and implantation of a second ovum sometime after the start of a pregnancy, resulting in two fetuses of different gestations" (p. 219). In one such case, the two fetuses (one male and one female) were about four weeks apart in their conception but were born on the same day as part of an "uneventful" delivery (p. 220).

Myth #8 The Chinese lunar calendar accurately predicts the sex of a baby

The Chinese lunar calendar is often used to predict the sex of a baby based on the mother's birthdate and the date of conception. It's one of the few sex prediction methods that can be used on the day of the conception! Some skeptical researchers [3] discuss the lunar calendar and point out a website that says this method is up to 93% effective, and they also indicate that part of the allure of the lunar calendar is that it was lost in a tomb for centuries. In what must be the largest study in our entire book, these same researchers analyzed data from almost three million births in Sweden and found that the method was no more accurate than flipping a coin.

Myth #9 — Female fetuses have faster heart rates than male fetuses

According to Perry et al. [4] many medical professionals believe that female fetuses have faster heart rates than male fetuses. They also suggest that "this assumption is probably based on the fact that boys are slightly larger, and larger individuals tend to have slower heart rates ..." (p. 173). Research has demonstrated, however, that there is not a significant difference in the heart rates of female as compared with male fetuses [5]. This same study also demonstrated that there is no difference in how variable the heart rates are for the different sexes. So, like the lunar calendar, fetal heart rate cannot be used to accurately predict the baby's sex.

Myth #10 — Epidurals create a high risk of harm during delivery

In the movie *Baby Mama* [6], a medical professional asks the pregnant women in her class the following questions: "How many of you are planning on doing natural childbirth? ... And how many of you are planning on using toxic, western medications to drug your baby?" In answering the questions, everyone in the class is planning to do natural childbirth, except for the woman (played by Amy Poehler) who has already demonstrated a pattern of selfish behavior in the movie. Similarly, in the movie *What to Expect When You're Expecting* [7], one of the mothers-to-be is asked if she is going to get an epidural, and her response is, "Do I look like somebody who wants to drug my baby?" Statements like these reflect the worries of a lot of future parents. Family doctor Harriet Hall [8] suggests that "The natural childbirth movement seems to view childbirth as an extreme sport or a rite of passage that is empowering and somehow enhances women's worth. Women who 'fail' and require pain relief or C-section are often looked down upon and made to feel guilty or at least somehow less worthy" (para. 4). However, research shows that women shouldn't feel guilty about using an epidural. A recent review of 38 studies involving nearly 10,000 women found that epidurals were *not* associated with negative outcomes such as lower scores of newborn health using the Apgar scale [9]. Although epidurals can be associated with some negative side effects (e.g., fever in the mother), the risk of complications is very low. Hall [8] points out that even Novocain has some risks "but can you imagine a dentist telling a male patient to 'man up' and have a root canal procedure without any anesthetic? Because it will be safer? Because embracing the pain will be empowering?" (para. 11). Based on logic like this, we believe this should be a personal choice for every woman, but we have to admit that we'd go straight for the epidural the moment we stepped in the hospital.

Myth #11

More babies are born during a full moon

According to the subtitle of a story in one popular news source "Experts say moon has gravitational pull on embryonic fluid around baby" [10]. Supposedly, the same forces that create a high tide cause a pregnant woman's waters to break. A study involving over 500,000 births, however, reported that there was no relation between the moon's cycle and births [11]. The study also debunked the related belief that moon cycles influence birthing complications. Lilienfeld et al. [12] also debunk the similar myth that full moons cause an increase in crimes and emergency room visits. This phenomenon is also called "The Lunar Effect," and terms such as "lunatic" and "looney" are derived from the Latin term for moon (i.e., *luna*). Lilienfeld and colleagues point out that the myths tied to The Lunar Effect persist due to selective perception and memory. For example, medical professionals might notice there was a full moon on a night when they delivered a large amount of babies. They easily remember the connection between the full moon and the high rate of births. However, they may be less likely to take notice of a night when there was a high number of births despite there being only a crescent moon. In addition to being an example of selective perception, this myth also provides an excellent example of an *illusory correlation* in which a person believes one event is connected to another event even though they are actually unrelated to each other [13].

Myth #12

Pre-chewing a baby's food has no known risks

The practice of pre-chewing a baby's food has been around for thousands of years. This appeal to tradition was part of actress Alicia Silverstone's reasoning for pre-chewing her 11-month-old son's food in a viral video posted on her website [14]. Pre-chewing food (also called "kiss feeding" or "premastication") is often described as being a part of weaning. Silverstone indicated that her son "literally crawls across the room to attack my mouth if I'm eating" (para. 1). Though this practice may be harmless at times, it also may be a method of disease transmission [15] and transfer of bacteria that can cause cavities [16] from mother to baby.

References

[1] Bruder, C. E., Piotrowski, A., Gijsbers, A. A., et al. (2008). Phenotypically concordant and discordant monozygotic twins display different DNA copy-number-variation profiles. *American Journal of Human Genetics*, 82(3), 763–771.

[2] Tuppen, G. D., Fairs, C., De Chazal, R. C., & Konje, J. C. (1999). Spontaneous superfetation diagnosed in the first trimester with successful outcome. *Ultrasound in Obstetrics & Gynecology*, 14, 219–221. doi:10.1046/j.1469-0705.1999. 14030219.x.

[3] Villamor, E., Dekker, L., Svensson, T., & Cnattingius, S. (2010). Accuracy of the Chinese lunar calendar method to predict a baby's sex: A population-based study. *Paediatric and Perinatal Epidemiology*, 24, 398–400. doi:10.1111/j.1365-3016. 2010.01129.x.

[4] Perry, D. F., DiPietro, J., & Costigan, K. (1999). Are women carrying "basketballs" really having boys? Testing pregnancy folklore. *Birth*, 26, 172–177. doi:10.1046/j. 1523 –536x.1999.00172.x.

[5] Ogueh, O. & Steer, P. (1998). Gender does not affect fetal heart rate variation. *BJOG: An International Journal of Obstetrics & Gynaecology*, 105, 1312–1314. doi:10.1111/j.1471–0528.1998.tb10011.x.

[6] Michaels, L., Goldwyn, J. (Producers), & McCullers, M. (Director) (2008). *Baby Mama* [Motion picture]. United States: Relativity Media.

[7] Medavoy, M., Messer, A., Thwaites, D. (Producers), & Jones, K. (Director) (2012). *What to Expect When You're Expecting* [Motion picture]. United States: Alcon Entertainment.

[8] Hall, H. (2011, February 15). Childbirth without pain: Are epidurals the answer? Retrieved from http://www.sciencebasedmedicine.org/childbirth-without-pain-are-epidurals-the-answer/ [accessed August 2014].

[9] Anim-Somuah, M., Smyth, R. M., & Jones, L. (2011). Epidural versus non-epidural or no analgesia in labour. *Cochrane Database Syst Rev*, 12. doi:10.1002/14651858. CD000331.pub3.

[10] Daily Mail Reporter (2013, July 22). So did the full moon send Kate into labour? Old wives tale proven in the timing of Royal baby delivery. Retrieved from http://www.dailymail.co.uk/news/article-2374345/Royal-babys-birth-Did-moon-send-Kate-Middleton-labour.html [accessed August 2014].

[11] Arliss, J. M., Kaplan, E. N., & Galvin, S. L. (2005). The effect of the lunar cycle on frequency of births and birth complications. *American Journal of Obstetrics and Gynecology*, 192(5), 1462–1464. doi:10.1016/j.ajog.2004.12.034.

[12] Lilienfeld, S. O., Lynn, S. J., Ruscio, J., & Beyerstein, B. L. (2010). *50 Great Myths of Popular Psychology: Shattering Widespread Misconceptions about Human Behavior*. Malden, MA: Wiley-Blackwell.

[13] Chapman, L. J. & Chapman, J. P. (1967). Genesis of popular but erroneous psycho-diagnostic observations. *Journal of Abnormal Psychology*, 72, 193–204.

[14] Silverstone, A. (2012, March 23). Home video: Breakfast with baby bear. Retrieved from http://thekindlife.com/blog/2012/03/home-video-breakfast-with-baby-bear/ [accessed August 2014].

[15] Gaur, A. H., Dominguez, K. L., Kalish, M. L., et al. (2009). Practice of feeding premasticated food to infants: A potential risk factor for HIV transmission. *Pediatrics*, 124, 658–666. doi:10.1542/peds.2008-3614.

[16] Douglass, J. M., Li, Y., & Tinanoff, N. (2008). Association of Mutans streptococci between caregivers and their children. *Pediatric Dentistry*, 30, 375–387. doi:10.1111/j. 1752–7325.2007.00050.x.

2 GROWTH, BODY, & MIND

Great Myths of Child Development, First Edition. Stephen Hupp and Jeremy Jewell.
© 2015 John Wiley & Sons, Inc. Published 2015 by John Wiley & Sons, Inc.

Myth #13

Letting babies "cry it out" during bedtime is harmful to their development

One of the first questions that family and friends ask about a new baby is, "Has she started sleeping through the night?" For many new parents it can be a long time before the answer to this question is "yes." A recent study of over 5000 parents showed that about 25% described their child's sleep as a problem [1]. This parental frustration is also (perhaps crudely) represented by Samuel L. Jackson's narration in the audio version of the provocatively named book *Go the F**k to Sleep* [2]. Pediatric sleep disturbance is associated with child behavior problems [3] and familial stress [4], often leading to pharmaceutical interventions designed to help with sleep [5]. The most commonly reported sleep problems in early childhood revolve around bedtime resistance and night wakings [6].

Letting babies and toddlers "cry it out" is a recommendation that has been around for over a century. In his 1894 book, *The Care and Feeding of Children* [7], the pediatrician Dr. L. Emmett Holt recommends letting babies "cry it out" if they're crying to be indulged (e.g., held or rocked). In the 1910 fifth edition of his book [8], Holt expands on this recommendation by saying that in response to night cries:

> One should get up and see that the child is comfortable – the clothing smooth under the body, the hands and feet warm, and the napkin not wet or soiled. If all of these matters are properly adjusted and the child is simply crying to be taken up, it should not be further interfered with ... It should simply be allowed to "cry it out". (pp. 161–162)

In this age-old approach (also called "extinction" or "systematic ignoring" by behavioral psychologists) parents are encouraged to place their little one in their crib while still awake, avoid rocking them to sleep, make sure they're safe, and then leave the bedroom until morning. Holt [8] warns that crying during the first night could last an hour or more but that over the subsequent nights the crying will be eliminated most of the time.

A variation of the cry-it-out approach was later popularized by Richard Ferber's book *Solve Your Child's Sleep Problems* [9]. This more gradual approach involves checking in briefly (1 or 2 minutes at a time) on the infant or toddler during predetermined time intervals. For example, this approach often starts with 5-minute intervals and works up to 15-minute intervals. Parents still avoid holding or rocking the child, and parents leave the room while the child is still awake. This graduated cry-it-out approach (also called "graduated extinction" or "progressive-waiting") became known as the Ferber method. Ferber himself discouraged parents from using Holt's original cry-it-out approach, which he referred to as the "cold turkey routine" because of how hard it can be on the parents to listen to their child cry without checking in on them.

Nevertheless, other parenting book writers have been critical of any cry-it-out approach. For example, in the book *The No-Cry Sleep Solution* [10], Elizabeth Pantley attacks the cry-it-out approach after failing to use it with her own child. She writes, "this was a simplistic and harsh way to treat another human being, let alone the precious little love of my life. To allow a baby to suffer through pain and fear until she resigns herself to sleep is heartless and, for me, unthinkable" (p. 5). Pantley even suggests that the cry-it-out approach will lead to life-long damage in the parent–child relationship.

William Sears and his co-authors are some of the most influential critics of the cry-it-out approach. In their book, *The Baby Sleep Book* [11], they suggest that the cry-it-out approach is "biologically and developmentally wrong" (p. 60); "can sabotage your parent-child relationship" (p. 70); may make your child "more likely to have Attention Deficit Hyperactivity Disorder, along with poor school performance and antisocial behavior" (p. 211); and may result in a "violent, impulsive, emotionally unattached child" (p. 212). Sears et al. cite several research studies that lead them to make these claims (which we will critique later). The cry-it-out controversy has also made its way into pop culture. For example, Sears et al. [11] describe a scene from the sitcom *Mad About You* in which:

> Jamie and Paul put their little one through the cry-it-out experience. The program showed every excruciating detail of the new parents' anguish as they sat outside baby's door and resisted the urge to go in and pick baby up. Predictably, just as mom was about to rush in, baby stopped crying and fell asleep. It worked! There was a big sigh of relief across the nation, but not for the TV mom. Jamie looked stricken as she said, "I'm afraid we've broken her little heart." (p. 208)

More recently, in the first season of the sitcom *Modern Family* [12], Cam and Mitchell had a difficult time trying to use the cry-it-out approach with their daughter, Lily. After calling the cry-it-out approach "torture" for Lily, Cam says that the approach is "hard if you happen to be a person who hates to hear another person suffer." Cam later says to Mitchell that there is "something wrong with you that the sound of our child in such distress doesn't bother you more." Even celebrity parents have been critical of the cry-it-out approach. Actress Salma Hayek shared on the *Rachel*

Ray Show that, based on the best advice she ever received from her own mother, she would never let her daughter cry it out even though it sometimes takes hours to put her to sleep, and Rachel Ray responded by saying "I like that a lot better than leaving a baby crying" [13].

Parents frequently receive conflicting advice from the experts. A recent review of self-help books for parents about childhood sleep problems indicates that 61% of these books endorse the cry-it-out approach as a useful technique for some families, whereas 31% of these books oppose it [14]. The remaining 8% didn't take a stance. Perhaps due to conflicting reports from self-help book writers, the public is also divided. An online poll asked the question "Would you – or do you – let your baby 'cry it out'" [15]. Of the 171,000+ votes cast, 41% responded "yes" and 59% responded "no." Also, in *The Baby Sleep Book* [11], Sears et al. report that 95% of the "several hundred" parents they surveyed in their practice indicated that "cry-it-out advice didn't feel right to them" (p. 206). Although both the online poll and the Sears family practice statistics could be criticized on a number of methodological grounds (i.e., they aren't well-controlled studies), our own research shows that 26% of students and 43% of parents agreed that "Letting 1-year-olds 'cry it out' at bedtime hurts their emotional development" [16].

Indeed, the risk of damage to emotional development is exactly the message that self-help book writers such as Pantley and Sears are sending. Before we examine whether the cry-it-out approach is damaging to a baby's emotional health, it's worth discussing whether the approach is effective at decreasing sleep disturbance. After all, if it doesn't work, then no one should be using it in the first place.

Researchers have examined both major variations of the cry-it-out approach. Several randomized controlled trials of the original cry-it-out approach (i.e., extinction) show that it's effective at decreasing pediatric sleep disturbance with infants, toddlers, and preschoolers (e.g., Rickert and Johnson [17]). The efficacy of the graduated cry-it-out approach is also supported by randomized controlled trials (e.g., Hiscock and Wake [18]). Using the American Psychology Association's Task Force's criteria (i.e., see Silverman and Hinshaw [19]), both variations of the cry-it-out approach meet the criteria for "well-established" evidence-based interventions [20]. Additionally, there is a growing research literature that indicates the cry-it-out approach can also work if the parent stays in the child's bedroom (but not the child's bed) while ignoring crying, and this variation (sometimes called "camping out") may be a little easier on the parents [21, 22]. Each night the parent moves closer and closer to the hallway until they're eventually out of the bedroom altogether.

What is the alternative to using one of the variations of the cry-it-out approach? Because Pantley and Sears are strongly opposed to the cry-it-out approach, they instead recommend immediately responding to cries from infants and pleas from toddlers [10, 11]. Thus, in the immediate-responding approach parents often rock babies to sleep, sleep in the same bed, or otherwise help their children fall asleep. Yet there are no well-designed studies that find the immediate-responding approach improves pediatric sleep disturbance [23].

To the contrary, the immediate-responding approach has the potential to prolong sleep disturbance and create a negative sleep association that makes matters worse. More specifically, if a baby is rocked to sleep in his parent's arms and then placed in his crib, this can become a negative sleep association because when he wakes up in the night, he is no longer being rocked in his parent's arms. He then may have a hard time falling back asleep and will cry out until rocked again.

What about the claims by Sears et al. [11] that the cry-it-out approach leads to emotional damage and more? We don't have the space to critique all of the studies listed in their book, but it would be informative to critique one as representative of them. For example, Sears et al. state, "researchers at Pennsylvania State and Arizona State universities found that infants with excessive crying during the early months showed more difficulty controlling their emotions and became even fussier when their parents tried to console them at ten months" (p. 212). The primary finding in the correlational study to which they refer [24] showed that babies who cried a lot (in general and not necessarily in the crib) at 6 weeks old were more likely to have a negative reaction to a frustrating stimulus in the laboratory when they were 10 months old. The study had absolutely nothing to do with the cry-it-out approach or even sleep for that matter, and yet Sears et al. [11] used it to suggest the cry-it-out approach leads to "difficulty controlling emotions" (p. 212). The goal of the study was to examine the relation between crying and self-regulation, and it basically showed that temperament is fairly consistent in a baby's first year across settings. The study is *not* evidence that the cry-it-out approach causes emotional damage. All of the other research studies cited by Sears et al. are subject to a similar critique.

Črnčec et al. [23] reviewed studies that directly examined the cry-it-out approach and reported that it does not harm babies' or toddlers' emotional health or attachment. A well-designed five-year study that followed children over time recently demonstrated that the cry-it-out approach is not harmful [22]. In fact, there are some indications that teaching infants how to sooth themselves to sleep by using the cry-it-out approach may actually *improve* their emotional health. For example, France [25] studied sleep-disturbed infants (ages 6–24 months old) treated with the cry-it-out approach and compared them to infants who weren't treated with this approach. Children treated with the cry-it-out approach scored better on measures of security, likeability, and emotional health; however, Price et al. [22] failed to replicate this finding.

To be clear, in many situations parents *should* immediately respond to their baby's cry (e.g., wet diaper, pain, illness). Nevertheless, so long as the child is safe and well-cared for, it's reasonable to stop responding to cries to be held or rocked during the night. Admittedly, it can be very difficult for loving parents to listen to their baby cry without immediately responding. However, as described above, some experts have responded to this challenge by providing variations of the original cry-it-out approach that include occasional quick checks (e.g., the Ferber method) or parental presence (e.g., camping out). Unfortunately, when other self-help book writers perpetuate the "damaging to development" myth, it makes it even harder for parents to implement any of the cry-it-out variations, which increases the likelihood that parents give up on this effective technique too early. Moreover, statements that the cry-it-out approach causes damage can play into another broader myth described by the book *One Nation Under Therapy* [26]. Specifically, this book describes "The Myth of the Fragile Child" (p. 11) in which many people believe children are so fragile that they cannot handle any stress; when, in fact, children are quite capable of dealing with much of the stress in their lives. Indeed, learning to deal with stress is an important life skill.

On a final note, the cry-it-out approach is typically not advocated before a baby is at least 5 or 6 months old. Also, proponents of the cry-it-out approach do not suggest that every parent should use this technique. Rather, they argue that it can be one helpful and safe choice for many families struggling with their children's sleep problems. Although parents feel good when they hold, rock, or feed a baby to sleep sometimes, routinely rocking or feeding a baby to sleep every time may set the baby up for future sleep problems. Thus, one of the best ways to avoid pediatric sleep disturbance in the first place is to give babies a chance to learn self-soothing skills by letting them fall asleep on their own.

What you need to know

An important point about the cry-it-out approach is that it's typically used along with other methods for improving "sleep hygiene." For example, sleep experts recommend making sure babies and toddlers have a consistent sleep schedule, follow a bedtime routine, and avoid having their child fall asleep to a television [27]. Accordingly, before the cry-it-out approach is used, these and other sleep hygiene issues should be addressed. Sleep experts also emphasize the value of making sure the crib follows safety guidelines. Additionally, a baby monitor can be used to help monitor crib safety. If you are currently trying to improve the sleep of a baby or toddler, we recommend the book *Sleeping Through the Night, Revised Edition* [28], which discusses the graduated cry-it-out approach as one option for improving sleep hygiene. Finally, it's important to add that parent educators often use proactive tactics by encouraging new parents (and daycare teachers), from the beginning, to place babies in their crib when they're *sleepy but not yet asleep.*

References

[1] Sadeh, A., Mindell, J. A., Luedtke, K., & Wiegand, B. (2009). Sleep and sleep ecology in the first 3 years: A web-based study. *Journal of Sleep Research*, 18, 60–73. doi:10.1111/j.1365-2869.2008.00699.x.

[2] Mansbach, A. (Author) & Jackson, S. L. (Narrator) (2011). *Go the F**k to Sleep*. Grand Haven, MI: Brilliance Audio.

[3] Pollock, J. I. (1992). Predictors and long-term associations of reported sleeping difficulties in infancy. *Journal of Reproductive and Infant Psychology*, 10, 151–168. doi:10.1080/02646839208403947.

[4] Meijer, A. M., Wittenboer, V. D., & Godfried, L. H. (2007). Contribution of infants' sleep and crying to marital relationship of first-time parent couples in the 1st year after childbirth. *Journal of Family Psychology*, 21, 49–57. doi:10.1037/0893-3200.21.1.49.

[5] Schnoes, C. J., Kuhn, B. R., Workman, E. F., & Ellis, C. R. (2006). Pediatric prescribing practices for clonidine and other pharmacologic agents for children with sleep disturbance. *Clinical Pediatrics*, 45, 229–238. doi:10.1177/ 000992280604500304.

[6] Kuhn, B. R. & Weidinger, D. (2000). Interventions for infant and toddler sleep disturbance: A review. *Child & Family Behavior Therapy*, 22, 33–50. doi:10.1300/J019v22n02_03.

[7] Holt, L. E. (1894). *The Care and Feeding of Children*. New York, NY: D. Appleton and Company.

[8] Holt, L. E. (1910). *The Care and Feeding of Children, 5th Edition*. New York, NY: D. Appleton and Company.

[9] Ferber, R. (1985). *Solve Your Child's Sleep Problems*. New York, NY: Simon & Schuster.

[10] Pantley, E. (2002). *The No-Cry Sleep Solution*. New York, NY: Contemporary Books.

[11] Sears, W., Sears, R., Sears, J., & Sears, M. (2005). *The Baby Sleep Book*. New York, NY: Little, Brown and Company.

[12] Levitan, S., Lloyd, C. (Writers), & Spiller, M. (Director) (2010). Up all Night [Television series episode]. In S. Levitan & C. Lloyd (Executive Producers), *Modern Family*. Los Angeles, CA: 20th Century Fox.

[13] Annino, J. (Producer) (2009, August 10). *Rachel Ray Show* [Television series]. United States: Watch Entertainment. Retrieved from http://www. rachaelrayshow.com/show/segments/view/salma-answers-audience-questions/ [accessed August 2014].

[14] Ramos, K. D. & Youngclarke, D. M. (2006). Parenting advice books about child sleep: Cosleeping and crying it out. *Sleep*, 29, 1616–1623. doi:10.1002/ icd.526.

[15] BabyCenter, LLC (2011). Do you let your baby cry it out? Retrieved from http://www.babycenter.com/viewPollResults.htm?pollId=1547 [accessed November 30, 2011].

[16] Hupp, S., Stary, A., & Jewell, J. (submitted). Beliefs about myths related to child psychology, development, and parenting: Which myths need the most debunking?

[17] Rickert, V. I. & Johnson, C. M. (1988). Reducing nocturnal awakening and crying episodes in infants and young children: A comparison between scheduled awakenings and systematic ignoring. *Pediatrics*, 81, 203–212.

[18] Hiscock, H. & Wake, M. (2002). Randomised controlled trial of behavioural infant sleep intervention to improve infant sleep and maternal mood. *British Medical Journal*, 324, 1062–1065. doi:10.1136/ bmj.324.7345.1062.

[19] Silverman, W. K. & Hinshaw, S. P. (2008). The second special issue on evidence-based psychosocial treatments for children and adolescents: A 10-year update. *Journal of Clinical Child and Adolescent Psychology*, 37, 1–7. doi:10.1080/15374410701817725.

[20] Kuhn, B. R. & Elliott, A. J. (2003). Treatment efficacy in behavioral pediatric sleep medicine. *Journal of Psychosomatic Research*, 54, 587–597. doi:10.1016/S0022-3999(03)00061-8.

[21] France, K. G. & Blampied, N. M. (2005). Modification of systematic ignoring in the management of infant sleep disturbance: Efficacy and infant distress. *Child & Family Behavior Therapy*, 27, 1–16. doi:10.1300/ J019v27n01_01.

[22] Price, A. M., Wake, M., Ukoumunne, O. C., & Hiscock, H. (2012). Five-year follow-up of harms and benefits of behavioral infant sleep intervention: Randomized trial. *Pediatrics*, 130, 643–651. doi:10.1542/peds.2011-3467.

[23] Črnčec, R., Matthey, S., & Nemeth, D. (2010). Infant sleep problems and emotional health: A review of two behavioural approaches. *Journal of Reproductive and Infant Psychology*, 28, 44–54. doi:10.1080/ 02646830903294995.

[24] Stifter, C. A. & Spinrad, T. L. (2002). The effect of excessive crying on the development of emotion regulation. *Infancy*, 3, 133–152. doi:10.1207/ S15327078IN0302_2.

[25] France, K. G. (1992). Behavior characteristics and security in sleep disturbed infants treated with extinction. *Journal of Pediatric Psychology*, 17, 467–475. doi:10.1093/jpepsy/17.4.467.

[26] Sommers, C. H. & Satel, S. (2005). *One Nation Under Therapy: How the Helping Culture is Eroding Self-reliance.* New York, NY: St Martin's Griffin.

[27] Mindell, J. A., Meltzer, L. J., Carskadon, M. A., & Chervin, R. (2009). Developmental aspects of sleep hygiene: Findings from the 2004 National Sleep Foundation Sleep in America poll. *Sleep Medicine*, 10, 771–779. doi:10.1016/j.sleep.2008.07.016.

[28] Mindell, J. A. (2005). *Sleeping Through the Night, Revised Edition.* New York, NY: HarperResource.

Myth #14 Sugar intake causes children to be hyperactive

On any given Saturday afternoon, countless children attend birthday celebrations with lots of birthday cake, sugary drinks, and possibly a candy-filled piñata at the center of events. At these times, it's common to hear one parent mutter to another, "These kids will all be bouncing off the walls after they eat all that sugar." Indeed, many parents do associate sugar intake with a child's level of activity. The idea harkens back to what many were told in a high school biology class: sugar is a quick energy source. Some parents have even reported that their child's behavioral reaction to sugar causes so much hyperactivity that they believe their child is "sugar reactive," and sugar has often been described by some as a cause of Attention-Deficit/Hyperactivity Disorder (ADHD). How did this idea become so popular?

The media has gladly played a part in the proliferation of this belief. In the theatrical trailer to the movie *Parental Guidance* (Figure 1) [1], grandfather Artie (played by Billy Crystal) and grandmother Diane (played by Bette Midler) are asked to babysit their three grandchildren. They're warned by the children's parents not to let them eat any food with sugar. The mother says, "They don't eat sugar," and their father adds, "We tried to introduce just a little bit of sugar, and it was like going off the rails of the crazy train." But grandpa Artie has different ideas. He offers cake to his grandsons as a bribe to not tell their mother he allowed them to watch a horror movie. The scene erupts in pandemonium soon afterward, as both children quickly grab cake by the handful and are found by their mother running around the kitchen babbling uncontrollably with cake smeared all over their hair, face, and shirts.

Similar scenes play out in many television shows as well. For example, in *The Simpsons* [2], Bart Simpson and his best friend, Milhouse, drink an "all syrup super squishy." Within seconds of tasting the drink, both characters begin hallucinating and then go on a hyperactive "bender" across their entire town. On another animated show, *Beavis and*

Figure 1   In the movie *Parental Guidance,* the children become very hyperactive after eating real cake (with sugar) for the first time.

Butt-Head [3], Beavis transforms into the hyperactive, uncontrollable "Cornholio" when he eats too much sugar.

These examples in the media, and many others like them, appear to have effectively established this belief in the public consciousness. A study by dosReis and colleagues [4] found that over half of parents surveyed believed that sugar affects children's hyperactive behavior. In our research, 82% of college students and 70% of parents agreed with the statement that "Too much sugar causes most children to be hyperactive" [5]. In other research, 42% of teachers believed that decreasing sugar would effectively reduce ADHD symptoms [6]. The medical community has also had a surprising role in the propagation of this belief. A study by Bennett and Sherman [7] surveyed 462 doctors across the state of Washington regarding their treatment recommendations for children referred for hyperactivity. The researchers surveyed general practitioners and family physicians in addition to pediatricians. They found that among other results, about 45% of these doctors had recommended a "low-sugar diet" as a treatment for hyperactivity.

Although a majority of the public believes that there is an established link between sugar and hyperactivity, the evidence against this belief is substantial. The most recent review of research analyzed 23 studies, only including those that met strict inclusion criteria [8]. For example, studies were only analyzed if they used a placebo condition and kept the parents, children, and research staff from knowing which group the child belonged to (sugar or no sugar) so that they would not be biased in their ratings. Results of the review found that most of the 23 studies found little to no difference between the sugar and the no sugar (placebo) groups. When the researchers corrected for the small number of subjects in most of the studies, they concluded that sugar was not associated with hyper-activity, either measured through direct observation or by the ratings of the parents or teachers. Moreover, a well-designed study by Wolraich and colleagues [9] compared the effects of sugar, aspartame (a controver-sial artificial sweetener), and saccharin (considered to be a placebo group) on children whose parents described them as "sugar sensitive" using a variety of measures including cognitive performance, motor activity, and subjective ratings of behavior by parents, teachers, and researchers. These researchers concluded that neither sugar nor aspartame was responsible for any effects in these children.

Researchers have even examined the potential link between sugar and attention-deficit/hyperactivity disorder (ADHD). For example, Milich and Pelham [10] compared the effects of ingesting sugar versus aspartame in a group of children diagnosed with ADHD (the disorder had a slightly different label at the time of the study). The study examined a number of potential effects in these children, including various behaviors reflecting compliance, attention, behaviors towards peers, performance on academic tasks, and ratings by teachers and counselors. The researchers reported that there was "no consistent evidence that sucrose ingestion adversely affects the learning or behavior of ..." boys with ADHD (p. 717). This type of research has led the Center for Disease Control and Prevention to note that "Research does not support the popularly held views that ADHD is caused by eating too much sugar ..." [11].

Despite the research showing no link between sugar and hyperactivity, why do so many parents continue to believe there is a connection? A study by Hoover and Milich [12] sought to understand a potential "expectancy effect" related to this myth. In this cleverly designed study, the researchers recruited 35 mothers of children who reported they believed that their child's behavior was affected by sugar. The mothers and children were split into two groups; one group was told their child would be given an artificially sweetened drink and the other group was told their child would be given a drink with a high dose of sugar. In reality, both groups consumed an artificially sweetened drink *without* sugar, thus testing whether the mothers' expectancy of their child's behavior would affect their ratings. Mothers and their children then participated in a structured play task together, and then the mothers completed questionnaires regarding their child's behavior. Results showed that mothers who were told that their child consumed sugar rated their child as being much more hyperactive than the other group; these mothers also showed many more controlling behaviors during the play interaction. Specifically, these mothers tended to be more physically close, criticize more, and give more commands than the other group. Given these results, it's important to interpret with great caution those studies that rely on parent measures of hyperactivity. The connection that parents make between sugar and hyperactivity is a good example of the illusory correlation that is described in the Introduction.

Importantly, we already have strong evidence for the most likely cause of ADHD. Research indicates that the heritability of ADHD is particularly high. That is, a person's genes largely affect how hyperactive, impulsive, and inattentive they act [13]. Just like every genetically influenced trait, the environment can still help shape the expression of these behaviors. However, sugar intake is not an important part of the environment when it comes to ADHD.

The myth that sugar makes kids hyperactive could be relatively harmless if it simply results in parents decreasing their child's sugar intake to some degree. Unfortunately, this simple association between sugar intake and children's hyperactivity has gone one step further in the minds of many, becoming a potential cause for ADHD. This myth has led to sugar elimination diets in which *all* sugar is removed from the child's diet. These types of diets are very time-intensive and disruptive to daily life because sugar is in a lot of foods. Sugar elimination diets draw time and energy from seeking evidence-based treatments. Moreover, a sugar elimination diet may lead parents to eliminate healthy foods containing sugar (e.g., fruit) which will disrupt a balanced diet.

In conclusion, it appears that with regard to ADHD, the public would likely benefit from a great deal more education regarding the symptoms and causes of ADHD as well as established treatments [14]. So, while restricting the amount of sugar in a child's diet may have some health benefits, it won't keep them from jumping on the couch, sprinting around the house, or talking a lot.

What you need to know

Behavioral interventions are consistently recommended as an evidence-based approach to treating children with ADHD. Pelham and Fabiano [15] provide a comprehensive review of three evidence-based variations of behavioral interventions: behavioral parent training, behavioral classroom management, and behavioral peer interventions in recreational settings.

Stimulant medications also have significant research support in terms of decreasing symptoms associated with ADHD [16]. Thus, the American Academy of Pediatrics recommends a combination of FDA-approved medications for ADHD in combination with behavior therapy [17]. Nevertheless, due to possible side effects of medications, and due to research showing that there are only short-term benefits of medication (and not long-term benefits [15]), behavioral interventions should also be considered as a stand-alone intervention. When medication is used, the addition of behavioral interventions should always be strongly considered.

In his book *Taking Charge of ADHD: The Complete, Authoritative Guide for Parents* [18], Russell Barkley discusses issues related to intervention for ADHD as well as issues related to the causes. The book discusses both behavioral interventions and medications.

References

[1] Fickman, A. (Director) (2012). Parental Guidance [Film]. Los Angeles, CA: Twentieth Century Fox Film Corporation.

[2] Groening, M. (1993). Boy Scoutz 'n the Hood. Kirkland, M. (Director), Silverman, D. (Producer), *The Simpsons*, Los Angeles, CA: Twentieth Century Fox.

[3] Brown, K. (Writer), Judge, M. (Writer & Director), & Kaplan (Director) (1994). The Great Cornholio [Television series episode]. *Beavis and Butt-Head*, New York, NY: MTV Networks.

[4] dosReis, S., Zito, J. M., Safer, D. J., et al. (2003). Parental perceptions and satisfaction with stimulant medication for attention-deficit hyperactivity disorder. *Journal of Developmental & Behavioral Pediatrics*, 24, 155–162. doi:10.1097/ 00004703-200306000-00004.

[5] Hupp, S., Stary, A., & Jewell, J. (submitted). Beliefs about myths related to child psychology, development, and parenting: Which myths need the most debunking?

[6] Sciutto, M. J., Terjesen, M. D., & Frank, A. S. B. (2000). Teachers' knowledge and misperceptions of attention-deficit/hyperactivity disorder. *Psychology in the Schools*, 37, 115–122. doi:10.1002/(SICI)1520-6807(200003)37:2<115:: AID-PITS3>3.0.CO;2-5.

[7] Bennett, F. C. & Sherman, R. (1983). Management of childhood "hyperactivity" by primary care physicians. *Journal of Developmental & Behavioral Pediatrics*, 4(2), 88–93.

[8] Wolraich, M. L., Wilson, D. B., & White, J. W. (1995). The effect of sugar on behavior or cognition in children. A meta-analysis. *Journal of the American Medical Association*, 274, 1617–1621. doi:10.1001/ jama.1995.03530200053037.

[9] Wolraich, M. L., Lindgren, S. D., Stumbo, P. J., et al. (1994). Effects of diets high in sucrose or aspartame on the behavior and cognitive performance of children.

New England Journal of Medicine, 330, 301–306. doi:10.1056/NEJM199402033300501.

[10] Milich, R. & Pelham, W. E. (1986). Effects of sugar on the classroom and playgroup behavior of attention deficit disordered boys. *Journal of Consulting and Clinical Psychology*, 54, 714–718. doi:10.1037/0022-006X.54.4.714.

[11] Center for Disease Control and Prevention (2013). Facts about ADHD. Retrieved from http://www.cdc.gov/NCBDDD/adhd/facts.html; para.7 [accessed August 2014].

[12] Hoover, D. W., & Milich, R. (1994). Effects of sugar ingestion expectancies on mother-child interactions. *Journal of Abnormal Child Psychology*, 22, 501–515. doi:10.1007/BF02168088.

[13] Kratochvil, C. J., Vaughan, B. S., Barker, A., et al. (2009). Review of pediatric attention deficit hyperactivity disorder for the general psychiatrist. *Psychiatric Clinics of North America*, 32, 39–56. doi:10.1016/j.psc.2008.10.001. Meredith Corporation (2012). Attitudes about children's mental health. Retrieved from http://www.parents.com/health/mental/child-mind-institute-survey-results [accessed August 2014].

[14] McLoed, J. D., Fettes, D. L., Jensen, P. S., et al. (2007). Public knowledge, beliefs, and treatment preferences concerning Attention-Deficit Hyperactivity Disorder. *Psychiatric Services*, 58, 626–631. doi:10.1176/appi.ps.58.5.626.

[15] Pelham, W. E. & Fabiano, G. A. (2008). Evidence-based psychosocial treatments for attention-deficit/hyperactivity disorder. *Journal of Clinical Child and Adolescent Psychology*, 37, 184–214. doi:10.1080/15374410701818681.

[16] American Psychiatric Association (2012). Children: Attention-Deficit/Hyperactivity Disorder. Retrieved from http://www.psychiatry.org/mental-health/people/children [accessed August 2014].

[17] American Academy of Pediatrics, Subcommittee on Attention-Deficit/Hyperactivity Disorder, Committee on Quality Improvement (2011). Clinical practice guideline for the diagnosis, evaluation, and treatment of attention-deficit/hyperactivity disorder in children and adolescents. *Pediatrics*, 128, 1007–1022. doi:10.1542/peds.2011-2654.

[18] Barkley, R. A. (2013). *Taking Charge of ADHD, Third Edition: The Complete, Authoritative Guide for Parents*. New York, NY: Guilford Publications, Incorporated.

Myth #15 Using a baby walker will help a toddler walk sooner

The term "toddler" commonly refers to children who are at least 1 year old, and this term is derived from the manner of walking, or toddling, that begins right around the first birthday. The child's first steps are a memorable and notable event for parents. In fact, right at this very moment, some toddler is taking her first steps toward her parent's open arms (or video-equipped smartphone). A quick Internet search of videos using the key term "baby's first steps" will undoubtedly make you a happier person.

It's no surprise that parents want to help their children learn to toddle as soon as possible. After all, future track competitions may be hanging in the balance. Moreover, parents frequently compare their children's milestone achievements with those of their neighbors' children. In order to get a leg up on the competition, many parents for a long time have used "baby walkers" to help their babies learn to walk (note: in this chapter "baby walker" does not mean "baby zombie" but rather a wheeled device that a baby can sit in and travel around by moving his or her feet). In fact, centuries ago doctors recommended the use of baby walkers to teach infants to walk. For example, Ferrarius, in the year 1577, is on record suggesting that baby walkers should be used to help teach walking [1]. Similarly, Doctor William Cadogan, in the 1700s, urged parents to explicitly teach their children to walk as soon as they could [2].

One reason for such an early push to get infants to walk is that some physicians once viewed "crawling on all fours, not as a natural stage of human development, but as a bad habit that, if not thwarted, would remain the baby's primary form of locomotion for the rest of its life" [2] (p. 65). Moreover, because crawling is the way many animals get around, there was a time when parents would not even let their children crawl for fear that the behavior was too animalistic [2]. Another reason parents once wanted their children to walk as soon as possible is that it was once believed that "it was unlucky for a child to learn to speak before it had begun to walk" [2] (p. 65). Both walking and talking tend to occur around the first birthday. Additionally, in some communities in the world, "couples are not allowed to have intercourse until their offspring learn how to walk" because this prevents parents from having too many children in a short amount of time [3]. Consequently, in these communities many parents are probably quite motivated to help their infants take their first steps as soon as humanly possible!

Works of art often served as reflections of a culture before there were television sets and movie theaters, and baby walkers commonly appear in older works of art. For example, baby walkers appear in artwork from medieval times with one example including "Joseph the Carpenter presenting a square wooden baby-walker to the infant Jesus" [4] (p. 148). In another centuries-old example, the artist Rembrandt completed a work called "The Walking Trainer" in 1646 in which a mother uses a baby walker to teach her child to walk, and this image was actually intended to be a metaphor for how Rembrandt's pupils needed to frequently practice in order to become great artists [5].

But it's not just medieval doctors and artists who long encouraged baby walker use in order to promote walking; there were also baby walker peddlers. A 1906 advertisement boasts "STRAIGHT LEGS and a strong, straight back developed if baby learns to walk with Glascock's Baby-Walker" and it also adds that the walker is "Endorsed by physicians as a perfect physical developer for children." Similar claims are being made today. A 2013 Internet sales pitch from Sears (the company, not the pediatrician) says "Give your kid a leg up with baby walkers. These handy contraptions on wheels encourage your baby to take the first steps while a comfy seat provides balance" [6]. One option for your child is the Elmo Tiny Steps walker that, according to the Sears website, will "Help build your little one's leg muscles …" [7]. Or perhaps your toddler would prefer the My Friend Pooh walker that "makes learning how to walk fun for child and parent both!" [8]. We could add a lot more, but you're probably getting the drift.

Researchers have examined claims like the ones found in these advertisements. Specifically, do baby walkers really help infants learn to walk more quickly? A review of studies on this topic concluded that baby walkers weren't associated with learning to walk sooner [9]. In fact, in all four studies in the review, the infants who used the baby walker actually learned to walk more *slowly* by a few weeks, though this was only a statistically significant difference in two of the four studies. While the studies did have some limitations (such as small sample size), by and large they also had some nice design characteristics, including the random assignment of twins to baby-walker and no-baby-walker groups.

Research on baby walkers has led the American Academy of Pediatrics (AAP) to state that "these devices do not help the process of learning to walk. They actually eliminate the desire to walk" [10]. Furthermore, baby walkers present an even bigger problem than the possibility of delayed walking; they can be dangerous. In the early part of the 1990s, there were approximately 25,000 baby walker injuries treated in American hospitals on a yearly basis, with some of these injuries resulting in death [11]. According to the American Academy of Pediatrics, some of the dangers include: falls down stairs, burns from pulling hot items off tables or stoves, drowning in a pool or tub, and poisoning [12]. The majority of these injuries occurred even when the parent was supervising the infant because infants can move very speedily in a baby walker.

Baby walker injuries led to a collaboration between the US Consumer Product Safety Commission and the baby walker industry to develop safer walkers. While baby walkers have become safer (for example, the newer models are not supposed to be able to fit through normal doorways), they continue to be associated with thousands of injuries every year, and the American Academy of Pediatrics still "strongly urges parents not to use baby walkers" [10]. In fact, since 2004 in Canada it has been "illegal to import, advertise for sale, or sell baby walkers ..." even at garage sales, making Canada the first country to institute this ban [13]. Interestingly, some parents like baby walkers so much that the Canadian ban has led to an underground black market, even though there can be a hefty fine (or even jail time) for getting caught. One reason that some Canadian parents refuse to give up their baby walkers might be because they think they will help their infants learn to walk. In one study in the USA, 77% of the parents reported using baby walkers even though they remembered talking to their pediatrician about safety warnings, and 72% believed that the baby walkers helped their children learn to walk earlier [14]. In our research, 78% of students and 76% of parents agree with the statement that "Baby walkers help young children learn to walk" [15].

It's easy to see why parents would believe baby walkers help their infants learn to walk. The infants are, after all, getting around while upright and moving their feet. Because the infants do end up walking, parents attribute the new skill to the walker. This is a good example of the post hoc, ergo propter hoc reasoning fallacy described in the "Sources of Psychological Myths" part of the Introduction. That is, just because one event happens after the other, it doesn't mean that the first event caused the second.

In conclusion, while the American Academy of Pediatrics discourages the use of baby walkers, they do suggest some alternatives to baby walkers that include occasional use of stationary activity centers, playpens, and high chairs [12]. Although these devices do not help teach infants to walk, they can be a safe place to keep a baby while nearby parents are trying to complete a chore or two.

What you need to know

Although most infants will learn to walk without any special training, learning to walk is challenging due to the coordination of different skills needed. The American Academy of Pediatrics describes everything that goes into learning to walk [10]. For example, infant movements begin strengthening important muscles in the first few months while the infant squirms around on her back or is given special supervised "tummy time" on her stomach. These early movements strengthen muscles that are important for eventually sitting up and crawling. One way parents can encourage crawling is to place preferred objects a little bit out of reach.

Crawling then helps the child develop the strength and balance that will lead to pulling herself up to a standing position. Holding onto a small table or chair while standing further prepares the soon-to-be toddler to take her first steps. Be careful, though, because even though she figures out how to stand, she may actually not know how to sit back down!

Once an infant begins moving around, parents need to start thinking about child safety. Baby walker or not, there are a lot of ways a moving infant can get hurt. The American Academy of Pediatrics also provides some safety tips related to locomotion [16, 17]. To prevent falls, parents can add gates to doorways and stairs as well as other guards for windows on the upper floors. Parents should also be careful not to put hot items, such as coffee cups, within reach on the edge of a table. Backyard swimming pools need to be fenced off, but parents should be aware that a child can drown in less than two inches of water which could include the bathtub, the toilet, or a bucket of water. Other household preparations include precautions to prevent poisoning (e.g., cleaners, medicines, etc.), choking (e.g., small objects, chunks of food, etc.), strangulation (e.g., cords from window blinds), suffocation (e.g., plastic bags), and even access to firearms in the home.

References

[1] Spaulding, M. & Welch, P. (1991). *Nurturing Yesterday's Child: A Portrayal of the Drake Collection of Paediatric History*. Toronto: Natural Heritage/Natural History.

[2] Calvert, K. (2003). Patterns in childrearing in America. In W. Koops & M. Zuckerman (Eds), *Beyond the Century of the Child: Cultural History and Developmental Psychology*. Philadelphia, PA: University of Pennsylvania Press.

[3] Callan, G. O. H. (1989). *The World of the Baby: A Celebration of Infancy through the Ages*. New York, NY: Doubleday.

[4] Kevill-Davies, S. (1991). *Yesterday's Children: The Antiques and History of Childcare*. Woodbridge, Suffolk: Antique Collectors' Club.

[5] Bevers, H. (2010). Drawing in Rembrandt's workshop. In H. Bevers, L. Hendrix, W. W., Robinson, & P. Schatborn (Eds), *Drawings by Rembrandt and his Pupils: Telling the Difference*. Los Angeles, CA: J. Paul Getty Museum.

[6] Walkers & Jumpers (n.d.). Retrieved from http://www.sears.com/baby-gear-walkers-jumpers/b-1020371 [accessed August 2014].

[7] Sesame Street Elmo Tiny Steps 2-in-1 Walker (n.d.). Retrieved from http://www.sears.com/sesame-street-elmo-tiny-steps-2-in-1/p-04919329000P?prdNo=2&blockNo=2&blockType=G2 [accessed August 2014].

[8] Disney Music & Lights Walker – My Friend Pooh (n.d.) http://www.sears.com/disney-music-lights-walker-my-friend-pooh/p-04901684000P?prdNo=3&blockNo=3&blockType=G3 [accessed August 2014].

[9] Burrows, P. & Griffiths, P. (2002). Do baby walkers delay onset of walking in young children? *British Journal of Community Nursing*, 7, 581–586.

[10] American Academy of Pediatrics (n.d.a). Movement: 8 to 12 Months. Retrieved from http://www.healthychildren.org/English/ages-stages/baby/pages/Movement-8-to-12-Months.aspx?nfstatus=401&nftoken=00000000-0000-0000-0000-000000000000&nfstatusdescription=ERROR%3a+No+local+token [accessed August 2014].

[11] Rodgers, G. B. & Leland, E. W. (2008). A retrospective benefit-cost analysis of the 1997 stair-fall requirements for baby walkers. *Accident Analysis & Prevention*, 40(1), 61–68. doi:10.1016/j.aap.2007.04.003.

[12] American Academy of Pediatrics (n.d.b). Baby Walkers: A Dangerous Choice. Retrieved from http://www.healthychildren.org/English/safety-prevention/at-home/pages/Baby-Walkers-A-Dangerous-Choice.aspx?nfstatus=401&nftoken=00000000-0000-0000-0000-000000000000&nfstatusdescription=ERROR%3a+No+local+token [accessed August 2014].

[13] Health Canada (n.d.). Consumer product safety. Retrieved from http://www.hc-sc.gc.ca/cps-spc/advisories-avis/out-ext/index-eng.php [accessed August 2014].

[14] Bar-on, M. E., Boyle, R. M., & Endriss, E. K. (1998). Parental decisions to use infant walkers. *Injury prevention*, 4, 299–300. doi:10.1136/ip.4.4.299.

[15] Hupp, S., Stary, A., & Jewell, J. (submitted). Beliefs about myths related to child psychology, development, and parenting: Which myths need the most debunking?

[16] American Academy of Pediatrics (n.d.c). Safety for Your Child: 6 to 12 Months. Retrieved from http://www.healthychildren.org/english/tips-tools/Pages/Safety-for-Your-Child-6-to-12-Months.aspx [accessed August 2014].

[17] American Academy of Pediatrics (n.d.d). Safety for Your Child: 1 to 2 Years. Retrieved from http://www.healthychildren.org/english/tips-tools/Pages/Safety-for-Your-Child-1-to-2-Years.aspx [accessed August 2014].

Myth #16 Showing cognitively stimulating videos to babies boosts their intelligence

In the book *50 Great Myths of Popular Psychology* [1], Lilienfeld et al. describe a long-lasting trend in parenting. Specifically, the 1980s were filled with parents trying to create "superbabies" by exposing their newborns to significant amounts of advanced mathematics and other languages [2]. Then, the 1990s were bursting with parents and teachers playing Mozart's music to their children, infants, and even fetuses with the hope of making their children smarter. Lilienfeld et al. thoroughly debunked the myth that, "Playing Mozart's Music to Infants Boosts Their Intelligence" (p. 45). Lilienfeld and colleagues also describe the 21st century version of this parenting trend. Namely, the 2000s have been jam-packed with parents buying cognitively stimulating videos (such as *Baby Einstein*) with the hope that they will help turn their children into geniuses. Instead of focusing on the

"Mozart Effect" myth that Lilienfeld et al. already skewered, we've decide to focus here on the latest version of this parenting trend. That is, we'll focus on what we're going to call the "Einstein Movement" (named after the proliferation of *Baby Einstein* products).

In the recent documentary *Race to Nowhere* [3], the filmmakers argue that excessive pressure can cause students to be "pushed to the brink by over-scheduling, over-testing and the relentless pressure to achieve … ." As one teen student in the film puts it, "School's just so much pressure that everyday I'd wake up dreading it." But many believe that this pressure to achieve does not start in middle school or high school. Rather, these pressures are in place at a much younger age. In the report *Crisis in Kindergarten: Why Children Need to Play in School* by the nonprofit organization Alliance for Childhood [4], the authors lament recent changes in typical Kindergarten classrooms when they state that "Skepticism about the value of play is compounded by the widespread assumption—promoted by hundreds of 'smart baby' products—that the earlier children begin to master the basic elements of reading, such as phonics and letter recognition, the more likely they're to succeed in school" (p. 7). And it's in this environment of pressure to help kids succeed that parents often seek products that will help their children get a "jump start" on the competition – even if the competition is just a few months old.

To help parents do this, there are a growing number of television shows, DVDs, and video programs that claim (or infer) that they can make infants and toddlers smarter. And surely many parents, somewhere in the back of their mind, hope that these products will help their future teenage child do just a little better on the SAT or ACT, allowing them to get into the prestigious college of their choice. This wave of television and videos geared directly for infants and toddlers burst onto the public market toward the end of the 1990s. For example, *Baby Einstein* products and television programs such as *Teletubbies* began to reach an international audience of parents and young children at this time [5]. According to the product's website, the *Baby Einstein* company was acquired by the Walt Disney Company in 2001 and was referred to by Oprah "as one of the hottest baby shower gifts" in 2002, which has ultimately contributed to *Baby Einstein* becoming "a world leader in developmental and entertainment products for babies and toddlers" [6].

Many other video-based educational products for infants and toddlers also exploded in the 2000s. In 2005 over three-quarters of all top-selling videos on the Amazon.com marketplace for children under 2 years old claimed to be educational [7]. Although some manufacturers of these products actually claim that their videos do not increase the IQ of infants watching them [7], the titles and descriptions of these products might give a different impression to parents. Titles such as *Left Brain: Inspires Logical Thinking* in the *Brainy Baby* series of DVDs certainly seems to imply that the product is focused on improving cognitive development, and the manufacturer describes the product as "the first video series that can help stimulate cognitive development" [7]. Programs such as these are big business as well. In 2004, DVDs designed to help with infant and toddler development reached an estimated $100 million dollars for that year [8].

In reaction to this increased media use in very young children, the American Academy of Pediatrics (AAP) Council on Communications and Media published a report that discouraged exposure to television and similar media in children under 2 years old [9]. Nevertheless, the prevalence of TV and DVD viewing in very young children has remained very high. In one of the largest surveys of media use and young children, Vandewater and colleagues [10] found that 63% of children ages 0 to 2 years watched television daily, and 30% watched a video on a typical day for over an hour. This is in contrast to the 66 minutes on average that they played outside or 39 minutes that they were read to by an adult.

Notably, 18% of infants and toddlers had a television in their bedroom [10]. Parents gave various reasons for putting a TV in their young child's bedroom including freeing up a television for adult viewing (47%), to keep the child occupied while the parent performs other activities (42%), or to help the child fall asleep (28%). Another large survey of parents also found that children as young as 3 months old are exposed to about 1 hour of television per day on average, with about 30 minutes of this being reported as "educational" programming and 15 minutes per day being videos designed for babies [11].

Although some may argue that many of these programs never claimed to make young children smarter, it appears that many parents assumed that to be the case. In a qualitative study of mothers of children ages 12 to 24 months, 68% reported that they owned "baby videos," and the majority of parents believed that the videos were marketed as being educational, with 55% of parents believing that there was in fact some educational benefit to viewing them [12]. Another study by Zimmerman et al. [11] confirmed that many parents believe that educational videos will make their child smarter. In this study, 29% of parents cited educational benefits or benefits for their child's brain as the most important reason for allowing their child's media use. Similar to the Ryan [12] study, results from the Zimmerman and colleagues [11] study found that the belief in the educational value of baby videos was endorsed more strongly than the simple use of these videos as a way to occupy their children while parents are busy. Also, in both of these studies, most of the parents didn't consistently watch the videos with their children, which contradicts most DVD manufacturer recommendations [11, 12]. Most recently, in our research, 85% of college students and 69% of parents agreed with the statement "Showing cognitively stimulating videos to infants boosts their intelligence" [13]. Moreover, this Einstein Movement myth is currently more widely believed than the popular Mozart Effect myth. That is, 60% of college students and 58% parents agreed with the statement "When Mozart's music is played to infants the music boosts their intelligence" [13].

Considering the widespread use and belief in baby learning videos, what does the research say about the intelligence-boosting potential of educational videos for infants? Courage and Setliff [14] reviewed a number of studies that provide evidence against the idea that videos marketed towards infants and toddlers provide benefits to their brain development. At the heart of this argument is a common research finding that has been termed the "video deficit" [5]. The deficit refers to the fact that "infants and toddlers do not readily imitate actions viewed on video media, although they will easily imitate the same actions viewed live" [14] (p. 74). This video deficit has been found in numerous research studies on spatial learning, word recognition, and language development [14]. The implication of this is that young children have the potential to learn, but they do so much more effectively when faced with live interaction as opposed to through media alone. One probable reason for this is the inability to translate meaning from a two-dimensional source (such as a television screen) compared to a three-dimensional interactive experience that they would have when relating to a parent or other adult [14].

Similarly, Barr and Hayne [15] discovered in a series of studies with 12- to 18-month-old children that live interaction was significantly more effective than video interaction for children's learning. Interestingly, a more recent study by Barr and colleagues [16] found that 12- to 18-month-olds were more responsive and imitative of infant videos if parents watched the videos with them and used questions or labeling during the videos. Although this is a thought-provoking research finding, it may have little real-world applicability considering that most parents don't do this [11, 12].

Another purported benefit of baby learning videos is that they improve language development and word learning. However, again the research on this topic has generally contradicted this assertion. For example, Robb and colleagues [17] studied the potential effects of the *Baby Wordsworth: First Words Around the House* DVD, which is part of the *Baby Einstein* series, on word learning in children between 12 and 15 months old. These researchers randomly assigned children into one of two groups. The DVD group was instructed to watch the video 15 times in a 6-week period while the control group was not given the video and told to follow their typical routines. At the end of the study the results indicated that multiple exposures to the DVD didn't produce any increases in word learning. However, the researchers also measured the amount of time that the children were read to by a parent, and this was strongly associated with word learning.

A similar study also investigated the potential effects of a similar DVD program on word learning in 12- to 18-month-old children [18]. This study grouped children slightly differently, with one group of children watching the DVD (at least 10 hours over 4 weeks) without parent interaction, a second group watching with parent interaction (at least 10 hours over 4 weeks), a third group being taught a list of words through parent interaction only (with no time requirements), and a control group (with no specified teaching or DVD instructions). Children in the parent-interaction-only group learned significantly more words, while both of the DVD-watching groups learned no more words than the control group. Thus, once again baby learning videos fail to be beneficial.

In a different type of study, Zimmerman and colleagues [11] surveyed over 1008 parents on their 8- to 24-month-old child's media use and language development over time. For children 8 to 16 months old, reading daily and storytelling daily by an adult predicted significantly higher language skills, while a similar trend was found for children ages 17 to 24 months. On the other hand, baby DVD programs were associated with significantly *lower* language skills in 8- to 16-month-olds, while educational programming, children's non-educational television, and adult programming had no relation to these children's language skills. For 17- to 24-month-olds, media use was unrelated to language development.

The research reviewed here is part of the basis for an update of the original American Academy of Pediatrics report on media use in children under 2 years old [19]. In this report, the authors reaffirm that media use should be discouraged in children under 2 years old, although the newer report also indicates that the original policy statement "is frequently *misquoted* by media outlets as *no media exposure* in this age group" (p. 1040, italics added). Thus, while the American Academy of Pediatrics does discourage television watching before age 2 years, they do not say that children under 2 years old should never see a television screen.

The "Sources of Psychological Myths" provide at least one good reason that parents tend to be influenced by the Mozart Effect and the more recent Einstein Movement. Specifically, the desire for easy answers probably motivates many parents. It's easy to show a video, and it has the side benefit of keeping a baby occupied during household chores or road trips. In fact, we don't blame parents for some occasional video use. To be fair, as parents, we've both been known to pop in a DVD or videotape for a baby or toddler from time to time. Some limited use of videos with infants is probably okay, as long as parents know that videos don't really teach babies what they need to know. Finally, the American Academy of Pediatrics [19] acknowledges that there is some evidence that high quality educational programs *after* the age of 2 years may have some educational benefits; however, nothing really beats interactions with other humans in real life!

What you need to know

The research on how to promote learning with infants and toddlers is clear. Adult interaction leads to the most effective learning in children and is far superior to "teaching" by videos. Furthermore, the American Academy of Pediatrics has recommended an alternative to television watching. That is, parents are encouraged to read with their baby every day starting at birth [20].

References

[1] Lilienfeld, S. O., Lynn, S. J., Ruscio, J., & Beyerstein, B. L. (2010). *50 Great Myths of Popular Psychology: Shattering Widespread Misconceptions about Human Behavior.* Malden, MA: Wiley-Blackwell.
[2] Clarke-Stewart, K. A. (1998). Historical shifts and underlying themes in ideas about rearing young children in the United States: Where have we been? Where are we going? *Early Development and Parenting,* 7, 101–117.
[3] Abeles, V. & Congdon, J. (Directors) (2010). *Race to Nowhere* [Documentary]. Lafayette: Reel Link Films.
[4] Miller, E. & Almon, J. (2009). *Crisis in the Kindergarten. Why Children Need to Play in School.* College Park, MD: Alliance for Childhood.
[5] Anderson, D. R. & Pempek, T. A. (2005). Television and very young children. *American Behavioral Scientist,* 48, 505–522. doi:10.1177/0002764204271506.
[6] How the Baby Einstein Company was conceived (n.d.). Retrieved from http://www.kidsii.com/babyeinstein/about/history [accessed August 2014].
[7] Kaiser Family Foundation (December, 2005). A teacher in the living room? Educational media for babies, toddlers and preschoolers. Kaiser Report.

[8] Khermouch, G. (2004). Brainier Babier? Maybe. Big Sales? Definitely. *Business Week*.

[9] American Academy of Pediatrics, Committee on Public Education (1999). Media education. *Pediatrics,* 104, 341–343. doi:10.1542/peds.104.2.341.

[10] Vandewater, E. A., Rideout, V. J., Wartella, E. A., et al. (2007). Digital childhood: Electronic media and technology use among infants, toddlers, and preschoolers. *Pediatrics*, 119, 1006–1015. doi:10.1542/peds.2006-1804.

[11] Zimmerman, F. J., Christakis, D. A., & Meltzoff, A. N. (2007). Television and DVD/video viewing in children younger than 2 years. *Archives of Pediatrics & Adolescent Medicine*, 161, 473–479. doi:10.1001/archpedi.161.5.473.

[12] Ryan, E. L. (2012). "They are kind of like magic": Why U.S. mothers use baby videos with 12- to 24-month-olds. *Journalism and Mass Communication*, 2, 771–785.

[13] Hupp, S., Stary, A., & Jewell, J. (submitted). Beliefs about myths related to child psychology, development, and parenting: Which myths need the most debunking?

[14] Courage, M. L. & Setliff, A. E. (2009). Debating the impact of television and video material on very young children: Attention, learning, and the developing brain. *Child Development Perspectives*, 3, 72–78. doi:10.1111/j.1750-8606. 2008.00080.x.

[15] Barr, R. & Hayne, H. (1999). Developmental changes in imitation from television during infancy. *Child Development*, 70, 1067–1081. doi:10.1111/1467-8624.00079.

[16] Barr, R., Zack, E., Garcia, A., & Muentener, P. (2008). Infants' attention and responsiveness to television increases with prior exposure and parental interaction. *Infancy*, 13, 30–56. doi:10.1080/15250000701779378.

[17] Robb, M. B., Richert, R. A., & Wartella, E. A. (2009). Just a talking book? Word learning from watching baby videos. *British Journal of Developmental Psychology*, 27, 27–45. doi:10.1348/026151008X320156.

[18] DeLoache, J. S., Choing, C., Sherman, K., et al. (2010). Do babies learn from baby media? *Psychological Science*, 21, 1570–1574. doi:10.1177/0956797610384145.

[19] American Academy of Pediatrics, Council on Communications and Media (2011). Media use by children younger than 2 years. *Pediatrics*, 128, 1040–1045. doi:10.1542/peds.2011-1753.

[20] Council on Early Childhood (2014). Literacy promotion: An essential component of primary care pediatric practice. *Pediatrics*, peds-2014. doi:10.1542/peds.2014-1384.

Myth #17 Using "baby talk" with an infant delays their ability to speak normally

Humans will stop using "baby talk" in the future. At least, based on the original *Star Trek* series [1], this is the fate of this soon-to-be-obscure type of communication. Consider the following interaction between the doctor, the first officer, and the captain of the Star Trek Enterprise. While Dr. McCoy holds a newborn baby on an alien planet he uses baby talk:

DR. MCCOY [TO A NEWBORN]:   "Ootchie-wootchie, cootchie-coo."
SPOCK [TURNING TO CAPTAIN KIRK]:   " 'Ootchie-wootchie, cootchie-coo,' Captain?"
CAPTAIN KIRK: "An obscure Earth dialect, Mister Spock, 'ootchie-cootchie, cootchie-coo.' If you're curious consult linguistics."

The above exchange takes place in a fictional 23rd century, so we may still have a few hundred years before baby talk becomes an "obscure Earth dialect." If Spock does decide to consult linguistics, he'll probably start with a definition. A basic definition of "baby talk" is any manner of speech directed to a baby that differs from how the person talks to an adult. Common characteristics of baby talk include: higher pitch; greater intonation; slower rate; stretched out syllables; longer pauses; simplified grammar; and changes to words that make them simpler, shorter, easier to say, or cuter (e.g., bye-bye, jammies, mama, doggie).

For a while, "motherese" was the technical term used to describe baby talk; however, because fathers and other caregivers also use baby talk, more recent technical terms include "parentese," "infant-directed speech," or "child-directed speech." Although these variations are commonly used interchangeably, they also can denote a specific period of life, especially considering that the word "infant" is Latin for "not" able "to speak" [2] (p. 222), and an "infant" becomes a "toddler" at the first birthday, around the time most children are starting to say their first words.

It's not just adults who use baby talk. When a 4-year-old child talks to a 2-year-old child, the older child often modifies the way the words are spoken [3], and when 2-year-old children talk to 1-year-old children, they even modify their speech [4]. Baby talk is also used commonly across many different cultures [5]. A form of baby talk has even been demonstrated when parents use sign language with their infants who are hearing impaired [6]. That is, the parents sign at a slower rate, exaggerate their movements, and use more repetition

Despite the widespread use of baby talk, Captain Kirk's indication that it will become an obscure dialect is possibly correct because here in the 21st century baby talk is already under attack. For example, in the movie *Meet the Fockers* [7] the main character, Greg (played by Ben Stiller), uses baby talk with his 1-year-old nephew. Greg's father-in-law (played by Robert De Niro) says, "Greg, Greg, Greg, don't infantilize him. Talk to him like an adult … just try to understand he's a little person. His communication skills aren't verbal yet, but he understands." Later in the movie, Greg notices his own father (played by Dustin Hoffman) using baby talk with the same toddler, and he repeats what his father-in-law told him: "Hey, dad, don't infantilize him. Just talk to him like a person."

Beyond the movies, some people in the real world also condemn baby talk. Actor Neil Patrick Harris (from the show *How I Met Your Mother*) told People magazine, "My parents always talked to my brother and myself like we were regular people and not babies" (although he probably doesn't really remember how they talked to him when he was a baby), and he also added that when it comes to his own children, "I don't talk down to them in baby talk" [8]. Even professional advice-givers have admonished baby talk. For example, the well-known advice columnist Abby (from Dear Abby) described baby talk as "annoying" and "condescending" [9]. Furthermore, Gold [10] went so far as to give a magazine article the title, "Baby Talk Hinders Learning," and the author specifically suggests that baby talk hurts language development. The attack on baby talk appears to be working, as a large number of people believe it's harmful. In our research, 50% of students and 52% of parents agreed with the statement that "Using 'baby talk' with an infant delays their ability to speak normally" [11].

Does baby talk really hinder language development? Several pieces of converging research suggest that baby talk is not harmful. Studies show that newborns actually prefer listening to infant-directed speech [12]. Infants who are hearing impaired also pay more attention to the baby talk version of sign language [6]. Interestingly, infants also stop preferring their mother's voice over a stranger's voice if their mother begins to speak in a monotone voice [13].

One possibility is that infants actually reinforce the use of baby talk in adults by paying more attention and looking happier when they hear baby talk [14]. That is, it may be the babies themselves that get the adults to engage in more baby talk. This preference for baby talk, however, may not occur at every age. For example, 4-month-olds prefer infant-directed speech, and this preference tends to dissipate by about 9 months old [15]. Some research suggests the preference for baby talk is based on the infant's preference for the happy emotion expressed because infants tend to stop preferring baby talk over adult talk when the adult-directed speech is done in a happy tone [16]. Thus, more research is needed to disentangle which other components of baby talk hold an infant's interest above and beyond the happy emotion conveyed.

Even solid evidence that infants prefer baby talk would not be enough to indicate that baby talk is harmless. Additional research, however, has actually shown some positive effects of learning from baby talk. For example, 7-month-old infants in one study were exposed to two words: one was delivered using baby talk and the other was delivered using "adult talk" [17]. Twenty-four hours later the babies had better word recognition (as measured by listening time) when the word was delivered in baby talk. Another study demonstrated that even adults learn a new language better if taught using some elements of child-directed speech [18].

While hardly definitive evidence that infants learn *more* through baby talk, the above studies, and others like them, tend to point more in the direction of babies learning more from baby talk rather than less. Soderstrom [19] summarized the research by suggesting that baby talk is "beneficial, rather than harmful – or at least neutral" (p. 520), and this seems to be a fair description of the overall body of research on baby talk. Thus, the idea that baby talk is harmful to language development is a myth.

With the available evidence and theory pointing in the direction of favorable benefits with infants, why do so many people think baby talk is harmful to language development? One important issue may be regarding the timing of when baby talk stops. We should first acknowledge that the ceasing of baby talk is likely a gradual process with perhaps some elements lasting longer than others. For example, as infants become toddlers it's possible that the adult's verbal pitch is gradually lowered to normal (i.e., this aspect of baby talk is on the decline) while at the same time childish derivatives of newly learned words may be increasing (e.g., potty, beddie-bye, blankie, binkie, sissy). At some point these types of words will decline again.

Certainly, many parents often use aspects of baby talk beyond when it would have any potential benefit, but that doesn't mean that baby talk is harmful. If there's a time when a child is using childish words more than his peers, it won't take long for the peers to shape up the more grown-up way of saying something. One thing is clear from our experience in working with youth: kids learn a lot of grown-up words from other kids. Even infants who hear a lot of baby talk are still generally exposed to a lot of adult-directed talk as well. That is, the majority of the language infants hear is adult-directed because they hear adults talking with each other [19].

The article with the title "Baby Talk Hinders Learning" [10] also helps explain why so many people are cynical about baby talk. This article describes research indicating that when caregivers use more complicated language, children tend to score better on tests of language [20]. Nevertheless, there are several problems with the assumptions in the article. First, the article focuses on preschool-aged children, but the article title appears to condemn all baby talk. Second, the article is based on research studies that do not really investigate baby talk per se, but rather quantity and complexity of language. Finally, the research is correlational, and one of the "Sources of Psychological Myths" is the error of assuming that a cause can be inferred from correlational research. Oftentimes when two variables are correlated, there are actually other sources at the root of the connection. For example, genes probably influence verbosity such that parents who have complicated language are more likely to have children with complicated language because they pass on their language genes. Moreover, parents often raise their children in an environment that is similar to the parent's childhood environment (e.g., the same school district) which can influence the language development of parents and their children in similar ways.

There's not really much research that specifically looks at the age at which different aspects of baby talk are faded out, but it's clearly okay for parents to feel comfortable using baby talk with babies. Everyone will develop their own communicative style with babies, and there's no one single right way to communicate with a baby. The most important thing is to do just that: communicate with the baby.

In the *Seinfeld* television show [21], when Seinfeld and Kramer finally get to "see the baby," they represent a split in attitudes related to baby talk. Kramer says in a very high pitched voice, "gootchie, gootchie, gootchie, goo." On the other hand, when Seinfeld talks to the baby, he uses a monotone voice and says, "Hello, how are you?" He later tells the baby, "You have a very nice place here." Both of these ways of interacting with a baby are okay, and neither will harm the baby. In fact, a little variety in communicative styles may be the best option for a baby, anyway. Parents need not worry too much about if they're using baby talk or not with infants; instead, they would do well to just focus on having fun interacting with the baby.

What you need to know

The American Speech-Language-Hearing Association (ASHA) provides some recommendations for promoting language development from birth to 2 years old (Activities to Encourage Speech and Language Development [22]). Among other recommendations, parents are encouraged to: (i) reinforce the baby's speech attempts by using eye contact and by talking back to the baby; (ii) imitate the baby's facial expressions and laughter; (iii) encourage the baby to imitate finger games and other actions; (iv) talk during most activities, such as meals and bathing; (v) incorporate gestures, like waving goodbye; (vi) expand on the words the baby says; (vii) raise voice pitch during questions; and (viii) read frequently with the baby or simply describe pictures from books. ASHA provides recommendations for ages 2 to 4 years old as well, which include fading out baby talk by beginning to pair diminutive forms of words (e.g., "din-din") with the original form of the word (e.g., "dinner") in the same sentence. Thus, while the use of baby talk is consistent with the ASHA recommendations for the first couple of years, there comes a time when it will be faded out. Another useful resource for parents is the book, *How Babies Talk: The Magic and Mystery of Language in the First Three Years* [23].

References

[1] Roddenberry, G. Fontana, D. C. (Writers), & Pevney, J. (Director) (1967). Friday's child [Television series episode]. In G. Roddenberry (Executive producer), *Star Trek*. Desilu Productions.

[2] Cresswell, J. & Oxford University Press (2010). *Oxford Dictionary of Word Origins*. New York, NY: Oxford University Press.

[3] Shatz, M. & Gelman, R. (1973). The development of communication skills: Modifications in the speech of young children as a function of listener. *Monographs of the Society For Research in Child Development*, 38, 1–38. doi:10.2307/1165783.

[4] Dunn, J. & Kendrick, C. (1982). The speech of two-and three-year-olds to infant siblings: "Baby talk" and the context of communication. *Journal of Child Language*, 9, 579–595. doi:10.1017/S030500090000492X.

[5] Fernald, A., Taeschner, T., Dunn, J., et al. (1989). A cross-language study of prosodic modifications in mothers' and fathers' speech to preverbal infants. *Journal of Child Language*, 16, 477–501. doi:10.1017/S0305000900010679.

[6] Masataka, N. (1996). Perception of motherese in a signed language by 6-month-old deaf infants. *Developmental Psychology*, 32, 874–879. doi:10.1037/0012-1649. 32.5.874.

[7] De Niro, R., Poll, J., Roach, J., et al. (Producers) & Roach, J. (Director) (2004). *Meet the Fockers* [Motion picture]. United States: TriBeCa Productions.

[8] O'Donnell, K. (2012, February 4). Neil Patrick Harris: There's no 'baby talk' in my house. Retrived from www.people.com [accessed August 2014].

[9] Van Buren, A. (Pen name) (2005, December 24). Dear Abby: Journals are priceless presents for families. Retrieved from http://www.ocregister.com/articles/dear-78229-abby-mother.html [accessed August 2014].

[10] Gold, S. S. (2003). Baby talk hinders learning. Retrieved from www.psychologytoday.com [accessed August 2014].

[11] Hupp, S., Stary, A., & Jewell, J. (submitted). Beliefs about myths related to child psychology, development, and parenting: Which myths need the most debunking?

[12] Cooper, R. P. & Aslin, R. N. (1990). Preference for infant-directed speech in the first month after birth. *Child Development*, 61, 1584–1595. doi:10.2307/1130766.

[13] Mehler, J., Bertoncini, J., Barrière, M., & Jassik-Gerschenfeld, D. (1978). Infant recognition of mother's voice. *Perception*, 7, 491–497. doi:10.1068/p070491.

[14] Smith, N. A. & Trainor, L. J. (2008). Infant-directed speech is modulated by infant feedback. *Infancy*, 13, 410–420. doi:10.1080/15250000802188719.

[15] Newman, R. S. & Hussain, I. (2006). Changes in preference for infant-directed speech in low and moderate noise by 4.5- to 13-month-olds. *Infancy*, 10, 61–76. doi:10.1207/s15327078in1001_4.

[16] Singh, L., Morgan, J. L., & Best, C. T. (2002). Infants' listening preferences: Baby talk or happy talk? *Infancy*, 3, 365–394. doi:10.1207/S15327078IN0303_5.

[17] Singh, L., Nestor, S., Parikh, C., & Yull, A. (2009). Influences of infant-directed speech on early word recognition. *Infancy*, 14, 654–666. doi:10.1080/15250000903263973.

[18] Golinkoff, R. M. & Alioto, A. (1995). Infant-directed speech facilitates lexical learning in adults hearing Chinese: Implications for language acquisition. *Journal of Child Language*, 22, 703–726. doi:10.1017/S0305000900010011.

[19] Soderstrom, M. (2007). Beyond babytalk: Re-evaluating the nature and content of speech input to preverbal infants. *Developmental Review*, 27, 501–532. doi: 10.1016/j.dr.2007.06.002.

[20] Huttenlocher, J. (1998). Language input and language growth. *Preventive Medicine*, 27, 195–199.

[21] Mehlman, P., Leifer, C. (Writers), & Cherones, T. (Director) (1994). The Hamptons [Television series episode]. In L. David, B. Scott, H. West. & G. Shapiro (Executive producers), *Seinfeld*. Castle Rock Entertainment.

[22] American Speech-Language-Hearing Association (n.d.). Activities to encourage speech and language development. Retrieved from www.asha.org [accessed August 2014].

[23] Golinkoff, R. M. & Hirsh-Pasek, K. (2000). *How Babies Talk: The Magic and Mystery of Language in the First Three Years of Life*. New York, NY: Plume.

Myth #18

Vaccines caused the rise in autism diagnoses

"Callous disregard," "retracted article," "ethical violations": these are just some of the provocative phrases you'll read in this chapter. In fact, this chapter covers perhaps the most heated, talked about, life-or-death myth covered in this book. Before we get to the controversy, however, we need to cover some basic information.

The latest edition of the *Diagnostic and Statistical Manual of Mental Disorders* (DSM-V) combined a few previous disorders (i.e., Autistic Disorder, Asperger's Disorder, and two others) into one diagnostic category that's now called Autism Spectrum Disorder [1]. This change reflects the view that these disorders already occurred on a continuum. The change also required some adjustments to criteria representing two primary diagnostic criteria: (i) impairments in social communication; and (ii) repetitive behaviors or interests. Big changes like this happen with every new edition of the DSM. For example, Asperger's Disorder was added to the DSM in 1994 [2] during the last major revision, and that change itself broadened the autism spectrum quite a bit. In fact, Autistic Disorder itself wasn't even added until 1980 (under the name Infantile Autism [3]). Prior to 1980, "autistic" behavior was subsumed under childhood schizophrenia [4].

The brief discussion of the DSM changes illustrates that: (i) disorders on the autism spectrum are relatively new editions to the DSM; (ii) the diagnostic criteria for autism keep changing; and (iii) it keeps getting easier to get diagnosed. In debunking the myth that "There's Recently Been a Massive Epidemic of Infantile Autism" [5] (p. 195) the authors further add that awareness of autism by professionals and parents has also led to the increase in diagnoses (from here on out, the word "autism" will represent the current Autism Spectrum Disorder label as well as previous labels for disorders on this spectrum). According to the Center for Disease Control [6], data from the year 2000 indicated that 1 out of 150 children met the criteria for Autism Spectrum Disorder, and by the year 2010 this number rose to 1 out of 68 children.

Autism Spectrum Disorder is largely caused by genes [7], although the environment clearly plays an important, although poorly understood, role. Nevertheless, the increasing rate of diagnoses has led many to look for other causes beyond genes, including the loosened definition of autism, and the heightened awareness of the disorder. Actress Jenny McCarthy (one of the co-hosts of *The View* [8]) has famously argued that vaccines caused the rise in autism diagnoses. She came to this conclusion after her son was diagnosed with autism and because "The rate of autism increased with the increase of vaccinations" [9] (p. 310). Interestingly, in the moments before her son received the MMR vaccine (MMR = measles, mumps, rubella), McCarthy asked the pediatrician, "Isn't this the autism shot or something like that?" [10] (p. 83).

Although McCarthy's original pediatrician told her there was no connection between vaccines and autism, she started finding doctors that did see a connection. One such doctor was Jerry Kartzinel who also indicates that the MMR vaccine caused autism for his own child [11]. Moreover, McCarthy has been influenced by other doctors such as Andrew Wakefield. Based on research with 12 children, Wakefield and his colleagues made a link between autism and the MMR vaccine. As described by Wakefield et al. [12]:

> In eight children, the onset of behavioural problems had been linked, either by the parents or by the child's physician, with measles, mumps, and rubella vaccination. Five had had an early adverse reaction to immunisation (rash, fever, delirium; and, in three cases, convulsions). In these eight children the average interval from exposure to first behavioural symptoms was 6·3 days (range 1-14). (p. 638)

As can be seen by the quote from this article, this autism–vaccine connection was not made by any type of controlled experiment or a sample of children large enough to infer a significant relationship between the vaccination and the onset of symptoms. This connection was made based on the parent or physician noticing that autism symptoms started occurring soon after the vaccination. Taken at first glance, though, one can see how this would seem like a concerning pattern worth investigating.

Indeed, since the publication of Wakefield's article, quite a few studies with thousands of children have been conducted. For example, over 500,000 children were studied in Denmark, and 82% had received the MMR vaccine [13]. This study compared autism rates in children that received the vaccine (at the average age of 17 months old) to those that didn't. Overall, both groups had equivalent rates of autism, strongly suggesting that the MMR vaccine doesn't cause autism. Many studies since then have reported similar findings. In fact, a recent meta-analysis (which is a larger study combining the results from several other studies) concluded that there's no link between the MMR vaccine and autism [14].

Paul Offit, author of *Autism's False Prophets* [15], suggests that as one vaccine theory of autism falls short, the anti-vaccine crowd quickly shifts attention to a new hypothesis [16]. Thus, another theory is that it's actually the preservatives in vaccines, rather than the vaccines themselves, that cause autism. One such preservative is called Thimerosal, which contains a very small amount of mercury. Because mercury poisoning can cause problematic symptoms for anyone, it's reasonable to wonder if the small amount of mercury included in Thimerosal causes problems for children. This concern led the CDC to discourage the use of Thimerosal in vaccines [17]. Nevertheless, even with significantly reduced levels of mercury in vaccines, autism rates have continued to increase, and research has consistently shown that there's *not* a link between Thimerosal and autism [18, 19]. The next shift in hypotheses has been that it's the accumulation of several vaccines, not any single vaccine, that causes autism; however, this hypothesis has also been refuted by research [16, 20].

The vaccine–autism hypothesis really began to unravel when 11 of the 13 co-authors from the Wakefield et al. [12] study released a statement *retracting* the interpretation that a "causal link was established between the MMR vaccine and autism as the data were insufficient" [21]. Of the two authors that weren't included on this retraction, one could not be contacted and the other was Andrew Wakefield. Wakefield continued to stand by the article even after the editors of the journal in which it was published actually retracted the original article [22]; we discovered the hard way that it's actually challenging to read the retracted article online now because of the big red "RETRACTED" written across every page.

The retraction came following a legal ruling that Wakefield had committed ethical violations for the way in which he conducted the study, partly for failing to disclose that he was being paid by the lawyers of parents who were suing makers of the MMR vaccine [23]. Moreover, the verdict suggested that he had acted with "callous disregard" by exposing the children in the study to unnecessary and painful medical procedures [24]. Despite all of the problems with Wakefield's research, Jenny McCarthy continues to stand by him, even writing in the foreword of Wakefield's book, "As the parent of a child who regressed into autism after his vaccinations, I have always considered Andy Wakefield to represent the kind of doctor and scientist who will ultimately help us end the epidemic of children with autism" [25] (p. iii).

Unfortunately, before Wakefield's research was discredited, the toothpaste was already out of the tube. The media had jumped on the story, and with help from the celebrity status of Jenny McCarthy, parents across the world became very worried about vaccines. Beliefs about an autism–vaccine connection still remain fairly high today. One recent study surveyed over 400 parents of children with autism [26]. Interestingly, 12% of these parents indicated that vaccines "are **known** to cause autism." While that percentage is not too shockingly high, 68% of the parents indicated that vaccines "are **suspected** to cause autism," which is only slightly less than the 75% of parents who correctly suspected that genes have a role in causing autism. This study had one other interesting question, and we just couldn't pass up the opportunity to report the results. Specifically, 16% of the parents indicated that they relied on Jenny McCarthy for "information about the possible causes of autism," and this percentage was higher than those relying on Andrew Wakefield (10%) and Paul Offitt (4%). Other recent research shows that 49% of parents of children with autism believe that vaccines and autism are related [27], and in our research, 23% of students and 24% of parents (in general) agreed with the statement that "Vaccines have been a common cause of autism" [28].

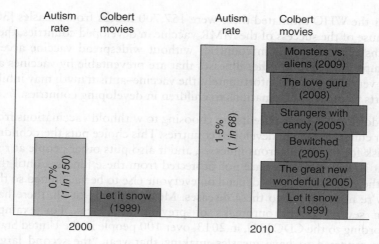

Figure 2   The autism rate is positively correlated with Stephen Colbert's movie success. The CDC (n.d.a) reported that in the year 2000, 1 out of every 150 children (or about 0.7% of youth) met the diagnostic criteria for autism. These numbers rose substantially in the years leading up to 2010, by which time Colbert had appeared in several movies.

Several of the "Sources of Psychological Myths" help explain why many people believe there's a vaccine–autism connection. First, regarding misleading media, under the guise of "balanced" reporting, news shows have often given equal time to both sides of the debate, even when evidence strongly contradicted Wakefield's side of the story. In the twelfth chapter of *Bad Science: Quacks, Hacks, and Big Pharma Flacks* [29], Ben Goldacre argues that the media is largely to blame for the vaccine scare. Second, parents often use post hoc, ergo propter hoc ("after this, therefore because of this") reasoning when autism symptoms are noticed. That is, parents often begin to notice autism symptoms between the first and second birthdays, and that also happens to be around the time children get the MMR vaccine. Finally, a third source relates to Jenny McCarthy's claim that the rise of autism correlates with the rise in the number of vaccinations, and she has a graph in her book that shows this connection [9] (p. 310); however, correlation does not equal causation. By that same logic we have created a very similar graph that actually shows that the rise of autism diagnoses corresponds with Stephen Colbert's movie acting success (Figure 2). Thus, it may actually be Stephen Colbert's success that is causing increased rates of autism!

Unfortunately, believing in this myth can result in fatal consequences. Measles is one of the most deadly illnesses a child can contract, and in

2011 the WHO estimated there were 157,700 deaths from measles [30]. Because of the success of the MMR vaccine in developed countries, these deaths typically occur in countries without widespread vaccine access. Mumps, rubella, and other illnesses that are preventable by vaccines are also very dangerous. Unfortunately, the vaccine–autism myth may inhibit efforts to provide vaccinations to children in developing countries.

Additionally, some parents are choosing to withhold vaccinations from their children, even in developed countries. This choice puts their children at risk for these dangerous illnesses, and it also puts other people at risk. That is, because babies are not protected from these illnesses until they get the vaccination, they depend on everyone else to be vaccinated so that they're not exposed to these diseases. Most troubling of all, there have been several recent outbreaks of preventable illness. For example, according to the CDC [31], in 2013, over 100 people in the United States were reported to have measles, making that year "the second largest number of cases in the U.S. since measles was eliminated in 2000." Similar outbreaks have occurred with mumps [32] and other illnesses resulting in deaths. These outbreaks are often traced to children who haven't been vaccinated [33].

In some ways Jenny McCarthy is an easy target when it comes to this myth, and we believe it's somewhat unfair to put too much blame on her. Parents probably wouldn't give much attention to McCarthy without the support of doctors like Jerry Kartzinel and Andrew Wakefield. Also, in an effort to be fair, there are some rare circumstances in which children can have negative reactions (but not autism) to vaccinations [34], so parents would be wise to discuss potential side effects with their pediatricians.

Finally, Lilienfeld et al. [35] describe one last dilemma that's an important part of this debate. Namely, "it's difficult to prove a negative in science" (p. 199). That is, while research very soundly fails to show a connection between autism and vaccines, no research study could ever investigate every contributing causal factor for every child with autism in the world. Although we have good evidence that autism is largely influenced by genes, potential environmental contributing factors should continue to be studied.

What you need to know

Applied Behavior Analysis (ABA) has been identified as a well-established comprehensive treatment for early autism [35]. Broadly speaking, ABA is an intensive intervention in which therapists develop a comprehensive plan to systematically reinforce specific adaptive behaviors (e.g., using language to ask for an object) that can replace maladaptive behaviors (e.g., using hitting to get an object). Social communication skills have a high priority, but ABA also targets many other behaviors as well (e.g., daily living skills, leisure skills). Some specific evidence-based variations of ABA include the Lovaas approach [36] (Lovaas, 1987) as well as Pivotal Response Training [37]. Additionally, The National Professional Development Center on Autism Spectrum Disorders [38] has identified many specific research-supported strategies that can be used as part of an ABA program, and their website provides a lot of useful updated information (www. autismpdc.fpg.unc.edu). Some examples include: the picture exchange communication system, functional behavior assessment, and task analysis, to name a few. One of the best resources for learning how to set up an ABA program is the book *Behavioral Intervention for Young Children with Autism: A Manual for Parents and Professionals* [39].

References

[1] American Psychiatric Association (2013). *Diagnostic and Statistical Manual of Mental Disorders: DSM-V*. Washington, DC: American Psychiatric Association.

[2] American Psychiatric Association (1994). *Diagnostic and Statistical Manual of Mental Disorders: DSM-IV*. Washington, DC: American Psychiatric Association.

[3] American Psychiatric Association (1980). *Diagnostic and Statistical Manual of Mental Disorders: DSM-III*. Washington, DC: American Psychiatric Association.

[4] American Psychiatric Association (1968). *Diagnostic and Statistical Manual of Mental Disorders: DSM-II*. Washington, DC: American Psychiatric Association.

[5] Lilienfeld, S. O., Lynn, S. J., Ruscio, J., & Beyerstein, B. L. (2010). *50 Great Myths of Popular Psychology: Shattering Widespread Misconceptions about Human Behavior*. Malden, MA: Wiley-Blackwell.

[6] Center for Disease Control (n.d.a). Autism Spectrum Disorders: Data & Statistics. Retrieved from http://www.cdc.gov/ncbddd/autism/data.html [accessed August 2014].

[7] Devlin, B. & Scherer, S. W. (2012). Genetic architecture in autism spectrum disorder. *Current Opinion in Genetics & Development*, 22, 229–237. doi: 10.1016/j.gde.2012.03.002.

[8] Walters, B. & Geddie, B.(Producers) (2013). *The View* [Television series]. New York: Barwell Productions.

[9] McCarthy, J. & Kartzinel, J. (2010). *Healing and Preventing Autism: A Complete Guide*. New York, NY: Plume.

[10] McCarthy, J. (2007). *Louder than Words: A Mother's Journey in Healing Autism*. New York, NY: Dutton.

[11] Kartzinel, J. J. (2007). Introduction. In J. McCarthy (Author), *Louder than Words: A Mother's Journey in Healing Autism*. New York, NY: Dutton.

[12] Wakefield, A. J., Murch, S. H., Anthony, A., et al. (1998). RETRACTED: Ileal-lymphoid-nodular hyperplasia, non-specific colitis, and pervasive developmental disorder in children. *The Lancet*, 351, 637–641.

[13] Madsen, K. M., Hviid, A., Vestergaard, M., et al. (2002). A population-based study of measles, mumps, and rubella vaccination and autism. *New England Journal of Medicine*, 347, 1477–1482. doi:10.1056/NEJMoa021134.

[14] Hobson, K. A., Mateu, P. F., Coryn, C. L., & Graves, C. (2012). Measles, mumps, and rubella vaccines and diagnoses of autism spectrum disorders among children: A meta-analysis. *World Medical & Health Policy*, 4(2), 1–14.

[15] Offit, P. A. & Columbia University (2008). *Autism's False Prophets: Bad Science, Risky Medicine, and the Search for a Cure*. New York, NY: Columbia University Press.

[16] Gerber, J. S. & Offit, P. A. (2009). Vaccines and autism: A tale of shifting hypotheses. *Clinical Infectious Diseases*, 48, 456–461. doi:10.1086/596476.

[17] Center for Disease Control (1999). Recommendations regarding the use of vaccines that contain Thimerosal as a preservative. *Morbidity and Mortality Weekly Report*, 48, 996–998. doi:10.1001/jama.282.22.2114-a.

[18] Hurley, A. M., Tadrous, M., & Miller, E. S. (2010). Thimerosal-containing vaccines and autism: A review of recent epidemiologic studies. *Journal of Pediatric Pharmacology and Therapeutics*, 15, 173–181.

[19] Price, C. S., Thompson, W. W., Goodson, B., et al. (2010). Prenatal and infant exposure to thimerosal from vaccines and immunoglobulins and risk of autism. *Pediatrics*, 126, 656–664. doi:10.1542/peds.2010-0309.

[20] Uno, Y., Uchiyama, T., Kurosawa, M., et al. (2012). The combined measles, mumps, and rubella vaccines and the total number of vaccines are not associated with development of autism spectrum disorder: The first case–control study in Asia. *Vaccine*, 30, 4292–4298. doi:10.1016/j.vaccine.2012.01.093.

[21] Murch, S. H., Anthony, A., Casson, D. H., et al. (2004). Retraction of an interpretation. *Lancet*, 363(9411), 750.

[22] Valentine, A., Davies, S. E., & Walker-Smith, J. A. (2010). Retraction— 'Ileal-lymphoid-nodular hyperplasia, non-specific colitis, and pervasive developmental disorder in children'. *The Lancet*, 375, 445.

[23] Boseley, S. (2010). Andrew Wakefield found 'irresponsible' by GMC over MMR vaccine scare. Retrieved from www.theguardian.com [accessed August 2014].

[24] Triggle, N. (2010). MMR scare doctor 'acted unethically', panel finds. Retrieved from www.news.bbc.co.uk/news [accessed August 2014].

[25] McCarthy, J. (2011). Foreword. In A. Wakefield (Author), *Callous Disregard: Autism Vaccines – The Truth Behind a Tragedy*. New York, NY: Skyhorse Publishing.

[26] Interactive Autism Network (2013). Autism knowledge and media questionnaire. Retrieved from https://www.ianresearch.org/pdfs/Community/IAN_Autism KnowledgeandMediaQuestionnaire01-28-2013.pdf [accessed August 2014].

[27] Bazzano, A., Zeldin, A., Schuster, E., et al. (2012). Vaccine-related beliefs and practices of parents of children with autism spectrum disorders.

American Journal on Intellectual and Developmental Disabilities, 117, 233–242. doi: 10.1352/1944-7558-117.3.233.

[28] Hupp, S., Stary, A., & Jewell, J. (submitted). Beliefs about myths related to child psychology, development, and parenting: Which myths need the most debunking?

[29] Goldacre, B. (2010). *Bad Science: Quacks, Hacks, and Big Pharma Flacks*. New York, NY: Faber and Faber.

[30] World Health Organization (n.d.). Measles. Retrieved from http://www.who.int/immunization_monitoring/diseases/measles/en/index.html [accessed August 2014].

[31] Center for Disease Control (n.d.b). Measles outbreaks. Retrieved from http://www.cdc.gov/measles/outbreaks.html [accessed August 2014].

[32] Center for Disease Control (n.d.c.). Mumps outbreaks. Retrieved from http://www.cdc.gov/mumps/outbreaks.html [accessed August 2014].

[33] Center for Disease Control (2013a). Measles – United States, January 1–August 24, 2013. Retrieved from http://www.cdc.gov/mmwr/preview/mmwrhtml/mm6236a2.htm [accessed August 2014].

[34] Center for Disease Control (2013b). Possible side-effects from vaccines. Retrieved from http://www.cdc.gov/vaccines/vac-gen/side-effects.htm#mmr [accessed August 2014].

[35] Rogers, S. J. & Vismara, L. A. (2008). Evidence-based comprehensive treatments for early autism. *Journal of Clinical Child & Adolescent Psychology*, 37, 8–38. doi:10.1080/15374410701817808.

[36] Lovaas, O. I. (1987). Behavioral treatment and normal educational and intellectual functioning in young autistic children. *Journal of Consulting and Clinical Psychology*, 55, 3–9. doi:10.1037/0022-006X.55.1.3.

[37] Koegel, R. L., O'Dell, M. C. & Koegel, L. K. (1987). A natural language teaching paradigm for nonverbal autistic children. *Journal of Autism and Developmental Disorders*, 17(2), 187–200. doi:10.1007/BF01495055.

[38] The National Professional Development Center on Autism Spectrum Disorders (n.d.). Evidence-based practice briefs. Retrieved from http://autismpdc.fpg.unc.edu/content/briefs [accessed August 2014].

[39] Maurice, C., Green, G. & Luce, S. C. (1996). *Behavioral Intervention for Young Children with Autism: A Manual for Parents and Professionals*. Austin, TX: Pro-Ed.

Speed busting for growth, body, & mind

Myth #19

A good response to stimulant medication is proof that a child has ADHD

Stimulant medications, such as Ritalin and Adderall, have been associated with short-term improvements in the attentive behavior of children with Attention-Deficit/Hyperactivity Disorder (ADHD) [1]. This effect has led some people to conclude that children must certainly have ADHD if they respond positively to a stimulant medication. Two primary lines of research, however, debunk this notion. First, stimulant medication is helpful for about 70–80% of children with ADHD, which means that up to 30% of children with ADHD do not respond favorably [2]. Second, stimulant medications "work similarly in people who do and do not have ADHD – they can help most children and adults achieve better focus and concentration" [3]. Taken together, the effectiveness or ineffectiveness of a stimulant medication shouldn't be used to confirm or dispute a diagnosis of ADHD. Because stimulant medications also work for children without ADHD, some undiagnosed children are being prescribed stimulant medication to help concentrate while studying for tests such as the ACT or SAT. This practice, called "pediatric neuroenhancement," has been strongly discouraged in a position statement endorsed by organizations such as the Child Neurology Society [4].

Myth #20 Requiring children to "clean their plates" promotes healthy eating habits

As part of a national effort to conserve resources in America during World War I, the "Clean Plate Club" campaign was designed to conserve food [5]. That is, it was unpatriotic to leave food on your plate. Today many children are still encouraged to eat every bit of food on their plate. However, these days portion sizes are considerably larger than they were in 1917 which makes the "clean your plate" philosophy a little more risky. With research showing a connection between binge eating and frequent parental statements like "clean your plate" [6], better advice for today is for parents to say, "stop eating when you're full."

Myth #21 Dyslexia's defining feature is letter reversal

Lilienfeld et al. [7] debunk the myth that "The Defining Feature of Dyslexia Is Reversing Letters" (p. 89), and they provide several pieces of evidence against this myth. For example, letter reversals are common among emerging readers, and research often fails to find significantly more letter reversals in children with dyslexia as compared with other groups of children [8]. Furthermore, letter reversals only contribute to a small amount of the errors of children with dyslexia [8]. Although some children with dyslexia may reverse letters, many children with dyslexia frequently do *not* reverse letters, and the mere act of reversing letters doesn't indicate a child has dyslexia. Thus, in *The Cosby Show*, Clair Huxtable didn't quite have it right when she said that Theo's dyslexia was simply defined as "a disorder in which people see letters backwards or in a different sequence" [9].

Myth #22
Most babies can learn to read with the right learning program

Prior to August of 2012, you may have been exposed to advertisements for a product that could teach a baby how to read. In fact, Robert Titzer's, *Your Baby Can Read!*® program [10] grossed an estimated 185 million dollars between 2008 and 2012 [11]. Targeting babies as young as 3 months old, the program uses flash cards, books, and videos to teach reading skills. The advertisements also claimed that research proved the program worked. However, the Federal Trade Commission [11] disagreed, and Titzer ultimately agreed to a 185 million dollar legal settlement for making false claims. Although some children can learn to read at a young age, no research has shown that a specific reading program can teach the typical baby to read.

Myth #23
Educational kinesiology promotes learning in children

Educational kinesiology is based on the idea that certain exercises activate the brain in a way that promotes learning. Brain Gym® is one name-brand version of educational kinesiology that is gaining in popularity [12]. Examples of the types of "exercises" that are a part of Brain Gym® include: purposefully yawning, tracing imagined symbols with a finger, and crawling on the floor. The idea behind these exercises is that they're said to improve coordination among different parts of the brain (e.g., front-to-back). After an extensive literature search, Hyatt [13] found only five peer-reviewed studies on Brain Gym® and discovered many serious credibility problems and methodological issues. For example, in one of the studies the study author was also one of the study's participants. The majority of the other studies were all published in the same journal in which the authors paid to have their work published. Overall, Hyatt reports that "these studies clearly failed to support claims that Brain Gym® movements were effective interventions for academic learning" (p. 122).

Myth #24
Facilitated communication is effective for children with autism

Many children with autism have never spoken a word. Nevertheless, they often can learn to use augmentative communication such as speech generating devices [14]. With speech generating devices, the child presses pictures or letters and the device produces words. These devices are an excellent resource for many children. However, another type of alternative communication is called *facilitated communication*, and it was developed in the last few decades of the 20th century. With facilitated communication children point to letters to spell words, much like the augmentative communication described earlier. However, the big difference between facilitated communication and effective augmentative communication is that with facilitated communication an adult holds on to the child's hand during the communication. That is, the adult is helping to "steady" the hand because the child is thought to have difficulty with fine motor control [15]. Using this method, children who had never spoken before were suddenly communicating in sentences. Unfortunately, after well-controlled research was conducted, it became apparent that the adults were actually controlling the child's hand [16].

The adult control may at times be intentional; however, some research also suggests an ideomotor response [17]. An ideomotor response involves adults having the child spell out words without even realizing that they're in control, much like how a Ouija board works. Thus, although there are some effective forms of augmentative communication, facilitated communication is not one of them. This is especially concerning when you consider that facilitated communication has been used to accuse some adults of sexual abuse [18]. Thanks to skeptics of facilitated communication, the practice has somewhat decreased in the 21st century. Unfortunately, a new variation is gaining steam. As described by one recent news story, "'Rapid Prompting Method' helps boy with autism communicate" [19]. Like facilitated communication, the rapid prompting method involves children pointing to letters [20]; however, instead of an adult steadying the child's hand, the adult often holds on to the letter sheet. The adult also makes a determination about which letter the child actually pointed to and chooses which finger movements to count as official pointing movements. Other aspects of the rapid prompting method include having the teacher sit on the student's right side, which is said to aid in left-brain learning (see Zane [21] for a description and critique). The documentary *A Mother's Courage: Talking Back to Autism* [22], narrated by actress Kate Winslet, promotes the rapid prompting method.

Myth #25 Dolphin-assisted therapy effectively treats children with special needs

Factually speaking, dolphins are awesome. They're beautiful, elegant, and intelligent. But are they therapeutic? In an interview, Betsy Smith, an associate professor and anthropologist, stated that "The dolphins' high intelligence and surprising sensitivity to the needs of the disabled, as well as their apparent delight in spontaneous, nonverbal play, makes them ideal 'companion therapists'" [23] (p. 386). Proponents argue that dolphin-assisted therapy (DAT) can help increase the adaptive functioning (e.g., language and social skills) of children with special needs, such as children with autism, Down's syndrome, cerebral palsy, and other conditions [24, 25]. There are several theories for how dolphins can provide therapeutic effects, with one theory focusing on the idea that "the ultrasound emitted by dolphins could have an effect on biological tissue ..." [26] (p. 99). Nevertheless, scientific evidence contradicts this possibility. Still others claim that dolphins possess telepathic (mind-reading) powers. In one of the most recent studies, 37 parents of children with special needs completed a questionnaire at pretest. After their child received dolphin-assisted therapy, the parents also completed the questionnaire as a posttest [24]. At the posttest, parents rated their children as improved on three of the four subscales (i.e., aggressive/acting out, irresponsible/inattentive, and socially withdrawn). However, Marino and Lilienfeld [27] point out serious flaws that are often included in research like this. Some of the biggest limitations include the lack of a control group, the parents' expectancy of improvement, and the effect of the general excitement during this fun intervention. Marino and Lilienfeld review several other studies with very questionable results, and they also describe several more common problems regarding the design of the studies.

References

[1] Pelham Jr, W. E. & Fabiano, G. A. (2008). Evidence-based psychosocial treatments for attention-deficit/hyperactivity disorder. *Journal of Clinical Child & Adolescent Psychology*, 37, 184–214. doi:10.1080/ 15374410701818681.

[2] Swanson, J. M., McBurnett, K., Christian, D. L., & Wigal, T. (1995). Stimulant medications and the treatment of children with ADHD. In T. H. Ollendick & J. R. Prinz (Eds), *Advances in Clinical Child Psychology*, 17, p. 265. New York, NY: Plenum Press.

[3] American Academy of Pediatrics (2013). What you need to know about stimulant medication. Retrieved from http://www.healthychildren.org/English/health-issues/conditions/adhd/pages/What-You-Need-to-Know-About-Stimulant-Medication.aspx [accessed August 2014].

[4] Graf, W. D., Nagel, S. K., Epstein, L. G., et al. (2013). Pediatric neuroenhancement: Ethical, legal, social, and neurodevelopmental implications. *Neurology*, 80, 1251–1260. doi:10.1212/WNL.0b013e318289703b.

[5] American Institute for Cancer Research (2004, February). Resign from the clean plate club. Retrieved from http://preventcancer.aicr.org/site/News2?page=NewsArticle&id=7598&news_iv_ctrl=0&abbr=pr_ [accessed August 2014].

[6] Puhl, R. M. & Schwartz, M. B. (2003). If you are good you can have a cookie: How memories of childhood food rules link to adult eating behaviors. *Eating Behaviors*, 4, 283–293. doi:10.1016/S1471-0153(03)00024-2.

[7] Lilienfeld, S. O., Lynn, S. J., Ruscio, J., & Beyerstein, B. L. (2010). *50 Great Myths of Popular Psychology: Shattering Widespread Misconceptions about Human Behavior*. Malden, MA: Wiley-Blackwell.

[8] Terepocki, M., Kruk, R. S., & Willows, D. M. (2002). The incidence and nature of letter orientation errors in reading disability. *Journal of Learning Disabilities*, 35, 214. doi:10.1177/002221940203500304.

[9] Leeson, M., Weinberger, E. (Writers), & Sandrich, J. (Director) (1989). Theo's gift [Television series episode]. In M. Carsey & T. Werner (Executive producers), *The Cosby Show*. New York: NBC Broadcasting.

[10] Titzer, R. C., Dozier, B., & Dozier, L. (2005). *Your Baby Can Read!* Carlsbad, CA: Penton Overseas.

[11] Federal Trade Commission (2012, August 28). Ads touting "Your Baby Can read" were deceptive, FTC complaint alleges. Retrieved from http://www.ftc.gov/opa/2012/08/babyread.shtm [accessed August 2014].

[12] Dennison, P. E. & Dennison, G. E. (1994). *Brain Gym*. Ventura, CA: Edu-Kinesthetics.

[13] Hyatt, K. J. (2007). Brain Gym®: Building stronger brains or wishful thinking? *Remedial and Special Education*, 28, 117–124. doi:10.1177/07419325070280020201.

[14] The National Professional Development Center on Autism Spectrum Disorders (n.d.). Evidence-based practice briefs. Retrieved from http://autismpdc.fpg.unc.edu/content/briefs [accessed August 2014].

[15] Biklen, D. (1993). *Communication Unbound: How Facilitated Communication is Challenging Traditional Views of Autism and Ability-Disability*. New York, NY: Teachers College Press.

[16] Jacobson, J. W., Mulick, J. A., & Schwartz, A. A. (1995). A history of facilitated communication: Science, pseudoscience, and antiscience science working group on facilitated communication. *American Psychologist*, 50, 750–765. doi:10.1037/ 0003-066X.50.9.750.

[17] Burgess, C. A., Kirsch, I., Shane, H., et al. (1998). Facilitated communication as an ideomotor response. *Psychological Science*, 9, 71–74. doi:10.1111/1467-9280.00013.

[18] Bligh, S. & Kupperman, P. (1993). Brief report: Facilitated communication evaluation procedure accepted in a court case. *Journal of Autism and Developmental Disorders*, 23, 553–557. doi:10.1007/BF01046056.

[19] Perry, T. (2013, June 30). "Rapid prompting method" helps boy with autism communicate. Retrieved from http://fox6now.com/2013/06/30/rapid-prompting-method-helps-boy-with-autism-communicate/ [accessed August 2014].

[20] Rapid Prompting Method (n.d.). Retrieved from http://www.asatonline.org/treatment/treatments/rpm [accessed August 2014].

[21] Zane (2012, February 15). A review of the Soma rapid prompt method. Retrieved from http://www.operationautismonline.org/blog/a-review-of-the-soma-rapid-prompt-method/.

[22] Friðrik, Þ. F. (Director) (2010). *A Mother's Courage: Talking Back to Autism* [Documentary]. New York, NY: First Run Features.

[23] Smith, B. (1987). Dolphins plus autistic children. *Psychological Perspectives*, 18, 386–397. doi:10.1080/00332928708410866.

[24] Dilts, R., Trompisch, N., & Bergquist, T. M. (2011). Dolphin-assisted therapy for children with special needs: A pilot study. *Journal of Creativity in Mental Health*, 6, 56–68. doi:10.1080/15401383.2001.557309.

[25] Nathanson, D. E., de Castro, D., Friend, H., & McMahon, M. (1997). Effectiveness of short-term dolphin-assisted therapy for children with severe disabilities. *Anthrozoos: A Multidisciplinary Journal of the Interactions of People & Animals*, 10, 90–100. doi:10.2752/089279397787001166.

[26] Brensing, K., Linke, K., & Todt, D. (2003). Can dolphins heal by ultrasound? *Journal of Theoretical Biology*, 225, 99–105.

[27] Marino, L. & Lilienfeld, S. O. (2007). Dolphin-assisted therapy: More flawed data and more flawed conclusions. *Anthrozoos: A Multidisciplinary Journal of the Interactions of People & Animals*, 20, 239–249. doi:10.2752/089279307X224782.

3 EMOTIONS & BEHAVIOR

Great Myths of Child Development, First Edition. Stephen Hupp and Jeremy Jewell.
© 2015 John Wiley & Sons, Inc. Published 2015 by John Wiley & Sons, Inc.

Bed-wetting is a sign of serious emotional problems

Parenting consists of a long series of "firsts": first steps, first words, and first dry night of sleep. Toilet training practices vary widely from one culture to the next and also throughout history [1]. While toilet training schedules for some cultures are a strictly controlled practice, other cultures are more lax, believing that this milestone will occur with only moderate encouragement and support from parents and others.

Mastering bladder control throughout the night can be one of the most challenging aspects of toilet training. Because it's so common for preschool-aged children to wet their beds, a child must be at least 5 years old before being diagnosed with problem bed-wetting or, as it's called, nocturnal enuresis [2]. Moreover, nocturnal enuresis is not diagnosed if the bed-wetting can be explained by a medical condition. But when problems with bed-wetting do occur, many parents are concerned that the bed-wetting reflects an underlying emotional or psychological problem.

Current parental worries about bed-wetting may have roots in Sigmund Freud's theories. Freud, a physician and founder of psychoanalysis, proposed that children's development was based on their achievement of milestones at various stages of psychosexual development. In *Three Essays on the Theory of Sexuality* [3], Freud describes three stages of "infantile masturbation," and he suggests that the function of bed-wetting is similar to nocturnal emissions (i.e., wet dreams). In this work and others, he frequently connects excessive masturbation with the later development of neuroses. With regard to bed-wetting, Freud states that "Most of the so-called bladder disorders of this period are sexual disturbances: nocturnal enuresis, unless it represents an epileptic fit, corresponds to a nocturnal emission" (p. 68). In the famous case study, *Dora: An Analysis of a Case of Hysteria* [4], Freud states that "Bed-wetting of this kind has, to the best of my knowledge, no more likely cause than masturbation, a habit whose importance in the aetiology of bed-wetting in general is still insufficiently appreciated" (p. 93). In Freud's analysis, these behaviors of bed-wetting and masturbation, both of which Dora admitted to doing, were early symptoms of her eventually diagnosed hysteria. Hysteria (from the root "hystera," or "uterus"), in that time period, was commonly used as a broad diagnosis to cover a range of emotional issues and was more frequently diagnosed in women [5].

Followers of Freud continued to elaborate on the connection between bed-wetting and emotional problems well into the 20th century. For example, in a review of psychoanalytic evaluation and treatment of enuresis, Mishne [6] states that "Those [psychoanalytic theorists] who view nocturnal enuresis as a symptom of emotional disturbance conclude that bed-wetting may be interpreted as a psychologically understandable reaction of the child; a reaction emanating from emotional conditions in the home and primarily from a deficient mother/child relationship" (pp. 475–476). Mishne describes the psychoanalytic theory that bed-wetting is predictive of later bisexuality because "the enuretic act is conceived as both, active and passive, masculine and feminine …" (p. 474), and Mishne also adds that "The psychodynamic perspective [on enuresis] also emphasizes distortion of body image, castration fantasies, and conflicts related to sexual identification" (p. 474). Wow, bed-wetting sounds to be a pretty powerful predictor, indeed!

Others, such as pediatrician Benjamin Spock [7], focus on the child's general anxieties as being the cause of bed-wetting. He states that "Happy, outgoing children seldom continue to wet the bed" (p. 430), and the most likely cause is "tenseness of various sorts in a child's feelings" (p. 429). Specifically, Dr. Spock suggests some possible causes of this tenseness could be moving into a new house, attending an exciting birthday party, feeling pressure at school, dealing with sibling rivalry, or experiencing the birth of a sibling. The last example includes the child's "longing in his dreams to go back to the good old days when he was a baby himself, when his mother took care of all his bodily needs without complaint, and he had nothing to worry about" (p. 429). As you might expect, Spock was influenced by the Freudian perspective.

However, the belief that bed-wetting is caused by psychological problems is surprisingly new when considering the expanse of history. In fact, for most of recorded history, many cultures have understood nighttime wetting to have some sort of physiological cause, similar to views held by the medical community today. For example, in *An Historical Account of Enuresis* [8], Glicklich notes that "It's not known when enuresis became a medical problem, but it has been recognized as a disturbance of childhood necessitating medical treatment since the time of the Papyrus Ebers which is dated 1550 B.C." (p. 859). Interestingly, the author notes that the ancient Egyptian treatment for incontinence required Juniper berries, Cyprus, and beer. Other remedies from the 15th to 19th centuries included eating or drinking tonics made from various plant or animal products, improving the child's diet and exercise regimen, or having the child avoid drinking before bedtime. Additionally, a number of more unusual and sometimes painful therapies were also employed. These included applying blisters to parts of the genital area or wearing various mechanical devices, such as an iron yoke worn around the crotch [8]. By the 19th century, but prior to Freud, most professionals treating children believed that enuresis was caused by some sort of physiological problem, including the child being a heavy sleeper, having poor local muscle control, or poor bedtime routines [8]. Thus, before Freud, professionals had a better idea of the causes of bed-wetting (but worse ideas for how to treat the issue).

Freud's influence, however, has continued to shape beliefs of many people today. In our research, 43% of students and 43% of parents agreed with the statement that "Children who frequently wet the bed usually have underlying emotional issues" [9]. A study of parents seeking treatment for their child's bed-wetting reported that 25% of the parents believed that their "Child could control wetting if [they] tried harder" [10] (p. 342). Similarly, another survey found that only 62% of parents failed to correctly identify enuresis as having a physical cause, and 26% of parents specifically thought bed-wetting has a psychological cause [11].

Regarding research on the causes of bed-wetting, two reviews found that children with a history of frequent bed-wetting tend to have problems with higher than normal urine production at night and a greater likelihood of dysfunction in the bladder or muscles controlling bladder release [12, 13]. Also, some researchers suggest problems with sleep arousal (being a deep sleeper) can contribute to bed-wetting [12, 14]. Therefore, medical research has found a variety of physiological explanations for bed-wetting [12, 14], with one expert on the topic making the definitive conclusion that "the research community has generally abandoned psychoanalytic speculations that enuresis is a problem caused by thoughts or feelings of children" [13] (p. 140).

Although there are a number of physiological explanations for bed-wetting, what does the research say specifically about underlying emotional problems? An initial research question would be to examine if children that wet the bed are more likely to have serious emotional problems. To answer this question, Friman and colleagues [15] administered a child behavior problems questionnaire to the parents of three groups of children: those with bed-wetting, those with behavioral clinical problems, and a control group of children who weren't referred for any problems. The study controlled for potential confounds such as age and sex of the child. Results indicated that the clinical group had significantly more problems and more intense problems than the bed-wetting group and the control group. The authors concluded that children with a history of frequent bed-wetting "do not necessarily have clinically significant behavioral comorbidity" (p. 539).

In another study, Fergusson and Horwood [16] followed a group of children in New Zealand for over 15 years. When they examined the relationship between bed-wetting and behavior problems they found very small correlations for symptoms of ADHD, anxiety, and conduct problems. When the researchers controlled for more important variables related to these problems, such as family history of bed-wetting and socioeconomic status, the relation between bed-wetting and emotional behavioral problems diminished even further. The authors concluded that "the associations between delays or difficulties with nocturnal bladder control and later adjustment are generally quite weak and there is little evidence to suggest that children with these problems are at a markedly increased risk of psychological problems during adolescence" [16] (p. 667).

While the study by Fergusson and Horwood [16] indicates that bed-wetting is not caused by serious underlying emotional problems, other studies have found that this relationship may actually work in the opposite direction. In other words, bed-wetting itself may cause some stress in the child. To gain the child's view of bed-wetting, Butler and Herron [17] administered questionnaires regarding the problem to several thousand 9-year-old children. Out of 21 possible childhood difficulties, bed-wetting was ranked as the 8th most difficult, and was ranked more difficult than other problems such as being "often ill," "worrying a lot," and being "shy." So it may be no wonder that bed-wetting might cause some distress in children [18]. Relatedly, one would expect that distress in children would decline after they were provided with effective treatment to curb bed-wetting. This possibility was investigated in a randomized controlled study of children in treatment for bed-wetting compared with a waitlist control group of children [19]. From the results of their study, the authors concluded that children felt less distressed after receiving treatment.

Like many of the other myths in this book, one might wonder – what's the big deal? So what if someone believes bed-wetting is caused by a psychological problem; does this belief really hurt anyone? An accurate diagnosis of the cause of bed-wetting should lead directly to evidence-based treatment. If a child's parent and physician were to assume that their bed-wetting was caused by psychological problems, then this could lead to unnecessary psychological treatment that would potentially be a waste of time, money, and effort [15] and also lead to undue blame being placed on the child, causing even greater shame and embarrassment.

A dramatic example of unnecessary shame from bed-wetting is depicted in the movie, *The Loneliest Runner* [20], by Michael Landon, who reportedly made the movie based on his own childhood problem with bed-wetting. In the movie, the main character's mother views bed-wetting as a sign of weakness and laziness, and she hangs her son's urine-stained sheets outside of his bedroom window for the whole neighborhood to see. A similar scenario was described in the autobiography *The Duck Commander Family* [21] by Willie and Korie Robertson, stars of the television show *Duck Dynasty*. In the book Willie Robertson states that his father "used to get on me for peeing in the bed and would threaten to spank me …" (p. 20).

Another celebrity publicly shared the pride associated with overcoming bed-wetting. Rapper Sean "P Diddy" Combs shared with talk show host Ellen DeGeneres [22] that as a child he "went on a quest to stop wetting the bed, and the first day I had a sleepover and I didn't wet the bed, it was one of the greatest days of my life, and it gave me the swagger that I have today because I stopped wetting the bed." Ultimately bed-wetting doesn't reflect a character flaw, or deeply entrenched emotional issues. Instead it deserves evidence-based treatment and compassion.

What you need to know

A urine alarm is a research-supported intervention for bed-wetting. Mowrer [23] studied this type of device in one of the first applied behavioral treatment studies. A urine alarm consists of a small sensor attached to the child's underwear. The alarm is intended to wake the child upon urination and is thought to work through classical conditioning in which the child begins to associate a full bladder feeling with the need to awaken [24]. According to a review by Gimpel and colleagues [24], "The enuresis alarm may be the most effective treatment for PNE [primary nocturnal enuresis], with estimated success ranging up to 70% …" (p. 26). Additionally, research has found that the urine alarm is much better than medication for attaining long-term effectiveness [25]. Although the urine alarm appears to be the most effective treatment in the long term, there are a number of obstacles to its implementation. Because of the necessary disturbance in sleep when the urine alarm is used, both parents and children must have an adequate level of motivation and patience; otherwise, the treatment may be discontinued too early [25]. An additional advantage of the urine alarm, however, is that it's relatively inexpensive compared with medication [24].

References

[1] Luxem, M. & Christophersen, E. (1994). Behavioral toilet training in early childhood: Research, practice, and implications. *Journal of Developmental & Behavioral Pediatrics*, 15(5), 370–378. doi:10.1097/00004703-199410000-00009.

[2]   American Psychiatric Association (2013). *Diagnostic and Statistical Manual of Mental Disorders: DSM-V*. Washington, DC: American Psychiatric Association.

[3]   Freud, S. (1949). *Three Essays on the Theory of Sexuality*. London: Imago.

[4]   Freud, S. & Rieff, P. (1963). *Dora: An Analysis of a Case of Hysteria*. New York, NY: Collier.

[5]   Scull, A. (2011). *Hysteria: The Disturbing History*. Oxford: Oxford University Press.

[6]   Mishne, J. M. (1993). Primary nocturnal enuresis: A psychodynamic clinical perspective. *Child and Adolescent Social Work Journal*, 10(6), 469–495. doi:10.1007/bf00757431.

[7]   Spock, B. (1946). *The Common Sense Book of Baby and Child Care*. New York, NY: Duell, Sloan and Pearce.

[8]   Glicklich, L. B. (1951). Special reviews: An historical account of enuresis. *Pediatrics*, 8, 859–876.

[9]   Hupp, S., Stary, A., & Jewell, J. (submitted). Beliefs about myths related to child psychology, development, and parenting: Which myths need the most debunking?

[10] Landgraf, J. M., Abidari, J., Cilento, B. G., et al. (2004). Coping, commitment, and attitude: Quantifying the everyday burden of enuresis on children and their families. *Pediatrics*,113, 334–344. doi:10.1542/peds.113.2.334.

[11] Huling, U., Siegelberg, T., & McDermott, E. (2003). Healthcare providers need to be more proactive in discussing bedwetting. Retrieved from http://www.thefreelibrary.com/Healthcare+Providers+Need+to+Be+More+Proactive+in+Discussing... -a0106030624 [accessed August 2014].

[12] Hjalmas, K., Arnold, T., Bower, W., et al. (2004). Nocturnal enuresis: An international evidence based management strategy. *Journal of Urology*, 171, 2545–2561. doi: 10.1097/01.ju.0000111504.85822.b2.

[13] Houts, A. C. (1991). Nocturnal enuresis as a biobehavioral problem. *Behavior Therapy*, 22, 133–151. doi:10.1016/s0005-7894(05)80173-x.

[14] Butler, R. J. (1998). Annotation: Night wetting in children: Psychological aspects. *Journal of Child Psychology and Psychiatry*,39,453–463.doi:10.1111/1469-7610.00342.

[15] Friman, P. C., Handwerk, M. L., Swearer, S. M., et al. (1998). Do children with primary nocturnal enuresis have clinically significant problems? *Archives of Pediatrics and Adolescent Medicine*,152,537–539. doi:10.1001/archpedi. 152.6.537.

[16] Fergusson, D. M. & Horwood, L. J. (1994). Nocturnal enuresis and behavioral problems in adolescence: A 15-year longitudinal study. *Pediatrics*, 94, 662–668.

[17] Butler, R. & Herron, J. (2007). An exploration of children's views of bed-wetting at 9 years. *Child: Care, Health and Development*, 34, 65–70. doi:10.1111/ j.1365-2214.2007.00781.x.

[18] Hägglöf, B., Andren, O., Bergström, E., et al. (1998). Self-esteem in children with nocturnal enuresis and urinary incontinence: Improvement of self-esteem after treatment. *European Urology*, 33(Suppl. 3), 16–19. doi:10.1159/000052236.

[19] Moffatt, M. E. K., Kato, C., & Pless, I. B. (1987). Improvements in self-concept after treatment of nocturnal enuresis: Randomized controlled trial. *Journal of Pediatrics*, 110, 647–652. doi:10.1016/s0022-3476(87)80572-3.

[20] Landon, M. (Producer & Director) (1976). *The Loneliest Runner* [Motion Picture]. USA, NBC.

[21] Robertson, W. & Robertson, K. (2012). *The Duck Commander Family: How Faith, Family, and Ducks Created a Dynasty*. New York: Howard Books.

[22] DeGeneres, E. (2013, March 1). Diddy wet the bed [Video file]. Retrieved from http://www.ellentv.com/2013/03/01/diddy-wet-the-bed/ [accessed August 2014].

[23] Mowrer, O. H. (1938). Apparatus for the study and treatment of enuresis. *American Journal of Psychology*, 51, 163–165.

[24] Gimpel, G. A., Warzak, W. J., Kuhn, B. R., & Walburn, J. N. (1998). Clinical perspectives in primary nocturnal enuresis. *Clinical Pediatrics*, 37, 23–29. doi: 10.1177/000992289803700104.

[25] Monda, J. M. & Husmann, D. A. (1995). Primary nocturnal enuresis: A comparison among observation, imipramine, desmopressin acetate and bed-wetting alarm systems. *Journal of Urology*, 154, 745–748. doi:10.1016/s0022-5347(01)67152-0.

Myth #27 Most antidepressants for children with depression are approved by the FDA

If you've noticed that fish seem happier these days, it may be related to chemicals from antidepressant medications. How do the fish get the antidepressant chemicals? Americans are taking so many antidepressants that chemicals, like fluoxetine hydrochloride (most commonly marketed with the brand name of Prozac), pass from human urine through the sewage system to lakes and rivers. This information was reported in a news story in which antidepressant chemicals were found in bluegills [1].

The World Health Organization [2] estimates that globally over 350 million people experience clinical depression, making it one of the leading causes of disability in the world. Although rates of depression are higher among teens and adults, a study of children in the USA (ages 8 to 15 years old) found that almost 4% experienced depression, with most of these children being severely impaired [3]. Unfortunately, less than half of these children had received any kind of treatment for the disorder in the past year. Depression becomes more prevalent as kids get older, as a similar report by the Substance Abuse and Mental Health Services Administration [4] found that rates of diagnosed depression increased from 4% at age 12 to over 10% by age 17, with only about a third of those children receiving any kind of treatment in the past year.

To combat this monumental public health problem, many physicians prescribe antidepressant medications (e.g., Prozac, Celexa, and Zoloft). The National Center for Health Statistics recently conducted a national survey regarding antidepressant use in America [5]. The authors found that about 11% of the US population (ages 12 years and older) is currently taking antidepressants, an increase in use by almost 400% from data about 15 years earlier [6]. For adolescents between 12 and 17 years old, almost 4% were taking antidepressants [5]. Although the rate of antidepressant use in younger children is more difficult to estimate, Cox and colleagues [7] found that about 0.5% of children between 5 and 9 years old and 1.4% between ages 10 and 14 years old had been prescribed an antidepressant from 2002 to 2005 [7]. Nevertheless, these rates may be declining, as earlier data from 1994 indicated the rate for antidepressant use ranged from 1.5% in 10- to 14-year-olds enrolled in an HMO to about 3.5% in 10- to 14-year-olds covered by Medicaid [8]. Researchers examining antidepressant use in children as young as 2 years old have noted a need for increased research in this age group as well [9].

With antidepressants being commonly used in youth, many people assume that these medications are approved by the US Food and Drug Administration (FDA) for use in children. In our research, 68% of students and 68% of parents agreed with the statement that "Most antidepressants used for kids are approved by the Food & Drug Administration" [10]. Nevertheless, at the time of this writing, there is only one antidepressant, fluoxetine (known by brand names such as Prozac and Sarafem), that is approved for the treatment of depression in children [11]. That is, none of the other commonly used antidepressants are FDA approved to treat depression in children.

Approval from the FDA is an important issue for two reasons. Medications receive FDA approval if they're safe and effective. Thus, lack of FDA approval indicates that a particular medication either has safety concerns or the medication has limited research regarding efficacy in children. One potential safety issue moved front and center in 2004 when the FDA directed drug companies to add a "black box" warning on all antidepressants prescribed to children and adolescents [12]. This imperative came after FDA committees and advisory boards heard testimony from the public and also reviewed numerous studies indicating antidepressant use was related to increased suicidality [12]. For example, a meta-analysis revealed that youth had higher rates of suicidal thoughts and suicide attempts when taking an antidepressant as compared to a placebo; however, it is worth noting that there were no suicide completions in any of the studies included in the analysis [13]. While this FDA "black box" warning does not prohibit the prescribing of most antidepressants to children, it does note that "There was considerable variation in risk of suicidality among drugs, but a tendency toward an increase in the younger patients for almost all drugs studied" [14]. This FDA announcement actually came a few months after the Medicines and Healthcare Products Regulatory Agency (MHRA) in the United Kingdom [15] announced a stronger response against antidepressant use. Currently, the MHRA advises physicians on two classes of antidepressants known as SSRIs (such as Prozac and many others) and SNRIs (such as Effexor and others). For SSRIs the MHRA states that they "are not for use in children …," with the exception of fluoxetine, and simply that "SNRIs are not for use in children or adolescents aged less than 18 years" [16].

Since the application of these "black box" warnings, some have come forward to criticize this move, citing perceived flaws in the research [17]. However, since then, better designed research has also found that the odds of a suicide attempt increased by 52% for children and adolescents that were taking antidepressants compared to a matched control group that weren't taking antidepressants [18]. Beyond suicidality, other researchers have examined what are termed as psychiatric adverse events (PAE), such as declines in the mood or behavior of the child and their relationship with SSRI antidepressant use in kids. For example, Wilens and colleagues [19] found that 22% of their sample experienced a psychiatric adverse event, which typically emerged about three months after SSRI treatment and usually disappeared fairly quickly after the child stopped taking the SSRI.

So, what effect has all of this research and the FDA "black box" warnings had on the choices made by physicians and parents? A large scale study found that after the FDA "black box" warning in 2004, antidepressant prescriptions in the USA significantly declined for adolescents (age 13 to 17) and young adults (age 18 to 24) but no decline was seen in children 12 years old and younger [20]. Another study found a similar decline in the prescription of most antidepressants for children (age 5 to 17) after the FDA "black box" warning; however, this study also showed a significant increase in prescriptions of fluoxetine, the only FDA-approved antidepressant for depression in children [21]. Although physicians appeared to heed the FDA on these two related issues, the results of this study also indicated that the recommendation to increase monitoring of these young patients didn't increase as hoped.

Although the belief that most antidepressants are FDA approved for childhood depression is inaccurate, some critics of the FDA have raised concerns that the imposition of the "black box" warnings has kept physicians from prescribing sorely needed medications to children with depression and in doing so has done more harm than good [22]. However, there is actually considerable controversy in the medical community as to whether most antidepressants are even effective in treating the symptoms of depression in children [23, 24]. For example, in the three large studies of fluoxetine's effectiveness reviewed by Cheung and colleagues [23], those receiving the drug compared to a placebo were often rated less depressed by clinicians, but no such improvements were reported by the children themselves. The results of effectiveness studies for the other antidepressants that are not FDA approved are often much worse. For example, three studies of parox-etine (e.g., Paxil) showed no significant differences between the group treated by the drug and the group receiving a placebo on the primary outcome measures [23]. Although some authors noted methodological problems with studies of the effectiveness of antidepressants in kids [23], a more serious problem with the research on these drugs is the problem of selective publication. This problem refers to the possibility that studies on antidepressant effectiveness with positive outcomes are more likely to be published than studies showing a lack of antidepressant effectiveness. For example, a review by Turner and colleagues [25] published in the *New England Journal of Medicine* concluded that "Not only were positive results more likely to be published, but studies that weren't positive, in our opinion, were often published in a way that conveyed a positive outcome" (p. 256). Garland [26], a physician-researcher involved in some of the studies on antidepressant use in kids, notes that researchers "who *did* see results of neg-ative paroxetine industry trials were prohibited by nondisclosure contracts from discussing them" (p. 490). Unfortunately, the file drawer problem [27], in which researchers do not even try to publish research with non-significant findings, is common in most areas of research, but it's especially concerning when forced by contract.

In closing, we aren't arguing that children should never take antidepres-sants. Rather, parents should be aware of the inherent issues surrounding medications for depression, which also include other possible concerning side effects beyond the suicidality issue. In fact, we look toward the future and hope that parents' options for treatment improve. This is one myth that could change over time. That is, the day may come when most of the antidepressants taken by children are FDA approved. Luckily, the section below describes another alternative.

What you need to know

Clinical depression in children is a very serious issue that requires careful and effective treatment. Therefore, parents of children with depression should work closely with their healthcare providers to weigh the risks and benefits of any treatment option. But for those parents who are hesitant to use antidepressants, there's another effective treatment that can be used instead of, or in addition to, medication. Cognitive-behavioral therapy (CBT) is perhaps the most researched psychosocial intervention and is currently the treatment of choice for a variety of problems in youth [28]. Cognitive-behavioral therapy for depression often focuses on helping the child challenge maladaptive patterns of thinking and focus on engaging in adaptive activities. Well-controlled studies on CBT have found it to be a well-established intervention for children and adolescents [29].

Parents appear to hold favorable beliefs regarding counseling, as one recent study found that "among a group of parents seeking mental health care for their children, counseling was perceived as beneficial and having few risks, whereas antidepressant medications were perceived as both beneficial and risky" [30] (p. 295). One potential misconception regarding psychological treatments such as CBT is that treatment must be lengthy and expensive. For example, in an episode of *The Simpsons* [31] the mental health professional treating Lisa Simpson tells her parents that "she'll be fine after years of expensive treatment." However, the length of CBT treatment is usually only ten sessions or less [32]. In fact, a recent economic study on the cost-effectiveness of psychosocial treatment (primarily CBT) concluded that "Screening children for signs of depression and the provision of a psychological intervention to prevent a diagnosable case of MDD [Major Depressive Disorder] represents very good value for money" [33] (p. e729).

References

[1] Streater, S. (2003, October 17). Traces of antidepressant found in bluegills in Texas creek. Retrieved from http://www.baylor.edu/mediacommunications/index.php?id=10747 [accessed August 2014].

[2] World Health Organization (2012, October). *Depression* (Fact Sheet No. 389). Retrieved from http://www.who.int/mediacentre/factsheets/fs369/en/index.html [accessed August 2014].

[3] Merikangas, K. R., He, J. P., Brody, D., et al. (2010). Prevalence and treatment of mental disorders among US children in the 2001–2004 NHANES. *Pediatrics*, 125(1), 75–81. doi:10.1542/peds.2008-2598.

[4] Substance Abuse and Mental Health Services Administration (2007). *Results from the 2006 National Survey on Drug Use and Health: National Findings* (Office of Applied Studies, NSDUH Series H-32, DHHS Publication No. SMA 07-4293). Rockville, MD.

[5] National Center for Health Statistics (2011a). *NCHS Data Brief, 76, October 2011. Antidepressant use in persons aged 12 and over: United States, 2005–2007.* Hyattsville, MD.

[6] National Center for Health Statistics (2011b). *Health, United States, 2010: With special feature on death and dying. Table 95.* Hyattsville, MD.

[7] Cox, E. R., Halloran, D. R., Homan, S. M., et al. (2008). Trends in the prevalence of chronic medication use in children: 2002–2005. *Pediatrics,* 122, e1053–1061. doi:10.1542/peds.2008-0214.

[8] Zito, J. M., Safer, D. J., dosReis, S., et al. (2002). Rising prevalence of antidepressants among US youths. *Pediatrics,* 109, 721–27. doi:10.1542/peds.109.5.721.

[9] Zito, J. M., Safer, D. J., dosReis, S., et al. (2000). Trends in the prescribing of psychotropic medications to preschoolers. *JAMA: Journal of the American Medical Association,* 283(8), 1025–1030. doi:10.1001/jama.283.8.1025.

[10] Hupp, S., Stary, A., & Jewell, J. (submitted). Beliefs about myths related to child psychology, development, and parenting: Which myths need the most debunking?

[11] Food and Drug Administration (2007). *Questions and answers on antidepressant use in children, adolescents, and adults: May 2007.* Retrieved from http://www.fda.gov/Drugs/DrugSafety/InformationbyDrugClass/ucm096321.htm [accessed August 2014].

[12] Food and Drug Administration (2004a). *FDA launches a multipronged strategy to strengthen safeguards for children treated with antidepressant medications* (Press Release). Retrieved from http://www.fda.gov/NewsEvents/Newsroom/PressAnnouncements/2004/ucm108363.htm [accessed August 2014].

[13] Bridge, J. A., Iyengar, S., Salary, C. B., et al. (2007). Clinical response and risk for reported suicidal ideation and suicide attempts in pediatric antidepressant treatment: A meta-analysis of randomized controlled trials. *JAMA: Journal of the American Medical Association,* 297(15), 1683–1696.

[14] Food and Drug Administration (2004b). *Revisions to product labeling.* Retrieved from http://www.fda.gov/downloads/Drugs/DrugSafety/Information byDrugClass/UCM173233.pdf [accessed August 2014].

[15] Medicines and Healthcare Products Regulatory Agency (2003). *Safety review of antidepressants used by children completed* (Press Release). Retrieved from http://www.mhra.gov.uk/NewsCentre/Pressreleases/CON002045 [accessed August 2014].

[16] Medicines and Healthcare Products Regulatory Agency (2013). *Selective serotonin reuptake inhibitors and serotonin and noradrenaline reuptake inhibitors: Patient summary.* Retrieved from http://www.mhra.gov.uk/Safetyinformation/Generalsafetyinformationandadvice/Product-specificinformationandadvice/Product-specificinformationandadvice%E2%80%93M%E2%80%93T/Selectiveserotoninre-uptakeinhibitors/Patientsummary/index.htm [accessed August 2014].

[17] Klein, D. (2006). The flawed basis for FDA post-marketing safety decisions: The example of anti-depressants and children. *Neuropsychopharmacology,* 31, 689–699. doi:10.1038/sj.npp.1300996.

[18] Olfson, M., Marcus, S. C., & Schaffer, D. (2006). Antidepressant drug therapy and suicide in severely depressed children and adults. *Archives of General Psychiatry,* 63, 865–872. doi:10.1001/archpsyc.63.8.865.

[19] Wilens, T. E., Biederman, J., Kwon, A., et al. (2003). A systematic chart review of the nature of psychiatric adverse events in children and adolescents treated with selective serotonin reuptake inhibitors. *Journal of Child and Adolescent Psychopharmacology*, 13, 143–152. doi:10.1089/104454603322163862.

[20] Pamer, C. A., Hammad, T. A., Wu, Y., et al. (2010). Changes in US antidepressant and antipsychotic prescription patterns during a period of FDA actions. *Pharmacoepidemiology and Drug Safety*, 19, 158–174. doi:10.1002/pds.1886.

[21] Busch, S. H., Frank, R. G., Leslie, D. L., et al. (2010). Antidepressants and suicide risk: How did specific information in FDA safety warnings affect treatment patterns? *Psychiatric Services*, 61, 11–16. doi:10.1176/appi.ps.61.1.11.

[22] Brent, D. A. (2004). Antidepressants and pediatric depression – The risk of doing nothing. *New England Journal of Medicine*, 351, 1598–1601. doi:10.1056/NEJMp048228.

[23] Cheung, A. H., Emslie, G. J., & Mayes, T. L. (2005). Review of the efficacy and safety of antidepressants in youth depression. *Journal of Child Psychology and Psychiatry*, 46, 735–754. doi:10.1111/j.1469-7610.2005.01467.

[24] Raz, A. (2006). Perspectives on the efficacy of antidepressants for child and adolescent depression. *PLoS Medicine*, 3(1), e9. doi:10:1371/journal.pmed.0030009.

[25] Turner, E. H., Matthews, A. M., Linardatos, E., et al. (2008). Selective publication of antidepressant trials and its influence on apparent efficacy. *New England Journal of Medicine*, 358, 252–260. doi:10.1056/NEJMsa065779.

[26] Garland, E. J. (2004). Facing the evidence: Antidepressant treatment in children and adolescents. *Canadian Medical Association Journal*, 170, 489–491.

[27] Rosenthal, R. (1979). The file drawer problem and tolerance for null results. *Psychological Bulletin*, 86(3), 638–641. doi:10.1037/0033-2909.86.3.638.

[28] Compton, S. N., March, J. S., Brent, D., et al. (2004). Cognitive-behavioral psychotherapy for anxiety and depressive disorders in children and adolescents: An evidence-based medicine review. *Journal of the American Academy of Child and Adolescent Psychiatry*, 43, 930–959. doi:10.1097/01.chi.0000127589.57468.bf.

[29] David-Ferdon, C. & Kaslow, N. J. (2008). Evidence-based psychosocial treatments for child and adolescent depression. *Journal of Clinical Child & Adolescent Psychology*, 37, 62–104. doi:10.1080/15374410701817865.

[30] Stevens, J., Wang, W., Fan, L., et al. (2009). Parental attitudes toward children's use of antidepressants and psychotherapy. *Journal of Child and Adolescent Psychopharmacology*, 19, 289–296. doi:10.1089/cap.2008.0129.

[31] Wilmore, M. (Writer) & Oliver, R. (Director) (2009). The good, the sad, and the drugly [Television series episode]. In Jean, A., Brooks, J. L., Groening, M., & Simon, S. (Producers), *The Simpsons*. Los Angeles: Fox Broadcasting.

[32] Klein, J. B., Jacobs, R. H., & Reinecke, M. A. (2007). Cognitive-behavioral Therapy for adolescent depression: A meta-analytic investigation of changes in effect-size estimates. *Journal of the American Academy of Child and Adolescent Psychiatry*, 46, 1403–1413. doi:10.1097/chi.0b013e3180592aaa.

[33] Mihalopoulos, C., Vos, T., Pirkis, J., & Carter, R. (2012). The population cost-effectiveness of interventions designed to prevent childhood depression. *Pediatrics*, 129, e723–730. doi:10.1542/peds.2011-1823.

Myth #28   Drawings contain specific signs useful in identifying subconscious problems

Before you read about this myth, it will be helpful if you can first carefully draw a picture of a person. Although you can draw the picture on a separate sheet of paper if you like, we'll also leave some space below. Go ahead and kindly draw your picture now:

This section will provide you with some tools to interpret your drawing, and this "projective drawing," also specifically referred to as a Human Figure Drawing, will possibly reveal some hidden truths about you. In fact, there's no shortage of suggestions in the psychological literature regarding the meaning of every little detail (or lack thereof) in your drawing. Freud himself liked the idea of using drawings as a means of accessing the subconscious, as evidenced by his interpretation of a memory from Leonardo da Vinci's childhood. According to Freud, "nature has given the artist the ability to express his most secret mental impulses, which are hidden even from himself, by means of the works that he creates" [1] (p. 57).

Interpreting the meaning of children's drawings has been of interest for over a century. In the 1926 book, *Measurement of Intelligence by Drawings* [2], Florence Goodenough briefly summarizes four decades' worth of children's drawings being a focus of psychological attention. Goodenough [2] also presents the Draw-a-Man test as an assessment of intelligence for children. The child's drawing received points for including correct details. For example, children earned more points for drawing body parts such as the basics, like legs and arms, as well as details like nostrils and fingers. Children also received more points for including clothing and another point if the man's costume didn't contain any incongruities (e.g., "a sailor's hat with a business suit," p. 99). Correct body proportions and other drawing skills, such as firmly drawn lines, were also considered.

Goodenough's description of the Draw-a-Man test was not a "projective" drawing technique. A projective technique is part of the psychodynamic tradition of assessment tools, and according to Machover [3] "Projective methods of exploring motivations have repeatedly uncovered deep and perhaps unconscious determinants of self-expression which could not be made manifest in direct communication" (p. 4). Thus, by this definition, a drawing used to evaluate intelligence is not a "projective" technique.

With Goodenough's urging, though, and consistent with the proliferation of dream interpretation and the Rorschach Inkblot Test to uncover hidden truths (see Myths 20 and 35 in Lilienfeld et al. [4]), others began using the Draw-a-Man test (also called the Draw-a-Person Test) in the projective sense to examine children's supposedly hidden, difficult to access, internal conflicts and emotions and to identify important personality traits. For example, researchers studied the test as an aid in diagnosing specific childhood problems such as behavior disorders, delinquency, maladjustment, and schizophrenia [5].

In particular, Machover [3] provided a detailed overview for how to interpret specific signs within projective drawings (also called the "sign approach"). For example, a large head in the drawing suggests the person may be "paranoid, narcissistic, intellectually righteous, and vain" (p. 38). In another example, "over-emphasis of the mouth is frequently tied up with food faddism and gastric symptoms, profane language, and temper tantrums" (pp. 43–44). Other signs include small eyes representing self-absorption, large eyes representing hostility, noticeable ears representing symptoms of schizophrenia, emphasized nostrils representing aggression, hands in pockets representing masturbation, large hands representing guilt, and buttons representing dependence on the mother (especially if drawn in the position of the belly button). Also, the following drawing components can have sexual significance: mouth, lips, hips, hair, hats, hands, nose, neck, Adam's apple, buttocks, pockets, shoulders, shoes, cigarettes, feet, ties, guns, canes, waistlines, and, of course, the drawing of the private parts.

Projective drawings were also expanded to include drawings of the whole family [6], sometimes called the Family Drawing Test. According to Hulse [7], children "project their deeper emotional feelings for the different members of their family into drawings which attain the importance of 'frozen dreams'… giving definite and permanent proof of the patient during a certain period of his emotional development" (p. 79).

More recently, therapists started using Kinetic Family Drawings [8] in which the family is drawn doing something. In a Kinetic Family Drawing, actions between family members, such as throwing a ball, are seen in "highly competitive or 'jealous' children" (p. 30). Parental activities like "mowing the lawn, chopping, cutting, etc. are seen with 'tough' or 'castrating' fathers" (p. 30) and sometimes mothers. Furthermore, if the drawing somehow includes an "X" (e.g., as in the crossing legs of an ironing board) then this "is a constant theme with children attempting to control the sexual impulse" (p. 98). In another interesting example, water in a Kinetic Family Drawing (e.g., fishing in a pond) is a potential sign of suicide because it's "more than a chance factor that many suicides leap into water" (p. 148). Some have suggested that interpreting specific projective signs in family drawings can be useful in the identification, prevention, and treatment of child abuse [9]. A computer scoring system for Kinetic Family Drawings has even been developed in recent years [10].

The Kinetic School Drawing [11] is another more recent development and includes interpretations such as these: (i) drawings of the outdoors (e.g., recess) represent children's dislike of academics; (ii) drawings that emphasize the classroom's structures represent social interaction avoidance; or (iii) emphasis on the teacher may represent a desire for warm interactions with the teacher.

The House-Tree-Person (H-T-P) was another major version of drawings and was clearly labeled as a projective device [12]. Specific signs could be found within the house's windows. For example, windows "drawn without panes at times seem to represent oral- and/or anal-eroticism, as well as feelings of hostility" (p. 369). The tree was also fertile material for interpretations. For example, "The Tree drawn upon the crest of an arc-like hill seems frequently to represent an oral-erotic fixation, often coupled with a need for maternal protection" (p. 369).

While this first detailed description of the H-T-P focused on adults, it was quickly applied to children. Jolles [13] collected about 1000 H-T-P drawings from school-aged children. Jolles suggested that "Buck's hypothesis that the sex of the drawn person tends to represent the felt sex role of the subject is applicable to children" (p. 118). Jolles [14] made other interesting assertions about phallic-looking trees, with the greatest psycho-sexual disturbance occurring in children that drew trees that looked a little bit like a phallus, as opposed to trees that clearly looked like a phallus. Furthermore, interpretations about drawings of phallic trees were often corroborated by drawings of phallic looking chimneys. Just for fun, here's some space for you to try and draw a chimney that does *not* look like a phallus:

Commonly, the house, tree, and person were drawn on separate pieces of paper, but Burns [15] emphasized the value of combining them on one sheet and adding "some kind of action" (p. 5), and he called this a Kinetic-House-Tree-Person drawing. One interpretative example includes Falling Fruit Syndrome, in which fruit drawn falling from the tree represents someone's fall from grace.

One major shift in the use of projective drawings was for some psychologists to move away from the sign approach in which individual signs in the drawings represented specific psychological deviancies. That is, the alternative "global approach" focused on the *number of* signs (or emotional indicators) in general. Koppitz [16, 17] identified about 30 emotional indicators of maladjustment in children. Examples of emotional indicators include: omission of the neck, a tiny head, shading of the face, and crossed eyes in the drawing. Influenced by Koppitz, others developed the *Draw A Person: Screening Procedure for Emotional Disturbance* [18], which included a 55-item scoring system with some of the same indicators from the Koppitz method.

As noted by Naglieri and colleagues [18], the individual sign approach of projective drawings didn't have research support (most of the examples presented in this chapter used the individual sign approach). Reviews of studies on the individual sign approach clearly demonstrated the lack of supporting research [19–22]. Debate in the 1990s turned to the value of using the global approach. In a paper that set off a heated debate, Motta, Little, and Tobin [23] critiqued over 100 years' worth of projective drawing use and ended with a critique of the latest version of the Draw-A-Person [18], saying that this technique:

> ... is evaluated by determining whether it can discriminate a seriously disturbed group of children attending a psychiatric day treatment program from a normal, matched, control group. Why anyone would use figure drawings to identify such an obviously disturbed group when simple behavioral observation would suffice, is left to the reader's imagination. Nevertheless, the data from Naglieri and Pfeiffer's own study clearly show that their scoring procedure identified less than half of the psychiatrically disturbed group ...We can only wonder about the accuracy rate of this procedure using less disturbed children in regular school environments. (p. 165)

The Motta et al. [23] article sparked an unusually heated debate across several articles within the same journal issue [24–29] with a final rebuttal by Motta et al. [30] in which they underscore the point that identifying less than half of the children with emotional disturbance is *"less than chance"* (p. 198). The one common thread across these articles was that all of the authors agreed the individual sign approach was not valid, though some still argued for the value of the global approach.

The Gresham [26] response summarized some of the arguments against both projective drawing approaches, as well as hypotheses for why projective drawing continued to be popular. Specifically, some psychologists perceive projective drawings to be useful because of the illusory correlation, or the tendency to see connections that are not really there, often because they share some other superficial connection. In terms of the "Sources of Psychological Myths," this tendency would be described as reasoning by representativeness. Second, the information provided by the projective drawing fails to add to incremental validity: that is, to provide new information above and beyond what is already known, or could be determined, through other assessment tools. It's useful to imagine that a parent brings a child to a psychologist for aggressive behavior, and the child draws a human figure with large hands. The drawing of the hands is superficially related to the actual behavior of hitting. When the psychologist uses the drawing to say the child has aggressive tendencies, this doesn't add any new information because we already knew the child was demonstrating aggressive behavior (see also Lilienfeld, Armmirati, & David [31] and Lilienfeld, Wood, & Garb [32] for detailed discussions). Also, one early critique of projective drawings suggests that clinicians are misled by the illusory correlation between the drawing signs and the client's symptoms [33]. This illusory correlation, influenced by selective perception, may help explain why this children's drawing myth has lasted for so many decades.

Despite longstanding critiques of projective drawings, they continue to make intuitive sense to the general public and be widely used by professionals. In our research, 87% of students and 79% of parents agreed with the statement that "A child's drawings provide insight into the subconscious cause of their problems" [34]. It appears that psychologists hold a similar view. One study surveyed 175 school psychologists and found that 44% used the House-Tree-Person, 41% used a Kinetic Family Drawing, and 27% used Draw-a-Person [35]. High percentages of these school psychologists also used these three projective drawing tests for most aspects of assessment, including diagnosis, eligibility determination, treatment planning, treatment monitoring, reevaluation, and developing hypotheses. In another survey study, 58% of child custody evaluators reported using projective drawings with children to help with the evaluation [36] even though a comprehensive recent review concluded they're not useful in the assessment of child abuse [37]. This rate was trending *up* from a previous study that reported a proportion of about 38% [38]. Also in the 2008 study, 27% of child custody evaluators also used projective drawings to evaluate the parents (also trending *up* from the 9% reported in the 1997 study).

Before we conclude, we would like to distinguish between the regular use of drawings during assessment from the projective use drawings described in this chapter. Many children like to draw, and incorporating drawing into an assessment can be a useful way to build rapport with children and provide a non-threatening stimulus to talk about. Some psychologists use drawings as a "springboard for discussion," which appears to be a reasonable use of drawings but which should not be confused with projective drawings. Even when used as a stimulus for discussion, therapists should be mindful of the potential of a confirmation bias in which they lead the child into talking about aspects of the drawing that already support their view of the child.

We'll close with a brief description of a scene from the movie, *Little Fockers* [39]. The son of Ben Stiller's character is being assessed for entry into a prestigious child development center. Part of the assessment includes a drawing, and the boy chooses to draw a picture of his father, who happens to be a medical professional, giving his grandfather (played by Robert De Niro) a shot in a very sensitive area because the grandfather took a pill that caused him to have an erection for more than four hours. The drawing itself would certainly be an excellent springboard for discussion.

What you need to know

Psychologists do have several methods for conducting a comprehensive assessment of children's social-emotional health [40]. Typically, assessment includes multiple informants and multiple methods. Assessment usually incorporates some combination of parent, child, and teacher interviews. Psychologists also use reliable and valid rating scales that can broadly assess a range of areas, followed by more narrowly focused question-naires. In many cases, behavioral observations are conducted.

One important distinction between these assessment tools and projective drawings is a focus on functional assessment. Returning to the example of a parent bringing in a child for aggressive behavior, the behavioral observation might confirm that the child does indeed exhibit aggressive behavior, which itself is not that valuable. The observation, though, can also help provide information regarding antecedents that prompt the behavior (e.g., what usually happens right before the hitting) and consequences that are maintaining the behavior (e.g., what happens right after the hitting). Furthermore, the observation can be used to quan-tify the behavior (e.g., number of hits in a certain time period), which can then be used to monitor the effectiveness of treatment.

References

[1] Freud, S. (1964). *Leonardo da Vinci and a Memory of his Childhood*. New York, NY: Norton.
[2] Goodenough, F. L. (1926). *Measurement of Intelligence by Drawings*. Yonkers-on-Hudson, NY, Chicago, IL: World Book Company.

[3] Machover, K. (1949). *Personality Projection in the Drawing of the Human Figure*. Springfield, IL: C.C. Thomas.

[4] Lilienfeld, S. O., Lynn, S. J., Ruscio, J., & Beyerstein, B. L. (2010). *50 Great Myths of Popular Psychology: Shattering Widespread Misconceptions about Human Behavior*. Malden, MA: Wiley-Blackwell.

[5] Harris, D. B. (1963). *Children's Drawings as Measures of Intellectual Maturity: A Revision and Extension of the Goodenough Draw-a-Man Test*. New York: Harcourt, Brace & World.

[6] Appel, K. E. (1931). Drawings by children as aids to personality studies. *American Journal of Orthopsychiatry*, 1, 129–144.

[7] Hulse, W. (1951). The emotionally disturbed child draws his family. *Quarterly Journal of Child Behavior*, 3, 152–174.

[8] Burns, R. C. & Kaufman, S. H. (1970). *Kinetic Family Drawings (K-F-D): An Introduction to Understanding Children through Kinetic Drawings*. Philadelphia, PA: Brunner/Mazel.

[9] Schornstein, H. M. & Derr, J. (1977). The many applications of kinetic family drawings in child abuse. *Child Abuse & Neglect*, 1, 297–300. doi:10.1016/ 0145-2134(77)90004-7.

[10] Kim, S., Han, J., Kim, Y., & Oh, Y. (2011). A Computer Art Therapy System for Kinetic Family Drawings (CATS_KFD). *The Arts in Psychotherapy*, 38, 17–28. doi:10.1016/j.aip.2010.10.002.

[11] Sarbaugh, M. E. A., Peterson, D. W., Wise, P. S., & Potkay, C. R. (1982). Kinetic Drawing-School (KD-S) technique. *Illinois School Psychologists Association Monograph Series*, 1, 11–70.

[12] Buck, J. N. (1948). The H-T-P technique. A qualitative and quantitative scoring manual. *Journal of Clinical Psychology*, 4, 317.

[13] Jolles, I. (1952a). A study of the validity of some hypotheses for the qualitative interpretation of the H-T-P for children of elementary school age: I. Sexual identification. *Journal of Clinical Psychology*, 8, 113–118. doi:10.1002/1097-4679(195204)8:2 < 113::aid-jclp2270080203 > 3.0.co;2-f.

[14] Jolles, I. (1952b). A study of the validity of some hypotheses for the qualitative interpretation of the H-T-P for children of elementary school age: II. The "phallic tree" as an indicator of psycho-sexual conflict. *Journal of Clinical Psychology*, 8, 245–255. doi:10.1002/1097-4679(195207)8:3 < 245::aid-jclp2270080305 > 3.0.co;2-j.

[15] Burns, R. C. (1987). *Kinetic-House-Tree-Person Drawings (KHTP): An Interpretative Manual*. Philadelphia, PA: Brunner/Mazel.

[16] Koppitz, E. M. (1968). *Psychological Evaluation of Children's Human Figure Drawings*. New York, NY: Grune & Stratton.

[17] Koppitz, E. M. (1984). *Psychological Evaluation of Human Figure Drawings by Middle School Pupils*. New York, NY: Grune & Stratton.

[18] Naglieri, J. A., McNeish, T. J., & Bardos, A. N. (1991). *DAP:SPED: Draw a Person, Screening Procedure for Emotional Disturbance*. Austin, TX: Pro-Ed.

[19] Roback, H. B. (1968). Human figure drawings: Their utility in the clinical psychologist's armamentarium for personality assessment. *Psychological Bulletin*, 70, 1.

[20] Sloan, W. (1954). A critical review of HTP validation studies. *Journal of Clinical Psychology*, 10, 143–148.

[21] Swenson Jr, C. H. (1957). Empirical evaluations of human figure drawings. *Psychological Bulletin*, 54, 431–466.

[22] Swenson Jr, C. H. (1968). Empirical evaluations of human figure drawings: 1957–1966. *Psychological Bulletin*, 70, 20–44.

[23] Motta, R. W., Little, S. G., & Tobin, M. I. (1993a). The use and abuse of human figure drawings. *School Psychology Quarterly*, 8, 162–169. doi:10.1037/h0088273.

[24] Naglieri, J. A. (1993). Human figure drawings in perspective. *School Psychology Quarterly*, 8, 170–176. doi:10.1037/h0088275.

[25] Bardos, A. N. (1993). Human figure drawings: Abusing the abused. *School Psychology Quarterly*, 8, 177–181. doi:10.1037/h0088268.

[26] Gresham, F. M. (1993). "What's wrong in this picture?": Response to Motta et al.'s review of human figure drawings. *School Psychology Quarterly*, 8, 182–186. doi:10.1037/h0088269.

[27] Kamphaus, R. W. & Pleiss, K. L. (1993). Comment on "The use and abuse of human figure drawings". *School Psychology Quarterly*, 8, 187–188. doi:10.1037/h0088271

[28] Holtzman, W. H. (1993). An unjustified, sweeping indictment by Motta et al. of human figure drawings for assessing psychological functioning. *School Psychology Quarterly*, 8, 189–190. doi:10.1037/h0088270.

[29] Knoff, H. M. (1993). The utility of human figure drawings in personality and intellectual assessment: Why ask why? *School Psychology Quarterly*, 8, 191–196.doi:10.1037/h0088272.

[30] Motta, R. W., Little, S. G., & Tobin, M. I. (1993b). A picture is worth less than a thousand words: Response to reviewers. *School Psychology Quarterly*, 8, 197–199. doi:10.1037/h0088274.

[31] Lilienfeld, S. O., Ammirati, R., & David, M. (2012). Distinguishing science from pseudoscience in school psychology: Science and scientific thinking as safeguards against human error. *Journal of School Psychology*, 50, 7–36. doi:10.1016/j.jsp.2011.09.006.

[32] Lilienfeld, S. O., Wood, J. M., & Garb, H. N. (2000). The scientific status of projective techniques. *Psychological Science in the Public Interest*, 1(2), 27–66.

[33] Chapman, L. J. & Chapman, J. P. (1967). Genesis of popular but erroneous psycho-diagnostic observations. *Journal of Abnormal Psychology*, 72, 193 –204.

[34] Hupp, S., Stary, A., & Jewell, J. (submitted). Beliefs about myths related to child psychology, development, and parenting: Which myths need the most debunking?

[35] Hojnoski, R. L., Morrison, R., Brown, M., & Matthews, W. J. (2006). Projective test use among school psychologists: A survey and critique. *Journal of Psychoeducational Assessment*, 24, 145–159. doi:10.1177/0734282906287828.

[36] Ackerman, M. J. & Pritzl, T. B. (2011). Child custody evaluation practices: A 20-year follow-up. *Family Court Review*, 49, 618–628. doi:10.1111/j.1744-1617.2011.01397.x.

[37] Allen, B. & Tussey, C. (2012). Can projective drawings detect if a child experienced sexual or physical abuse? A systematic review of the controlled research. *Trauma, Violence, & Abuse*, 13, 97–111. doi:10.1177/1524838012440339.

[38] Ackerman, M. J. & Ackerman, M. C. (1997). Custody evaluation practices: A survey of experienced professionals (revisited). *Professional Psychology: Research and Practice*, 28, 137. doi : 10.1037//0735-7028.28.2.137.

[39] Rosenthal, J., De Niro, R., Roach, J. Hamburg, J. (Producers), & Weitz, P. (Director) (2010). *Little Fockers* [Motion picture]. United States: Universal Studios.

[40] Sattler, J. M. & Hoge, R. D. (2006). *Assessment of Children: Behavioral, Social, and Clinical Foundations*. San Diego, CA: J.M. Sattler.

Myth #29

Most toddlers go through a "terrible twos" stage

According to Grumpy Bear, "Two is a terrible age." Cheer Bear supports Grumpy Bear's negativity about 2 year-olds but has some optimism. Cheer Bear says, "Cheer up! They won't be two forever!"

As can be seen from the above quotes (taken from *The Care Bears and the Terrible Twos* [1]), both Grumpy Bear and Cheer Bear agree: 2-year-olds are terrible! A parent reading this story with a toddler is probably not hearing about the "terrible twos" for the first time. Pediatrician Jay L. Hoecker [2] (para 1) explains that "terrible twos are a normal stage in a toddler's development characterized by mood changes, temper tantrums and use of the word 'no'." Family therapist John Rosemond adds that parents begin asserting authority over the 2-year-old child, and this developmental period "is known as the 'terrible twos' because as parents take on this task, the child pushes back with all of his emotional strength" [3] (p. vii). Indeed, when anyone is around a 2-year-old, the word "terrible" might come to mind sometimes. It's true that most 2-year-olds do throw some temper tantrums, say "no," get frustrated, exhibit aggression, and often have a hard time listening to reason. Is this, however, a developmental period unique to 2-year-olds? Before we answer that question, we'll first discuss where the idea of the terrible twos originates.

The *Oxford Dictionary of Word Origins* [4] indicates that an early use of the phrase "terrible twos" comes from the 1951 Canadian documentary titled *The Terrible Twos and the Trusting Threes* [5]. This documentary gives parents a sense of "what to expect" by describing the terrible twos as "the first time they're able to fight for what they want" and then describes all of the difficulties in the typical day of a 2-and-a-half-year-old. These challenges include: (i) waking up early; (ii) unrolling all of the toilet paper; (iii) drawing on the wall; (iv) tormenting a younger sibling; (v) having tantrums; (vi) smearing cream on the dresser; and (vii) refusing to go to bed. The documentary concludes by suggesting that it's "consoling to know that the Terrible Two becomes the Trusting Three" and indicates that a child is "so much better at three than she was at two."

A search of the phrase "terrible twos" by using Google books' Ngram Viewer (http://books.google.com/ngrams/; Figure 3) supports the notion that the phrase started to appear in print around the time of the Canadian documentary, but it didn't really begin to take off until the 1970s (Ngram Viewer is a fun research tool that anyone can use, so feel free to take a break and go search a word or phrase to find out how often it appeared in books over time).

The *idea* of the terrible twos actually dates further back to Arnold Gesell. Gesell was a student of G. Stanley Hall and arguably America's first school psychologist [6]. These days, most child development textbooks give brief mention to Gesell's maturational theory, which views child development as the unfolding of a biological plan. For example, Gesell [7] suggests that "It's doubtful whether the basic temperamental qualities of infants can be measurably altered by environmental influence" (p. 372). That is, maturational theory gives a limited role to aspects of the child's environment such as parenting style, and this theory contradicts behavioral theory (although some of his writings do suggest more of a transaction between nature and nurture [see Ames [8]). In fact, Gesell battled with behaviorist John B. Watson for the role of most influential parenting expert in the 1920s, and it was Gesell's book *Infancy and Human Growth* [7] that beat out Watson's *Psychological Care of Infant and Child* [9] for an award from *Parent's Magazine* that year [10].

As part of this predetermined biological plan, Gesell actually suggests that 2-year-olds were rather pleasant. On the other hand, it was the two-*and-a-half*-year-old that became terrible. Gesell and colleagues [11] suggest that this specific age (two-and-a-half years old) is "the most exasperating age in the preschool period" (p. 177), and "more disputes occur at this age than at any other" (p. 200). They also indicate that two-and-a-half years old is the transition between the easier ages of 2 years old and 3 years old. The focus on the specific age of two-and-a-half years old continued in the work of Ames and Ilg [12] as they suggest that "the year begins so gently that one is not at first aware of the hidden sources of dominating power that will be unleashed in its midstream" (p. 4), later adding that "your once-enchanting Two-year-old has now become a

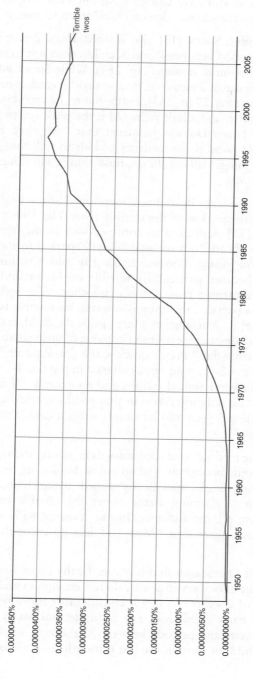

Figure 3   Google's Ngram Viewer shows the frequency of appearances of the phrase "terrible twos" in books from 1948–2008.

demon" (p. 15). If you still have Google's Ngram Viewer open, it might be fun to search when the phrase "demon child" starts to appear in books.

Pediatrician Benjamin Spock [13] also warned about 2-year-olds, suggesting that "in the period between 2 and 3, children are apt to show signs of balkiness and other inner tensions" (p. 284). While Spock admits that this begins before the age of 2 years old, he also says "it reaches new heights and takes new forms after 2" (p. 285). Furthermore, he even cites Gesell's idea that the age of two-and-a-half years old is the peak age of problems. Later, psychologist James Dobson indicated that "the most frustrating aspect of the 'terrible twos' is the tendency of kids to spill things, destroy things, eat horrible things, fall off things, flush things, kill things, and get into things" [14] (p. 50).

Pop culture, like the Care Bears book mentioned at the beginning has also helped spread the notion of the terrible twos. The 1990s television sitcom, *Dinosaurs* [15], dedicated an entire episode to the terrible twos. Quite possibly, the phrase "not the mama" will spark a memory of this popular show, as the young dinosaur frequently said it to his dinosaur father. This child became particularly terrible on his second birthday, right after this forewarning from his grandmother: "The second birthday's no cause for a party ... the baby is entering his terrible twos [lightning flashes outside] ... A strange evil force grips the child, transforming him into a deranged, destructive monster capable of unspeakable horrors. This is a dark, terrible day." Pretty quickly, the grandmother's warning becomes reality as the 2-year-old wreaks havoc in the family. A dinosaur pediatrician, a behavioral animal trainer, and an exorcist all fail to treat the terrible twos. The only intervention that works is tricking him into believing he is turning 3 years old by simply using a cake, three candles, and a birthday song.

The notion of the terrible twos continues to be strong today. A perusal through the electronic bookshelves of an online bookstore revealed over ten recent parenting books specifically aimed at surviving, stopping, taming, or otherwise claiming victory over the terrible twos. These books seem to have a large audience. In our research 85% of students and 83% of parents agree that "Most toddlers go through a 'terrible twos' stage" [16].

There's not a lot of research that has specifically compared the terribleness of different ages. Nevertheless, there's enough evidence to suggest that the age of 2 years old is not considerably more terrible than any other age of early childhood. For example, one study compared tantrums at different age periods between the ages 1 to 4 years old (technically the children were in the last 6 months of each age bracket)

[17]. The study found that tantrums were common in all age groups, with 87% of 1-year-olds and 91% of 2-year-olds having at least one parent-reported tantrum per month. This rate dropped to 59% for the 3-year-olds.

Although this higher percentage at age 2-years-old is noteworthy, one tantrum per month hardly qualifies as "terrible." The more interesting findings involve the number of tantrums per month and the duration of the tantrums. This same study demonstrated that 1-year-olds and 2-year-olds each average about eight tantrums per month, while 3-year-olds and 4-year-olds average nearly six tantrums per month. This is not a big difference. Also, tantrum duration got longer as children got older: 1-year-olds averaged 2-minute tantrums; 2-year-olds and 3-year-olds averaged 4-minute tantrums each; and 4-year-olds averaged 5-minute tantrums.

Another study of nearly 1000 parents in Norway demonstrated that children at age one-and-a-half years old had exactly the same amount of negative emotionality (e.g., mood changes) as children at two-and-a-half years old [18]. In fact, negative emotionality ticked up a bit at the next highest age period studied (i.e., 4- and 5-year-olds), although this was not a significant difference. Thus, negative emotionality was very stable between one-and-a-half and 5 years old in this study.

Taken together, these studies imply that the age of 2 years old is not more terrible than the ages of 1, 3, or 4. As described above, 1-year-olds and 2-year-olds have the *same* number of tantrums; 4-year-olds have longer tantrums, and they (along with 5-year-olds) have more negative emotionality than 2-year-olds. Moreover, many parents might argue that infants are more terrible than all of the other children combined. Infants cry, don't listen to reason, can't take care of themselves, and even though they can't say "no," you just know they're thinking it! Why doesn't anyone call infancy the "terrible zeros?"

The myth of the terrible twos has been propagated by a few of the "Sources of Psychological Myths." "Terrible twos" is a catchy term that resonates and is quickly spread by word-of-mouth. Another source of propagation includes the exaggeration of a kernel of truth. That is, perhaps a softer interpretation of the "terrible twos" is just a way of saying that some new challenging behaviors occur at age 2 years old. Even this interpretation falls flat, though, because new challenging behaviors really occur at different ages throughout childhood and adolescence. In fact, there are just as many prosocial and emotion management skills emerging at age 2 years old as there are challenging behaviors (see Thompson & Goodvin [19] for a summary of research). Thus, the terrible twos could just as well be termed the "tender twos" (which is a good point originally made by Ames & Ilg [12]).

It's hard to dispel the notion of the terrible twos partly because the definition of "two" keeps getting expanded. These days, references to the terrible twos often include the entire year of 2 years old with several months before and several months (or years) after. Any difficult behavior in the preschool years is now accounted for as being part of the terrible twos. For example, Rosemond [3] suggests "that some children enter 'the twos' earlier, some later," and he also adds that "the period of resolution varies from child to child, family to family" (p. viii). In a more recent book Rosemond [20] also speculates about one family, suggesting that "the parents had never fully cured the terrible twos, and the girl's ongoing tantrums were just a bad habit with four years of momentum behind it" [20] (p. 100). The child being referred to in this quote was 6 years old but still suggested to be in the terrible twos stage. It's also worth noting that this quote from Rosemond refers to the terrible twos as something that needs to be "cured."

Inherent in the idea of the terrible twos is the notion that almost all children will be terrible at around the age of 2 years old. The nice part about this myth is that it does help normalize some challenging behaviors in children, and all children do display some challenging behaviors. In fact, it's good for children to have oppositional behaviors sometimes (e.g., when someone tries to get them to do the wrong thing). Oppositional behaviors are not inherently problematic all of the time; they just seem terrible when they're used on us as parents.

While normalizing some challenging behaviors is a good thing, it can be taken too far. Some children, even at the age of 2 years old, are so oppositional that it begins to interfere with the quality of their lives and the lives of the people around them. In these cases, parents or teachers might need to think about doing something differently. It could be dangerous to assume all oppositional behavior is just part of the terrible twos, if that means taking no action.

What you need to know

There's no single "right way" to deal with "terrible" behavior in toddlers, but the book *Parenting the Strong-Willed Child* [21] describes one effective approach with children ages 2 to 6 years old. The book is based on the evidence-based strategy of behavioral parent training [22]. Some techniques included in this approach include positive attention, active ignoring, and giving effective instructions.

References

[1] Reich, A. & Bracken, C. (1983). *The Care Bears and the Terrible Twos*. New York, NY: Random House.

[2] Hoecker, J. L. (n.d.). I've heard a lot about the terrible twos. Why are 2-year-olds so difficult? Retrieved from http://www.mayoclinic.com/health/terrible-twos/AN02124 [accessed August 2014].

[3] Rosemond, J. K. (2013). *Making the "Terrible" Twos Terrific!*. Kansas City, MO: Andrews McMeel Publishing, LLC.

[4] Cresswell, J. (2010). *Oxford Dictionary of Word Origins*. New York, NY: Oxford University Press.

[5] Mackay-Smith, P. (Writer) & Crawley, J. (Director) (1951). *The Terrible Twos and the Trusting Threes* [Documentary]. Canada: National Film Board of Canada

[6] Fagan, T. K. (1987). Gesell: The first school psychologist: II. Practice and significance. *School Psychology Review*, 16(3), 399–409.

[7] Gesell, A. (1928). *Infancy and Human Growth*. New York, NY: The Macmillan Company.

[8] Ames, L. B. (1989). *Arnold Gesell: Themes of His Work*. New York, NY: Human Sciences Press.

[9] Watson, J. B. & Watson, R. A. R. (1928). *Psychological Care of Infant and Child*. New York, NY: W.W. Norton & Co.

[10] Weizmann, F., & Harris, B. (2012). Arnold Gesell: The maturationist. In. W. E. Pickren, D. A. Dewsbury, & M. Wertheimer (2012), *Portraits of Pioneers in Developmental Psychology* (pp. 1–20). New York, NY: Psychology Press.

[11] Gesell, A., Ilg, F. L., & Ames, L. B. (1943). *Infant and Child in the Culture of Today: The Guidance of Development in Home and Nursery School*. New York, NY: Harper & Row.

[12] Ames, L. B. & Ilg, F. L. (1976). *Your Two-Year Old: Terrible or Tender*. New York, NY: Delacorte Press.

[13] Spock, B. (1946). *The Common Sense Book of Baby and Child Care*. New York, NY: Duell, Sloan and Pearce.

[14] Dobson, J. C. (1978). *The Strong-Willed Child: Birth Through Adolescence*. Wheaton, IL: Tyndale House.

[15] Doyle, T. (Writer) & McCracken, J. (1994). Terrible twos [Television series episode]. In M. Jacobs & B. Hensen (Executive producers), *Dinosaurs*. Burbank, CA: Walt Disney Television.

[16] Hupp, S., Stary, A., & Jewell, J. (submitted). Beliefs about myths related to child psychology, development, and parenting: Which myths need the most debunking?

[17] Potegal, M. & Davidson, R. J. (2003). Temper tantrums in young children: 1. Behavioral composition. *Journal of Developmental & Behavioral Pediatrics*, 24, 140–147. doi:10.1097/00004703-200306000-00002.

[18] Janson, H. & Mathiesen, K. S. (2008). Temperament profiles from infancy to middle childhood: Development and associations with behavior problems. *Developmental Psychology*, 44, 1314–1328. doi:10.1037/a0012713.

[19] Thompson, R. A. & Goodvin, R. (2007). Taming the tempest in the teapot: Emotion regulation in toddlers. In C. A. Brownell & C. B. Kopp (Eds), *Transitions in Early Socioemotional Development: The Toddler Years* (pp. 320–344). New York: Guilford.

[20] Rosemond, J. K. (2012). *Parent-Babble: How Parents Can Recover From Fifty Years of Bad Expert Advice.* Kansas City, MO: Andrews McMeel Pub.

[21] Forehand, R. & Long, N. (2010). *Parenting the Strong-Willed Child: The Clinically Proven Five-Week Program for Parents of Two- To Six-Year-Olds* (Third edn). New York, NY: McGraw-Hill.

[22] Eyberg, S. M., Nelson, M. M., & Boggs, S. R. (2008). Evidence-based psychosocial treatments for children and adolescents with disruptive behavior. *Journal of Clinical Child & Adolescent Psychology,* 37, 215–237. doi:10.1080/15374410701820117.

Myth #30 Kids can be "scared straight" from delinquency

Many school districts throughout the nation have children in later elementary school and junior high visit their local juvenile detention center with the purpose of scaring the kids from a life of delinquency. In fact, strategies like this have been used for many decades. In 1978, television producer Andrew Shapiro brought an obscure prison inmate-run program to the attention of the entire nation with his documentary *Scared Straight!* [1]. The subject of the film was the "Lifers Group" in New Jersey's Rahway State Prison, which took youths (both male and female) and led them on a tour of the adult male prison facility with the culminating experience being an impromptu meeting between the youth and the "Lifers" (prisoners serving sentences greater than 25 years).

The Lifers take turns giving advice to the youth to stay in school, avoid drugs, and stop committing crimes. These prisoners don't hold anything back, and they also don't shy away from cursing, physical threats, and warnings about the daily difficulties of prison life, including rape. You could easily find a video clip from the documentary on your favorite video-viewing website, but we'll provide you a sense of the program with a quote. Talking directly to one of the youth, one of the Lifers says:

> You wanna be a smart guy? You wanna be a wise guy? Let me tell ya somethin', the police can make a thousand mistakes; you can only make one mistake and you're done ... Get that smile off your face, boy. Let me tell you somethin', I'll bite your f***in' nose off real quick, and if you think somebody's gonna stop me from doin' it, believe me, you're wrong. Cuz by the time they get here, it will be all over with. I got so much time they can't give me no more. Understand what I'm tellin' you? So when you sit there, you keep that smile off your face. Cuz I'm gonna hurt you, alright?

Perhaps partly due to provocative language like this, the 52-minute documentary went on to win an Academy Award in 1979 for Best Documentary. The original film concludes with individual interviews of youth reporting that the experience has changed their point of view on their own behavior. In the words of one youth, "It's just changed me all around the minute I stepped through that door." Shapiro followed up with the participants from his original documentary in two more films: *Scared Straight! 10 Years Later* [2] and *Scared Straight! 20 Years Later* [3], which were hosted by Danny Glover. Although the kids in the original *Scared Straight!* documentary were in their teens, similar programs since then have included children as young as 8 years old [4].

Scared Straight has made its way into pop culture several times. For example, "Prison Mike" is the alter ego of Michael Scott in the sitcom, *The Office* [5]. He tries to scare his employees into having a greater appreciation for their jobs. Also, several guest hosts on *Saturday Night Live* (SNL) [6] have helped Kenan Thompson scare kids straight in a recurring sketch for the show. It's difficult (but fun) to judge who makes the scariest inmate: Zach Galifianakis, Charles Barkley, Taylor Swift, or Betty White. The main difference between the *Scared Straight!* documentary and the SNL parody is that a prison guard tries to limit the sexually suggestive language … in the SNL parody!

Clearly, Scared Straight has become part of pop culture, but does it work? In the 20-year follow-up to the documentary, most of the participants reportedly went on to lead productive lives and credited the Scared Straight experience for helping send them on the right path. After viewing the anecdotal evidence presented in the documentary, the logic of why it should work is simple. The premise is that these kids have yet to receive a serious consequence. Thus, we can "give them a taste" of the consequence so they will change their behavior.

Although on some level this may make intuitive sense, it's more valuable to examine controlled and objective research on Scared Straight programs (we're using the term "Scared Straight programs" to refer to any program in which inmates try to counsel and scare youth, even though these programs actually have several different names). The research consistently shows these programs are not effective in deterring youth from reoffending [7–9]. In fact, the research results are actually very scary themselves, as these Scared Straight programs actually *increase* reoffending in participants – sometimes by a lot. A recent review of nine different research studies on Scared Straight programs found that participants were 1.6–1.7 times *more* likely to reoffend than those in control groups who didn't participate in these programs [7].

Although the greatest weight should be placed on the above controlled research studies, a recent news story provides an ironic twist on Shapiro's claims that the original cast of *Scared Straight!* benefited from the program [10]. Angelo Speziale, one of the juveniles from the original documentary, who was also featured as a success story in the follow-up *Scared Straight! 20 Years Later*, is now serving a sentence of 25 years to life after police used DNA evidence to solve the cold case murder and rape of his teenage neighbor. The actual murder and rape happened only about four years after he participated in the original Scared Straight program. Ironically, he was ordered to serve his sentence in the same prison that hosted his Scared Straight intervention.

But it seems that the idea of inmates scaring at-risk youth away from a life of crime continues to be publicly appealing, as a new television show *Beyond Scared Straight* [11] aired on A&E TV in January, 2011, and a record-breaking 2.6 million viewers watched the season 2 premiere, making it the network's "most-watched original series launch of all-time" (A&E TV Press Release [12]). A quick glance at the discussion board for *Beyond Scared Straight* suggests that a large percentage of viewers posting to the board are in favor of these Scared Straight programs and many want to know how to sign their own kids up for the show!

Although the intervention programs featured in *Beyond Scared Straight* are similar to the intervention from the original documentary, these newer versions have evolved in several ways – and might be even scarier! First, the role of the prison guards has become more similar to that of the adult inmates, as they're often physically and verbally intimidating toward the youth. In at least one episode the youth spend the night at the prison, whereas other episodes allow inmates and youth to have individual meetings together (supervised by a guard). Finally, in at least one episode the inmates encourage the youth to engage in self-talk, such as saying "I'm a loser."

What makes the show's incredible success most surprising is the equally publicized opposition to the new series by a variety of federal, state, and professional agencies. For example, two leading organizations in the field of juvenile justice, the Coalition for Juvenile Justice [13] and the National Council of Juvenile and Family Court Judges [14], issued press releases soon after the initial airing of *Beyond Scared Straight* condemning the network for misrepresenting the effectiveness of the program and propagating a program that is "neither developmentally appropriate nor trauma-informed" [13].

In fact, two high level administrators within agencies under the US Department of Justice went further in their criticism of the television series by actively discouraging states from implementing such programs and threatening to reduce federal funding if these programs continue, as they may violate the Juvenile Justice and Delinquency Prevention Act (1974) that does not allow youth to have contact with adult inmates [15]. Finally, in a report to the US Congress on crime prevention, researchers listed Scared Straight programs under the category of "What Does Not Work," discouraging the continued use of these programs [9]. And while A&E is continuing to film the series, two out of the three states whose programs were the subject of the filming (California and Maryland) have suspended these programs due to the ongoing controversy [16].

Considering all of the evidence against Scared Straight programs, why do they continue to be used? In a recent interview, Shapiro addresses the controversy by saying,

> There are critics of everything, and the only thing I can say to anybody who is skeptical or critical is I'm seeing it for myself. I'm not reading some study from 30 years ago that said these programs don't work. By the way, nobody has done any study in the 21st century. In fact, nobody's done any study in the last 20 years. There's no program that exists now that's ever been studied, and any study that was done of a program, it's a program that no longer exists. So it's totally irrelevant. But I'm seeing it with my own eyes, I'm there for every one of these shoots … It's a testimonial, I'm not a social scientist. I don't have a Ph.D. (Harrison, 2011 interview of Shapiro [17])

Although Shapiro suggests that the current research on Scared Straight programs may be outdated, there's another explanation, which is that researchers in the field of juvenile justice have stopped researching this program's effectiveness because so many studies have consistently determined its potential harm to participants. And given that several research studies already exist that indicate that these programs actually increase reoffending rates, it's logical to assume that new versions of the program (which are very similar and possibly worse) also have the potential to increase crime reoffending. Furthermore, even if a new study examined these new versions of the Scared Straight program and showed them to be ineffective, Shapiro could respond by saying that there are now even newer versions of Scared Straight that the "new" studies (which would suddenly become old studies) haven't yet examined. Shapiro's final response to the current research against Scared Straight is actually common, and it is the "I only believe what I personally see" view of programs that places little value in the scientific method. That is, Shapiro fails to realize that we all see the world through distorted lenses. The faulty assumption that our own eyes never deceive us has been termed *naïve realism* [18].

But why do Scared Straight participants actually have increased criminal behavior after the program when they're compared to youth who have not participated in the program? There are several theories (though few have been thoroughly tested). First, at-risk youth may see prison as a place that they actually fit in (Greater Egypt Regional Planning & Development Commission [19], as cited in Schembri [20]). Similarly, these youth may look up to the inmates in Scared Straight programs as role models [21], thus mimicking their criminal behavior while ignoring the verbal messages they're given during the program. It has also been suggested that the youth see the program as a personal challenge to commit crimes as a way to *prove* they weren't "scared" by the program [21].

Another group of researchers explain how programs that rely on inter-actions between antisocial peers may produce undesired effects. They suggest that in these programs deviant behavior is being reinforced through laughter and attention [22]. Indeed, during Scared Straight programs, laughter is often seen between peers during their initial tour of prison. An additional reason why Scared Straight programs may produce undesired effects is related to the concept of desensitization. In other words, by exposing at-risk youth to the environment and culture of the prison, they may become desensitized to prison as a serious deterrent, thus making them more likely to commit a crime in the future [20]. These types of explanations have also been referred to as "deviancy training" in group treatments; however, it is worth noting that these deviancy training effects typically do not occur within most settings in which there is actually an effective treatment that is being implemented [23].

Given the evidence that Scared Straight programs fail to work (and sometimes increase future criminality), it's somewhat surprising that they are so widely believed to be effective by so many people. In our research, 64% of students and 62% of parents agreed with the statement that "Programs like Scared Straight help prevent youth from breaking the law" [24]. So, what can explain the great popularity of these programs? Perhaps it comes down to the simplicity of Scared Straight programs. The original tour of the Lifer's Group at Rahway State Prison was a single three-hour experience that was based on a simple, though flawed, logic that's easy to understand. Unfortunately life's greatest problems are not so simple and easily fixed. The numerous programs that actually do reduce juvenile crime are much more complex, cost more, and often involve numerous professionals. In short, they're not simple. But sometimes simple and convenient answers turn out to be wrong, and to get real change we've got to invest in more than just what is convenient.

What you need to know

There are several interventions that are effective for at-risk youth. For example, both Multisystemic Therapy (MST) [25] and Multidimensional Treatment Foster Care (MTFC) [26] are evidence-based treatments that have been shown to be effective at decreasing delinquency in youth. Both of these approaches include several therapeutic components including individual therapy, academic interventions, modification of consequences, and support for caregivers. Sherman and colleagues [9] present an extensive review of the literature on crime prevention, and report that there are several important principles related to effective interventions. These include: (i) identifying and addressing specific criminogenic risks for youth (e.g., existing mental illness, substance use, associating with peers who also engage in delinquent behavior); (ii) using cognitive-behavioral interventions; (iii) delivering interventions as designed; and (iv) attempting to build skills in the youth. Other evidence-based interventions for disruptive behavior in youth include Anger Control Training [27], Problem Solving Skills Training [28], and the Oregon model of Parent Management Training (PMT) [29].

References

[1] Shapiro, A. (Producer) (1978). *Scared Straight!* [Documentary]. New Video Group.

[2] Shapiro, A. (Producer) (1987). *Scared Straight! 10 Years Later* [Documentary]. New Video Group.

[3] Shapiro, A. (Producer) (1999). *Scared Straight! 20 Years Later* [Documentary]. New Video Group.

[4] Arditi, L. (2011, January 29). Training school stops scared straight class. *Providence Journal*, p.6.

[5] Gervais, R., Merchant, S. (Writers), & Blitz, J. (Director) (2006). The Convict [Television series episode]. In G. Daniels et al. [Executive producers], *The Office*. Deedle-Dee Productions.

[6] Michaels, L. (Executive Producer). *Saturday Night Live* [Television series]. New York: NBC Studios.

[7] Petrosino, A., Turpin-Petrosino, C., & Buehler, J. (2005). Scared Straight and other juvenile awareness programs for preventing juvenile delinquency. *The Scientific Review of Mental Health Practice*, 4, 48–54. doi:10.1002/14651 858.CD002796.pub2.

[8] Petrosino, A., Turpin-Petrosino, C., & Finckenauer, J. O. (2000). Well-meaning programs can have harmful effects! Lessons from experiments of programs such as Scared Straight. *Crime & Delinquency*, 46, 354–379. doi:10.1177/ 0011128700046003006.

[9] Sherman, L.W., Gottfredson, D, MacKenzie, D. L., et al. (1997). Preventing Crime: What works, what doesn't, what's promising. A report to the United

States Congress. College Park, MD: University of Maryland, Department of Criminology and Criminal Justice.

[10] Schill, R. (2011a). Scared Straight! graduate plays starring role in cold case crime. Retrieved on December 1, 2011 from http://jjie.org/scared-straight-graduate-plays-starring-role/9285 [accessed August 2014].

[11] Shapiro, A. (Producer) (2011). *Beyond Scared Straight* [Television series]. A&E TV.

[12] A&E TV Press Release (2011). A&E network picks up a third season of the real-life series 'Beyond Scared Straight'. A&E TV. Retrieved from http://www.aetv.com/news/a-e-network-picks-up-a-third-season-of-the-real-life-series-%27beyond-scared-straight%27-17202302 [accessed November 22, 2011].

[13] CJJ News Release (2011). National juvenile justice experts criticize message of A&E's "Beyond Scared Straight": Coalition of State-based Juvenile Justice Leaders urges investments in proven strategies. Retrieved from http://juvjustice.org/media/resources/public/resource_538.pdf [accessed November 22, 2011].

[14] NCJFCJ News Release (2011). Scared Straight! programs not effective or appropriate interventions. Retrieved from http://www.ncjfcj.org/content/view/1372/347/ [accessed November 22, 2011].

[15] Robinson, L. O. & Slowikowski, J. (2011, January 31). Scary – and ineffective. Retrieved from http://articles.baltimoresun.com/2011-01-31/news/bs-ed-scared-straight-20110131_1_straight-type-programs-straight-program-youths [accessed August 2014].

[16] Schill, R. (2011b). "Scared Straight" programs suspended in California and Maryland.Retrievedfromhttp://jjie.org/beyond-scared-straight-scares-maryland-into-suspending-program/9439 [accessed November 22, 2011].

[17] Harrison (2011). "Beyond Scared Straight" producer shares secrets of A&E's hit series. Retrieved from http://www.channelguidemagblog.com/index.php/2011/08/15/beyond-scared-straight-producer-shares-secrets-of-aes-hit-series/ [accessed November 22, 2011].

[18] Ross, L. & Ward, A. (1996). Naive realism: Implications for social conflict and misunderstanding. In T. Brown, E. Reed, and E. Turiel (Eds), *Values and Knowledge* (pp. 103–135). Hillsdale, NJ: Lawrence Erlbaum Associates.

[19] Greater Egypt Regional Planning & Development Commission (1979). *Menard Correctional Center: Juvenile Tours Impact Study*. Carbondale, IL: Author.

[20] Schembri, A. (2006). Scared Straight: Jail and Detention Tours—A White Paper. Florida Department of Juvenile Justice. August 2006. www.djj.state.fl.us/Research/Scared_Straight_Booklet_Version.pdf.

[21] Finckenauer, J. O. *(1982). Scared Straight and the Panacea Phenomenon.* Englewood Cliffs, NJ: Prentice-Hall.

[22] Dishion, T. J., McCord, J., & Poulin, F. (1999). When interventions harm: Peer groups and problem behavior. *American Psychologist*, 54, 755–764. doi: 10.1037//0003-066x.54.9.755.

[23] Weiss, B., Caron, A., Ball, S., et al. (2005). Iatrogenic effects of group treatment for antisocial youths. *Journal of Consulting and Clinical Psychology*, 73(6), 1036.

[24] Hupp, S., Stary, A., & Jewell, J. (submitted). Beliefs about myths related to child psychology, development, and parenting: Which myths need the most debunking?

[25] Henggeler, S. W. & Lee, T. (2003). Multisystemic treatment of serious clinical problems. In A. E. Kazdin & J. R. Weisz (Eds), *Evidence-Based Psychotherapies for Children and Adolescents* (pp. 301–322). New York, NY: Guilford.

[26] Chamberlain, P. & Reid, J. B. (1998). Comparison of two community alternatives to incarceration for chronic juvenile offenders. *Journal of Consulting and Clinical Psychology, 66,* 624–633. doi:10.1037/0022-006x.66.4.624.

[27] Lochman, J. E., Barry, T. D., & Pardini, D. A. (2003). Anger control training for aggressive youth. In A. E. Kazdin & J. R. Weisz (Eds), *Evidence-Based Psychotherapies for Children and Adolescents* (pp. 263–281). New York: Guilford.

[28] Kazdin, A. E. (2003). Problem-solving skills training and parent management training for conduct disorder. In A. E. Kazdin & J. R. Weisz (Eds), *Evidence-Based Psychotherapies for Children and Adolescents* (pp. 241–262). New York, NY: Guilford.

[29] Patterson, G. R., Chamberlain, P., & Reid, J. B. (1982). A comparative evaluation of a parent-training program. *Behavior Therapy, 13,* 638–650. doi:10.1016/s0005-7894(82)80021-x.

Speed busting for emotions & behavior

Myth #31 Parents can usually tell when their child is depressed

Although most parents may feel they're "in tune" with their child's emotional state, this may not always be the case. In dozens of studies over the last several decades, research has shown that parents are fairly poor informants when it comes to identifying depression in their children. For example, parents tend to report many fewer symptoms of depression in their children (when the child is actually found to be depressed) compared to the level of symptoms that the children report themselves [1, 2]. Numerous studies have also found that symptoms of depression in parents were significantly related to the parents' rating of depression in their children (for a review see Treutler & Epkins [3]). In one study mothers with some depressive symptoms rated their own child's behavior from a video, and the videos were also independently rated by research assistants who didn't know the children [4]. As compared to the ratings of the research assistants, the mothers rated their child in the video as having more negative emotion. In other words, parents with depression may view their children through a "depressive lens" and see their children as depressed as well, even when they're not. Interestingly, researchers have found that parents are better informants when their children have disruptive behavior problems (e.g., aggression) as opposed to problems with their mood (e.g., anxiety and depression) [5]. This finding may make sense when you consider that disruptive behavior problems are much easier to observe, while observing feelings of depression is much more difficult.

Myth #32 Young girls are more likely to have clinical depression than young boys

When it comes to teens and adults, females are more likely to experience clinical depression than males; however, this is not the case when it comes to children [6]. In a ten-year longitudinal study, researchers assessed rates of depression in youth from age 11 years old through 21 years old [6]. At age 15 years old, 4% of girls and 1% of boys experienced clinical depression. However, at 11 years old, boys (at almost 2%) were significantly more likely to experience clinical depression than girls (less than 1%). These differences at both age groups were statistically significant. Boys and girls had equal rates of depression at age 13 years old (at about 2%). Thus, girls don't begin having more depression than boys until some time in adolescence.

Myth #33 Helping children avoid their fears is the best way to decrease their anxiety

Although parents naturally desire to protect children from their fears, continually helping a child to escape fears has the potential to make the fears grow bigger. For some children, fears are so severe that they disrupt their daily activities. For example, a child may fear a neighbor's barking dog that is on their way to school and insist on taking a longer route to avoid the dog. Or children may insist that the parent thoroughly search parts of their basement for spiders before venturing downstairs. To understand how parents should best react to their kids' fears and worries, let's consider what research shows to be most effective for clinically significant phobias. A review examined the 32 most rigorous and well-designed research studies evaluating the effectiveness of treatment for phobias and other anxiety disorders in kids [7]. They found that cognitive-behavioral therapy programs showed significant effectiveness in decreasing anxiety and fear in children. These programs typically have a standard set of procedures that include gradually exposing children to what they fear, building skills to cope with the fear, and rewarding themselves for facing their fears. Also, programs that include parents in the treatment were found to provide additional benefit [8]. An example of parent-focused components of these programs includes training parents to reward their child for facing their fear by either simple praise and encouragement or by providing more tangible rewards, as well as helping the parent cope with his or her anxiety. Research by Rapee and colleagues [9] found that children of parents who used the book *Helping Your Anxious Child: A Step-by-Step Guide* [10] showed greater improvements in facing their fears than a control group, though children who went through group treatment with a therapist experienced the greatest improvement of all three groups. Overall, the best way to decrease anxiety is to face the fear rather than avoid the anxiety. If it's one thing we learned from the movie *Frozen* [11], it's that "conceal, don't feel" is really bad advice!

Myth #34 Adults can usually tell if a child is lying

As adults we often fancy ourselves as being able to read children pretty well. Nevertheless, we might not be able to determine children's truthfulness as well as we think. Studies show that adults are not very good at determining whether or not children are telling the truth. In one interesting study, a researcher told preschool-aged children not to peek at a toy and then left the room while the child was being video recorded [12]. The researcher then returned and asked the child whether or not he or she peeked. Sometimes when children said "no" it was the truth, and other times it was a lie. The videos of the children saying "no" were then shown to college students who had to determine which children were telling the truth and which were lying. The college students had a 41% accuracy rating, which is less than chance. Overall, there were a lot of false alarms (i.e., truth-telling children being accused of lying) as well as a lot of mistaken trust (i.e., children getting away with the lie). As an interesting side note, of the children that did peek, 78% of them lied about it. Other research has shown similar results [13, 14]. The take-home point is this: children can't always be trusted.

Myth #35 Seeing other people be aggressive will decrease children's aggressive drive

Part of Albert Bandura's motivation for doing the classic Bobo doll experiments came from a commonly believed myth. That is, according to Bandura, "It was once widely believed that seeing others vent aggression would drain the viewer's aggressive drive" [15]. Lilienfeld et al. [16] trace this idea of *catharsis* back to the philosopher Aristotle (i.e., viewing tragic plays was thought to be cathartic) and later Sigmund Freud [17] and his followers. Across several studies, however, Bandura demonstrated that when children observe an adult exhibiting aggressive acts with a Bobo doll they're actually more likely (not less likely) to also exhibit aggressive acts with the Bobo doll [18]. Thus, Bandura debunked the myth that seeing aggression decreases aggression in children.

Myth #36
School homicides are on the rise

According to the Center for Disease Control [19] homicides are the second most common cause of death for children and adolescents (ages 5 to 18 years old). You are probably able to recall a few recent school shootings without too much effort. When school shootings do occur, they understandably make national news and headlines for months. These high profile cases, however, often give us the impression that school homicides are on the rise. The Center for Disease Control [19] has been tracking the frequency of school homicides for the last few decades. For example, in the 1992 school year, there were 34 youth homicides in United States' schools (elementary and secondary). Through most of the 1990s, the youth homicide rate in schools was 28 or higher. More recently, however, in the 2009 school year (the most recent year in which the information is reported by the CDC), there were 17 youth homicides in schools, and this is lower than the rates in the 1990s. In fact, over the last decade, each year has had lower rates of school youth homicides than most of the years in the 1990s. Thus, the available data suggest that school homicides aren't on the rise and may even be on the decline.

Myth #37
Drug Abuse Resistance Education (DARE) prevents drug use

Drug Abuse Resistance Education (DARE) has been very popular for several decades, and the program uses police officers to teach children lessons aimed at preventing drug abuse (including alcohol abuse). The program has traditionally focused on children in fifth and sixth grade, but more recently the prevention efforts of DARE have expanded to children of a broader age range (including children in kindergarten). Despite the popularity of DARE, research has consistently shown that it is not effective across several studies [20]. In a critique of DARE, Lynam et al. [21] point out that DARE advocates often argue that these studies examined an out-of-date version of DARE and that there is now a newer DARE curriculum. Although this is a possibility, it is very reasonable to be skeptical of DARE until research provides support for the newer curriculum.

References

[1] Angold, A., Weissman, M. M., John, K., et al. (1987). Parent and child reports of depressive symptoms in children at low and high risk of depression. *Journal of Child Psychology and Psychiatry*, 28(6), 901–915.

[2] Weissman, M. M., Wickramaratne, P., Warner, V., et al. (1987). Assessing psychiatric disorders in children: Discrepancies between mothers' and children's reports. *Archives of General Psychiatry*, 44(8), 747.

[3] Treutler, C. M. & Epkins, C. C. (2003). Are discrepancies among child, mother, and father reports on children's behavior related to parents' psychological symptoms and aspects of parent–child relationships?. *Journal of Abnormal Child Psychology*, 31(1), 13–27.

[4] Youngstrom, E., Izard, C., & Ackerman, B. (1999). Dysphoria-related bias in maternal ratings of children. *Journal of Consulting and Clinical Psychology*, 67(6), 905.

[5] Edelbrock, C., Costello, A. J., Dulcan, M. K., et al. (1986). Parent-child agreement on child psychiatric symptoms assessed via structured interview. *Journal of Child Psychology and Psychiatry*, 27(2), 181–190.

[6] Hankin, B. L., Abramson, L. Y., Moffitt, T. E., et al. (1998). Development of depression from preadolescence to young adulthood: Emerging gender differences in a 10-year longitudinal study. *Journal of Abnormal Psychology*, 107, 128–140. doi:10.1037//0021-843x.107.1.128.

[7] Silverman, W. K., Pina, A. A., & Viswesvaran, C. (2008). Evidence-based psychosocial treatments for phobic and anxiety disorders in children and adolescents. *Journal of Clinical Child & Adolescent Psychology*, 37, 105–130. doi:10.1080/ 15374410701817907.

[8] Rapee, R. M., Schniering, C. A., & Hudson, J. L. (2009). Anxiety disorders during childhood and adolescence: Origins and treatment. *Annual Review of Clinical Psychology*, 5, 311–341. doi:10.1146/annurev.clinpsy.032408.15 3628.

[9] Rapee, R. M., Abbott, M. J., & Lyneham, H. J. (2006). Bibliotherapy for children with anxiety disorders using written materials for parents: A randomized controlled trial. *Journal of Consulting and Clinical Psychology*, 74, 436. doi:10.1037/ 0022-006x.74.3.436.

[10] Rapee, R. M., Spence, S., Cobham, V., & Wignall, A. D. (2000) *Helping Your Anxious Child: A Step-by-Step Guide for Parents*. Oakland, CA: New Harbinger.

[11] Del Vecho, P. (Producer), Buck, C. (Co-director), & Lee, J. (Co-director) (2013). *Frozen* [Motion picture]. United States: Walt Disney Studies.

[12] Crossman, A. M. & Lewis, M. (2006). Adults' ability to detect children's lying. *Behavioral Sciences & the Law*, 24, 703–715. doi:10.1002/bsl.731.

[13] Edelstein, R. S., Luten, T. L., Ekman, P., & Goodman, G. S. (2006). Detecting lies in children and adults. *Law and Human Behavior*, 30, 1–10. doi:10.1007/s10979-006-9031-2.

[14] Westcott, H. L., Davies, G. M., & Clifford, B. R. (1991). Adults' perceptions of children's videotaped truthful and deceptive statements. *Children & Society*, 5, 123–135. doi:10.1111/j.1099-0860.1991.tb00378.x.

[15] Bandura (n.d.). Albert Bandura Bobo Doll experiment 1. Retrieved from http://www.youtube.com/watch?v=YclZBhn40hU.

[16] Lilienfeld, S. O. (2010). *50 Great Myths of Popular Psychology: Shattering Widespread Misconceptions About Human Behavior*. Chichester, West Sussex: Wiley-Blackwell.

[17] Freud, S., Strachey, J., & Gay, P. (1930/1989). *Civilization and its Discontents*. New York: W.W. Norton.

[18] Bandura, A. (1973). *Aggression: A Social Learning Analysis*. Englewood Cliffs, NJ: Prentice-Hall, Inc.

[19] Center for Disease Control (n.d.). School-associated violent death study. Retrieved from http://www.cdc.gov/violenceprevention/youthviolence/schoolviolence/savd.html [accessed August 2014].

[20] West, S. L. & O'Neal, K. K. (2004). Project DARE outcome effectiveness revisited. *American Journal of Public Health*, 94(6), 1027–1029.

[21] Lynam, D. R., Milich, R., Zimmerman, R., et al. (1999). Project DARE: No effects at 10-year follow-up. *Journal of Consulting and Clinical Psychology*, 67(4), 590–593.

4

SOCIAL ENVIRONMENT

Great Myths of Child Development, First Edition. Stephen Hupp and Jeremy Jewell.
© 2015 John Wiley & Sons, Inc. Published 2015 by John Wiley & Sons, Inc.

Myth #38

An "only child" is likely to be selfish, spoiled, and socially incompetent

After having their first child, parents are faced with the question of whether to have more. Parents make that decision based on a number of important considerations related to their family, finances, and life goals. For many parents, the decision is also influenced by the fear that, without siblings, an "only child" (also called a *singleton*) will be selfish, spoiled, and socially incompetent. This international fear extends all the way from North America to Asia. In China, for example, the only child is feared to become a "little emperor," and this fear likely causes anxiety for parents given China's 1979 policy strongly encouraging one-child families [1].

The idea of the spoiled only child is longstanding and traces its roots back over a century to G. Stanley Hall, a central figure in the history of psychology. Hall is the founder of the child study movement and also known for being a key scholar in defining adolescence as a distinct developmental period separate from childhood and adulthood [2]. He was also the first president of the American Psychological Association, and was instrumental in bringing Sigmund Freud to speak at Clark University, which would be the only visit to America that Freud ever made [3].

It was actually one of Hall's doctoral students, E. W. Bohannon, who (under Hall's supervision) wrote the *Study of Peculiar and Exceptional Children* [4]. As studied in Hall's child research laboratory, Bohannon describes categories of children according to physical or psychological traits. Examples of physical traits used to categorize children included agile, heavy, tall, ugly, and clumsy, to name a few; whereas examples of psychological traits included timid, talkative, cruel, orderly, and dirty. Within his data, Bohannon noticed interesting trends regarding these traits as they relate to the only child.

Specifically, he describes five characteristics that distinguish singletons from children with siblings by suggesting that singletons "have imaginary companions, do not go to school regularly, if at all, do not get along with other children well, as a rule, are generally spoiled by indulgence, and have bad health in most cases" [4] (p. 36). Bohannon explains the origin of these negative traits as he observed that one or both parents of singletons appeared to be "below the standard in vitality, and perhaps that sterility begins early with them" [4] (p. 37). Thus, he asserts that the fact that a couple has only one child is proof of some sort of physical deficiency that would presumably be passed on to the child.

Bohannon also explains that singletons are not able to socialize with their peers because "they do not understand each other" [4] (p. 37). Bohannon expands on this idea two years later when, in his dissertation, he indicates that singletons have "much the same longing for society as the children of other families, but their isolated home life had failed to give them equal skill and ability in realizing their social interests" [4] (p. 24). With regard to the typical personality traits of an only child, he states that their "worst traits ... were selfishness, 'spoiled', temper, jealousy, untruthfulness, stubbornness and haughtiness" [4] (p. 24), although he also acknowledges the best traits of singletons include affection and obedience. Perhaps most notably, Hall himself, the founder of the child study movement, is commonly credited as saying in a 1907 lecture that "Being an only child is a disease in itself" [5] (p. 547).

Alfred Adler continued pairing singletons with selfishness. For example, Adler stated that an "only child usually insists on being the center of attention ..." [6]. Additionally, Adler [7] suggests that singletons have "difficulties with every independent activity and sooner or later they become useless for life" (p. 155), and he also adds that "Their life approaches that of a parasite who does nothing but enjoys life while the rest of the world cares for his wants" (p.155). Similar descriptions continue today, with psychologist and best-selling author Kevin Leman stating that "Lonely onlies tend to be critical – and even more than a bit self-centered" [8] (p. 131). Thus, Bohannon's original assertions about singletons continue to influence some parenting advice-givers over 100 years later.

There are many examples of television characters that continue to propel the notion that singletons are selfish, spoiled, and lonely. For example, Jan Brady from the 1970s television show *The Brady Bunch* [9] becomes jealous of her friend Donna who is an only child, but after Jan's siblings purposefully ignore her (in order to allow her to actually experience what it's like to be an only child) she regrets her jealousy and tells her siblings "Once you've been pushed around by brothers and sisters like you, you sure do miss it." The episode ends when Jan invites her friend Donna to a family event so that "she won't be an only child either." More recently, Rachel Berry, a lead character on the television show *Glee* [10], sings a solo called "Only Child" that describes the personal suffering from being an only child (with lyrics like, "I'm an only child, more than enough for them, but not enough for me") as well as typical stereotypes of an only child (with lyrics like, "Never learned to share my Cher CDs"). In another pop culture example, a *New York Times* article emphasized the fact that Snooki is an only child after describing the reality TV star as self-centered and spoiled [11].

The spoiled only child character has been prominent in media aimed at even younger audiences as well. These include the character Angelica in the television series *Rugrats* [12] and the debutante Charlotte from Disney's *The Princess and the Frog* [13]. Thus, children are exposed to the spoiled only child narrative from a young age.

Public opinion polls reflect the strength of this belief in the public consciousness as well. Research over several decades asked the public whether being an only child was an advantage or disadvantage [14], with the majority of respondents choosing "disadvantage" in research spanning the time from 1950 (76%) through 1977 (67%). Similarly, Baskett [15] found that parents rated singletons as more spoiled and unlikeable compared to firstborns or youngest children. Herrera and colleagues [16] (1993) surveyed college undergraduates about their perceptions of various birth orders (e.g., first born, last born, singletons) and found that participants tended to rate singletons as the most disagreeable, whereas Nyman [17] found that the African American and Hispanic college students in their study tended to view singletons as self-centered and spoiled. Most recently, in our research, 79% of college students and 54% of parents agreed with the statement "Most 'only children' (without siblings) are more likely to be selfish and spoiled" [18]. While this myth appears to be intractable in the minds of the general public, it's even more startling that clinicians appear to ascribe to this myth as well. Recently, Stewart [19] conducted a survey of over 300 clinicians regarding how their beliefs about birth order might affect their judgment about a client's prognosis. When presented with a vignette of a fictitious client that was described as being an only child, clinicians rated that client's prognosis as poorer and also believed that they had "additional personal problems" (p. 174) compared to firstborn and middleborn children.

Even though the notion of singletons being selfish and spoiled is a widely held belief, research suggests that this belief is indeed just a myth. The most thorough review of the literature on this topic found 141 studies comparing singletons to three other family groups: small families (with two children), medium families (three or four children), and large families (five or more children) [20]. Results of this meta-analysis indicated that singletons (compared to all other family groups) had higher achievement motivation, self-esteem, and positive relations with parents. Other than these positive personality traits, there were no other significant differences for the other 11 personality categories. For example, singletons were found to be similar to all other family groups when it came to maturity, cooperativeness, self-control, emotional stability, social participation, extraversion, and peer popularity. Additionally, in one of the most recent studies to date, as part of a national survey, thousands of youth were asked to make friendship nominations about other children from their school [21]. Singletons received just as many friendship nominations as children with siblings.

The above studies were composed mostly of samples from the United States. Therefore, one might wonder whether these results are generalizable to other cultures. To answer this, Falbo and Poston [22] gathered data from four different provinces in China. Given China's 1979 policy encouraging families to have only one child, the question of whether singletons are at a disadvantage is one that is critical to that country. When examining various personality variables, the authors concluded that, "these results indicate that in the area of personality, there is no single only-child effect" (p. 32). Other research also debunks the spoiled singleton myth with children in the Netherlands [23].

Given that there's no evidence that singletons are selfish, spoiled, and socially incompetent, why do people continue to believe the myth? Falbo and Polit [1] summarized the cumulative theory on the topic of singletons in the context of birth order and reduced them to a few different theories. One theory emphasizes that singletons are deprived of the social lessons provided by sibling relationships, so they become less socially skilled, more self-centered, and less liked by peers. Another theory is that singletons experience a unique family structure where they're the recipients of an over-abundance of parental attention, leading to self-centeredness and spoiling.

Although these ideas make intuitive sense, they aren't supported by the research. Lilienfeld et al. [24] describe this issue by suggesting that common sense is not always right. That is, many people think that psychology is little more than a collection of facts that were already common sense, but Lilienfeld et al. advocate the position "that the essence of science is 'uncommon sense'... because it often requires us to override our gut hunches and intuitions about the natural world ..." (p. 13). Several of the "Sources of Psychological Myths" also help propagate the notion of the spoiled singleton. These include word-of-mouth, selective perception, and misleading media.

Falbo and Polit [1] also make some interesting historical points. Specifically, for much of history, it was relatively rare for parents to have only one child. Moreover, contributing factors that led families to have only one child included economic hardship, war, divorce, and women entering the work force. Thus, for many people having only one child may have been a sign of problems or changes in society of which they didn't approve, and singletons may have been viewed by some as a symptom of other issues.

Mancillas [25] argues that there are three primary reasons that the spoiled singleton myth is harmful. First, the myth may be harmful to singletons themselves, especially if this myth is communicated directly or indirectly to them. Second, the myth may impact the parents of an only child in the way that they perceive their child or interact with them. Third, parents who currently have only one child may feel undue pressure to have another child, leading them in some cases to have a second child when other personal or financial factors would have guided them otherwise. In addition to these potential harms, another problem may occur if therapists are biased in their dealing with a client who is an only child [19].

Interestingly, some research does find that singletons do display some differences compared with children with siblings. For example, a study of children in the Netherlands found that, although singletons appeared to have similar levels of happiness and self-esteem compared with children with siblings, they did also indicate lower ratings regarding the importance they placed on sports [23]. They also were more likely to agree with their parents' and peers' perceptions that they were less proficient in sports. So while it's not fair to avoid picking singletons for your playgroups, some evidence suggests that it might be advisable to avoid picking them for your dodgeball team.

What you need to know

Although there are books focused on raising singletons, parents probably really don't need any special tips for raising children without siblings. Moreover, some of the other sections of this book provide resources for dealing with the behavior problems associated with selfish or spoiled behavior (both for singletons as well as for children with siblings). Regarding children that are lonely (whether singletons or siblingtons), they may have social anxiety or social skills deficits. One book that may be helpful is, *Overcoming Your Child's Shyness & Social Anxiety: A Self-Help Guide using Cognitive Behavioral Techniques* [26]. Additionally, the end of Myth 43 (about imaginary friends) further discusses resources for social skills.

References

[1] Falbo, T. & Polit, D. F. (1986). Quantitative review of the only child literature: Research evidence and theory development. *Psychological Bulletin*, 100, 176–189. doi:10.1037/0033-2909.100.2.176.
[2] Thorndike, E. L. (1925). Biographical memoir of Granville Stanley Hall 1846–1924. *National Academy of Sciences Biographical Memoirs*, 12(5), 133–180.

[3] Clark University (2013). *Archives and Special Collections: The Sigmund Freud and Carl Jung lectures at Clark University*. Retrieved (March 14, 2013) from http://www.clarku.edu/research/archives/archives/FreudandJung.cfm.

[4] Bohannon, E. W. (1896). A study of peculiar and exceptional children. *The Pedagogical Seminary*, 4, 3–60.

[5] Fenton, N. (1928). The only child. *The Pedagogical Seminary and Journal of Genetic Psychology*, 35, 546–556.

[6] Adler, A. (1930). *The Pattern of Life*. New York, NY: Cosmopolitan Book Corporation.

[7] Adler, A. (1927). *Understanding Human Nature*. New York, NY: Greenberg.

[8] Leman, K. (2009). *The Birth Order Book* (revised and updated). Grand Rapids, MI: Revell.

[9] Schwartz, S. (1972). The Only Child. Duchowny, R. (Director), Schwartz, S. (Producer), *The Brady Bunch* [Television series]. Los Angeles, CA: Paramount Studios.

[10] Murphy, R. (2011). Original Song. Buecker, B. (Director), Murphy, R. (Producer), *Glee* [Television series]. Los Angeles, CA: Paramount Studios.

[11] Horyn, C. (2010, July 23). Snooki's Time. Retrieved from http://nytimes.com.

[12] Klasky, A., Csupo, G., & Coffey, V. (1991). *Rugrats* [Television series]. Burbank, CA: Nickelodeon Animation Studios.

[13] Clements, R. & Musker, J. (Directors) (2009) *The Princess and the Frog* [Film]. Burbank, CA: Walt Disney Animation Studios.

[14] Blake, J. (1981). The only child in America: Prejudice versus performance. *Population and Development Review*, 7, 43–54.

[15] Baskett, L. M. (1985). Sibling status effects: Adult expectations. *Developmental Psychology*. 21, 441–445. doi:10.1037/0012-1649.21.3.441.

[16] Herrera, N. C., Zajonc, R. B., Wieczorkowska, G., & Cichomski, B. (1993). Beliefs about birth rank and their reflection in reality. *Journal of Personality and Social Psychology*, 85(1), 142–150. doi:10.1037/0022-3514.85.1.142.

[17] Nyman, L. (1995). The identification of birth order personality attributes. *Journal of Psychology*, 129(1), 51–59. doi:10.1080/00223980.1995.9914947.

[18] Hupp, S., Stary, A., & Jewell, J. (submitted). Beliefs about myths related to child psychology, development, and parenting: Which myths need the most debunking?

[19] Stewart, A. (2004). Can knowledge of client birth order bias clinical judgment? *Journal of Counseling & Development*, 82, 167–176. doi:10.1002/j.1556-6678.2004.tb00298.x.

[20] Polit, D. F. & Falbo, T. (1987). Only children and personality development: A quantitative review. *Journal of Marriage and the Family*, 49, 309–325. doi: 10.2307/352302.

[21] Bobbitt-Zeher, D. & Downey, D. B. (2013). Number of siblings and friendship nominations among adolescents. *Journal of Family Issues*. doi: 10.1177/ 0192513X12470370.

[22] Falbo, T. & Poston Jr, D. L. (1993). The academic, personality, and physical outcomes of only children in China. *Child Development*, 64, 18–35. doi: 10.2307/1131435.

[23] Veenhoven, R. & Verkuyten, M. (1989). The well-being of only children. *Adolescence*, 24, 155–166.

[24] Lilienfeld, S. O., Ammirati, R., & David, M. (2012). Distinguishing science from pseudoscience in school psychology: Science and scientific thinking as safeguards against human error. *Journal of School Psychology*, 50(1), 7–36. doi: 10.1016/j.jsp.2011.09.006.

[25] Mancillas, A. (2006). Challenging the stereotypes about only children: A review of the literature and implications for practice. *Journal of Counseling and Development*, 84, 268–275. doi:10.1002/j.1556-6678.2006.tb00405.x.

[26] Willetts, L. & Creswell, C. (2007). *Overcoming Your Child's Shyness & Social Anxiety: A Self-Help Guide Using Cognitive Behavioral Techniques.* London: Robinson.

Myth #39

Divorce ruins most kids' lives

It's one of the greatest fears of many married couples with children – a divorce will ruin the kids' lives. This fear is realized in the television show *Mad Men*, which depicts life in the 1960s. In the Season 6 finale, Don Draper's daughter, Sally, is suspended from school, which prompts her mother to suggest this cause: "She's from a broken home" [1]. The movie *American Psycho* [2], set in the 1980s, gives audiences a glimpse of what can happen to children from a "broken home" as they turn into adults. The main character (played by Christian Bale), a serial killer, reveals "I'm a child of divorce, gimme a break."

Despite these rather negative glimpses in the media regarding the effect of divorce on children, most researchers estimate that about half of children in the USA will experience their parents' divorce by the time they turn 18 years old [3]. Given the prevalence of divorce and the fundamental changes that it brings to a family, one can see the power behind the fear that divorce ruins kids' lives.

The increasing divorce trend began in the decade of the 1970s, as children living in single mother households almost doubled from 1970 to 1980 [4]. This societal trend shocked many. Leading the charge against divorce was Judith Wallerstein, called the "Godmother of the Backlash Against Divorce" by *Time* magazine [5]. Wallerstein's research began with 131 children from 60 families living in Northern California who were seeking treatment from her clinic [6]. Qualitative results from the study pointed to severe consequences for children whose parents had divorced, stating that "Of the total sample studied, 44% (N = 15) of the children were found to be in significantly deteriorated psychological condition at the follow-up a year later" (p. 615).

The rhetoric of Wallerstein increased to a feverish pitch in the coming years. In a 1976 interview with the *New York Times* she stated, "I don't want to say don't divorce, but I think children might even prefer having an unhappy family" [7]. Wallerstein went on to write the national best seller, *Second Chances: Men, Women, and Children a Decade After Divorce* [8], as well as *The Unexpected Legacy of Divorce: A 25 Year Landmark Study* [9]. These books launched Wallerstein into the popular media, with interviews by Oprah and the PBS *Newshour* in 2000.

In an interview with Elizabeth Farnsworth from the PBS *Newshour* [10], Wallerstein describes the child participants from her original 1971 study who, in 2000, had entered young adulthood, "And they did feel that they sacrificed a lot to their parent's divorce." As young adults, Wallerstein notes about these participants, "They have a lot of trouble believing that they can love somebody, or that somebody is going to love them, and that it's going to be a relationship that's going to last."

Other political commentators have joined Wallerstein in criticizing divorce, including activist and author Phyllis Schlafly who stated in an interview that adults should put their happiness second to that of their child and only divorce in "extreme circumstances" such as abuse or addiction [11]. In the interview, Schlafly appears to also suggest that it's problematic that psychologists actually encourage divorce because it's a money-making process for the psychologists. Laura Schlessinger ("Dr. Laura") has also been a vocal advocate suggesting that divorce ruins kids' lives. Even though her doctoral degree is in physiology (instead of psychology), she became a family counselor, popular radio talk show host, and author of several bestselling books. For example, Schlessinger focuses on divorce as being one of the major "stupid things" in her book *Stupid Things Parents do to Mess up their Kids* [12].

Although the public at large tends to view divorce as being relatively more acceptable in recent years as compared to previous years [13], many people do worry about the impact it has on children. The Pew Research Center [14] recently undertook a comprehensive investigation of how the public views marriage and the family. Several interesting findings were revealed, with 61% agreeing with the statement that "a child needs a home with both a mother and a father to grow up happily." Surprisingly, this finding differed only slightly based on whether the respondents themselves grew up in an intact family (63%) compared with those whose parents were divorced (53%). Other factors also appear to influence how people view divorce's impact on children. For example, groups such as adults over 65 years old, men, those with relatively less education, and ethnic minorities tended to view divorce as more disruptive to children.

In our research, 40% of students and 47% of parents agreed with the statement that "Divorce tends to ruin the lives of most children that have to go through it" [15].

Given this research on opinions about divorce, it's clear that the fear of divorce's impact on children is a concern for many. But what does the research say? One of the most comprehensive reviews of the research on this topic was conducted in 2001 and extended a previous review from 1991 [16]. Amato [29] reviewed 67 studies from the 1990s and compared the differences between children who experienced divorce to those whose biological parents were still married. These studies found that children of divorce tended to have more conduct problems and concerns related to their psychological adjustment than those children living with both parents. Nevertheless, the size of this difference is relatively small. The study also revealed that children of divorce had more problems with academic achievement, self-concept, and social relationships. But the size of the difference was even smaller when these variables were considered. Other researchers have noted that when poverty levels are accounted for, these differences in academic achievement for children of divorce narrow even further [17].

More recent research has begun to focus on the possibility that some child adjustment problems after a divorce are actually better accounted for by existing family or parent variables that existed prior to the divorce (e.g., parent personality variables) and do not change. This more controlled research has found mixed results. About half of the studies found that when these variables are controlled for, the differences between children of divorce compared with children living with both parents virtually disappeared, while the other half of these studies continued to find differences of the same small magnitude as has already been reviewed in the previous research [18].

And herein lies the kernel of truth in this myth. Children who have experienced divorce do have a period of complications in various aspects of their life, though the true effect appears to be relatively small. In regards to the "Sources of Psychological Myths," this myth is easily spread due to word-of-mouth as it is often a tantalizing topic for neighborhood gossip.

It's also interesting to note the research findings that children's functioning post-divorce was highly dependent on the amount of conflict that existed in the marriage [19]. For couples in low-conflict marriages, divorce appeared to have mild negative effects on their children as they may have lost the benefits of a stable family structure (from the child's perspective). However, children from a high-conflict marriage experienced either no change in some areas of functioning, or improvement in other areas. The authors hypothesize that children perceive living with a single parent as superior to a very high stress family environment where both parents co-exist with a great deal of conflict.

As researchers have examined this issue more closely, they have turned away from the initial question of whether divorce is harmful to children and spent more time focusing on the family processes that occur before, during, and after the divorce that provide both risk and protective factors for the child [20, 21]. This focus leads us to perhaps the most important question surrounding the myth, which is: What can parents do to help children cope with a divorce?

One of the first challenges that children face during a divorce is the shock of the initial separation [21]. One study that interviewed children of divorce found that 23% didn't recall any discussion at all about their parents' separation or divorce, while 45% only received a one- or two-sentence statement from one parent with no reason for the divorce given [22]. Given these circumstances, it's understandable how children might struggle with the initial separation of their parents. Ideally, when parents decide to divorce, they should typically have a discussion with their children where both parents are present, discuss the reasons for divorce in developmentally appropriate terms, and allow the child to ask questions.

Another important risk factor to address is the amount of parental conflict that occurs during and after the divorce (for a review see Kelly & Emery [21]). Parents who express a high amount of conflict during and after the divorce process, especially in front of children, appear to have a negative effect on those children. These harmful family processes also include having children send negative messages between parents and vilifying the other parent in front of the children. Therefore, parent education, communication training, or other programs that encourage negotiation and conflict resolution and discourage involvement of the children in these negative interactions will likely benefit those children.

A decline in the quality of parenting is another significant factor for children during a divorce [23]. With divorce often comes parental anger, depression, and a general emotional upset that can interfere with good parenting practices. Additionally, parents may begin to initiate or increase drug and alcohol use in order to cope with the divorce, which again negatively impacts their parenting and discipline practices. Thus, improving parents' appropriate coping in this stressful time can provide an indirect positive effect on children's functioning as well.

One protective factor for children of divorce is the frequency and quality of the contact between the child and noncustodial parent. Recent research has shown that joint custody appears to be superior to sole custody when it comes to children's functioning in a number of domains [24]. For cases in which one parent has sole custody, frequent contact with the noncustodial parent (in which positive parenting experiences occur) is a strong protective factor for those children. Nevertheless, this is only true if the child's involvement with the noncustodial parent is positive; if not, this contact can be detrimental to the child (see Kelly & Emery [21]).

But what is the harm in believing the myth? There are several circumstances in which it would be harmful for people to actually believe this myth. First, for adults who are in a violent or abusive relationship with their spouse, this myth could prevent them from divorcing and seeking safety for themselves and their children. Second, parental divorce is often more beneficial to children in those marriages that are highly conflictual. Thus, the myth might create expectations from parents that their children will have serious problems following a divorce, which might lead the parents to begin viewing their children more negatively. Worse yet, because of this myth, children might start viewing themselves in a less positive light after their parents have divorced.

In conclusion, the belief that divorce will *ruin* a child's life appears to be a lasting and entrenched myth, though a myth nonetheless. While children's functioning in some domains appears to decline after parental divorce, this is not the case in all circumstances, as some children's functioning actually improves after a divorce. Also, the decline in functioning tends to be relatively small [3] and only exists in the short term for many children [25]. While we agree that all married couples should work hard to keep a marriage together when doing so is a healthy option, we disagree with the notion that a family is "broken" or that a child's life is "ruined" simply because of a divorce.

What you need to know

The book, *The Truth About Children and Divorce: Dealing With The Emotions So You and Your Children Can Thrive* [26], provides additional evidence for why divorce does not ruin children's lives. It also provides useful information for how parents can help their children cope with a divorce. Some of the specific topics include practical challenges, legal issues, parenting plans, as well as how to talk to children at different ages about the separation.

References

[1] Way, C. (Writer) & Weiner, M. (Writer & Director) (2013). In Care Of [Television series episode]. In M. Weiner, S. Hornbacher, A. Jacquemetton, et al. (Executive Producers), *Mad Men*. New York, NY: AMC Studios

[2] Solomon, C., Hanly, C., Pressman, E. R. (Producers), & Harron, M. (Director) (2000). *American Psycho* [Motion picture]. United States: Lions Gate Films.

[3] Amato, P. R. (2001). Children of divorce in the 1990's: An update of the Amato and Keith (1991) meta-analysis. *Journal of Family Psychology*, 15, 355–370. doi: 10.1037/0893-3200.15.3.355.

[4] U.S. Census Bureau (2000–2010). *Children under 18 years old by presence of parents: 2000–2010* [Current population survey table of 69 families and living arrangements]. Retrieved from http://www.census.gov/compendia/statab/2012/tables/12s0069.pdf [accessed August 2014].

[5] Van Beima, D. (1995, February). The price of a broken home. *Time*, 145(8), 53.

[6] Wallerstein, J. S. & Kelly, J. B. (1975). The effects of parental divorce: Experiences of the preschool child. *Journal of the American Academy of Child Psychiatry*, 14, 600–616.

[7] Grady, D. (2012, June 25). Judith S. Wallerstein, psychologist who analyzed divorce, dies at 90. *The New York Times*, p. A12.

[8] Wallerstein, J. S. & Blakeslee, S. (1989). *Second Chances: Men, Women and Children a Decade after Divorce*. New York: Tickner & Fields.

[9] Wallerstein, J. S., Lewis, J. M., & Blakeslee, S. (2000). *The Unexpected Legacy of Divorce: A 25 Year Landmark Study*. New York, NY: Hyperion.

[10] Farnsworth, E. (2000). Judith Wallerstein discusses her latest book, "The Unexpected Legacy of Divorce," an analysis of the long-term effect of divorce on children. Retrieved from http://www.pbs.org/newshour/conversation/july-dec00/wallerstein_12-19.htm.

[11] Willett, B. (2011, February 22). Feminists love divorce! [Web blog post]. Retrieved from http://www.huffingtonpost.com/beverly-willett/feminists-love-divorce_b_825208.html [accessed August 2013].

[12] Schlessinger, L. (2000). *Stupid Things Parents do to Mess up their Kids*. New York, NY: Harper.

[13] Gallup Inc. (2008). [Telephone interviews May 8–11, 2008 from chart illustrations]. Cultural tolerance for divorce grows to 70%. Gallup. Retrieved from http://www.gallup.com/poll/107380/Cultural-Tolerance-Divorce-Grows-70.aspx [accessed August 2014].

[14] Pew Research Center (2010). [Nationwide survey October 1–21, 2010 from chart illustrations]. The decline of marriage and rise of new families. Pew Social and Demographic Trends. Retrieved from http://www.pewsocialtrends.org/2010/11/18/the-decline-of-marriage-and-rise-of-new-families/5/#v-children [accessed August 2014].

[15] Hupp, S., Stary, A., & Jewell, J. (submitted). Beliefs about myths related to child psychology, development, and parenting: Which myths need the most debunking?

[16] Amato, P. R., & Kieth, B. (1991). Parental divorce and the well- being of children: A meta-analysis. *Psychological Bulletin*, 110, 25–46.

[17] McLanahan, S. S. (1999). Father absence and children's welfare. In E. M. Hetherington (Ed.), *Coping with Divorce, Single Parenting, and Remarriage: A Risk and Resiliency Perspective* (pp. 117–146). Mahwah, NJ: Lawrence Erlbaum.

[18] Amato, P. R. (2010). Research on divorce: Continuing trends and new developments. *Journal of Marriage and the Family*, 72, 650–666. doi:10.1111/j.1741-3737.2010.00723.x.

[19] Booth, A. & Amato, P. R. (2001). Parental predivorce relations and offspring postdivorce well-being. *Journal of Marriage and the Family*, 63, 197–212. doi: 10.1111/j.1741-3737.2001.00197.x.

[20] Arnett, J. J. (2010). *Adolescence and Emerging Adulthood: A Cultural Approach.* (4th edn). Upper Saddle River, NJ: Prentice-Hall.

[21] Kelly, J. & Emery, R. (2003). Children's adjustment following divorce: Risk and resilience perspectives. *Family Relations*, 52, 352–362. doi:10.1111/j.1741-3729.2003.00352.x.

[22] Dunn, J., Davies, L., O'Connor, T., & Sturgess, W. (2001). Family lives and friendships: The perspectives of children in step-, single-parent, and nonstop families. *Journal of Family Psychology*, 15, 272–287. doi: 10.1037/0893-3200.15.2.272.

[23] Hetherington, E. M. (1999). Should we stay together for the sake of the children? In E. M. Hetherington (Ed.), *Coping with Divorce, Single Parenting, and Re-marriage* (pp. 93–116). Mahwah, NJ: Lawrence Erlbaum.

[24] Bausermann, R. (2002). Child adjustment in joint-custody versus sole-custody arrangements: A meta-analytic review. *Journal of Family Psychology*, 16, 91–102. doi:10.1111/j.1741-3729.2003.00352.x.

[25] Chase-Lansdale, P. L. & Hetherington, E. M. (1990). The impact of divorce on life-span development: Short and long term effect. In P. B. Baltes, D. L. Featherman, & R. M. Lerner (Eds), *Life Development and Behavior* (Vol. 10, pp. 105–150). Hillsdale, NJ: Lawrence Erlbaum.

[26] Emery, R. E. (2006). *The Truth about Children and Divorce: Dealing with the Emotions so you and your Children can Thrive.* New York, NY: Penguin.

Myth #40

If you "spare the rod" you will "spoil the child"

Examples of child misbehavior are all around us: in movies, television, as well as in our own lives. How many times have we seen a child running amok on a playground, pushing other children and throwing rocks, with a beleaguered parent running behind, trying to get their attention? And as one parent whispers to another, "Well, if you spare the rod, you spoil the child," what they really mean is, "That kid needs a good spanking!" It seems that many parents often look to this relatively quick answer to take care of a variety of challenging child behaviors.

Although many parents are familiar with the abbreviated "spare the rod" proverb, it's likely that most are less familiar with the full biblical text from which it comes. In the New King James Version of the Bible [1], the applicable scripture from Proverbs 13:24 reads, "He who spares his rod hates his son, But he who loves him disciplines him promptly." And many appear to have translated the "rod" in this scripture to mean a paddle meant for spanking. But in fact, modern day translations of the passage often suggest a much different meaning. For example, the New Living Translation of the Bible [2] includes a version of the scripture that reads, "If you refuse to discipline your children, it proves you don't love them …," whereas the New International Reader's Version of the Bible [3] states that, "Those who don't correct their children hate them … ." In both translations, the concept of a "rod" has been replaced with a more general concept of "discipline." Interestingly, scholars believe that the translation referring to the rod was, in fact, likely referring to a staff that shepherds used to gently guide their sheep [4, 5]. This makes sense when one thinks of a parent guiding children as a shepherd would guide sheep, gently nudging them along the right path. As Fortune and Hertz [5] put it, "A shepherd uses his staff to guide the sheep where they should go. The staff is not used as a cudgel" (p. 77; "cudgel" is another word for "club").

So what do practicing clergy themselves say about the "spare the rod" proverb? A survey recently asked over 14,000 practicing American clergy about their views on corporal punishment [6]. The term "corporal punishment" includes spanking in addition to other forms of physical discipline. The study found that less than half of the clergy agreed with the idea of using the "spare the rod" proverb as justification for spanking. Also, a majority of the clergy agreed that parents "too often use the Bible to justify abuse." The authors conclude that "clergy support for corporal punishment is decidedly tepid, compared with attitudes expressed in the general US population in recent surveys and polls" (p. 543). Therefore, it appears that the link between the biblical scripture and the mandate to spank is most likely a misunderstanding of biblical scripture, and a majority of clergy don't support the "spare the rod" proverb as most people understand it.

Some parenting experts have long promoted the importance of spanking as a form of discipline. James Dobson, for example, author of several parenting books, has been an outspoken spanking advocate. Dobson [7] suggests that "Two or three stinging strokes on the legs or bottom with a switch are usually sufficient to emphasize the point, 'You must obey me'" (p. 47), and he adds that "a small amount of pain for a young child goes a long way" (p. 47). In response to a parent's question about what to do if a child won't stop crying after a spanking, Dobson [8] suggests he would offer "him a little more of whatever caused the original tears" (p. 52). That is, for Dobson, a second spanking appears to be the solution for crying too much after the first spanking. More recently, he answers a similar question the same way and adds that "real crying usually lasts two minutes or less but may continue for five" [9] (p. 135). He also emphasizes that spankings "should be confined to the buttocks, where permanent damage is very unlikely" [9] (p. 135).

But what does the general public think of the necessity of spanking? A public opinion poll surveyed over 1,000 adults in the USA and asked them "Do you think spanking is sometimes necessary to maintain discipline with children or do you think spanking is not necessary" [10]. Of those surveyed, 69% reported that spanking is sometimes necessary while 25% reported it's not. Similarly, in one study parents were asked if "It's sometimes necessary to discipline a child with a good, hard spanking," and almost 80% agreed with this sentiment [11]. In our research, 45% of students and 39% of parents agreed with the statement that "When kids are never spanked for their misbehavior, they are likely to be spoiled" [12].

Spanking continues to be a common practice. Straus and Stewart [13] examined data from a parent survey on the use of corporal punishment. They found that parents' use of corporal punishment peaked at age 5 years old, with over 90% of parents reporting that they had used corporal punishment in the past year, and did so about once a month on average. Notably, about half of parents reported spanking their infants monthly, and 40% spanked their 15-year-old children almost once a month [13]. A similar study surveyed parents with children under the age of 3 years old regarding their discipline practices [14]. Again, spanking was found to be relatively common in even very young children, with 26% of parents of children age 19 to 35 months old, and 11% of parents of children age 10 to 18 months old, reporting frequent spankings.

Although the use of spanking has gradually decreased in the last several decades [14, 15], there's been a backlash to this trend. For example, the introduction to survey results from readers of *Men's Health* ponders this question: "is the movement against corporal punishment just another instance of society going soft, and the precursor to a generation of spoiled, unruly children?" [16] (p. 31). Indeed, there are many examples in the media that seem to long for the "good old days" when spanking was a more commonplace way to get a child to behave. In a reality TV example, one of the stars (nicknamed "Tickle") from the show *Moonshiners* [17] indicated that:

> There's a big difference in how I was raised and how kids are raised now. The biggest difference is: parents don't whoop their kids no more. They let them do whatever they want to do. They just let them run wild, and

that's gonna bring up a generation of children that is never gonna be able to run this country.

Television dramas and comedies also provide pop culture representations of spanking being required for discipline. In the TV drama *Mad Men* [18], set in the 1960s, Don Draper returns home from work, and his wife, Betty, informs him that their son had been misbehaving. When Don accepts the boy's apology without any further discipline, Betty chastises him saying, "He needs a spanking. How else is he going to learn the difference between right and wrong?" When Don replies that, "it doesn't work that way," his wife becomes angry saying, "You think you'd be the man you are today if your father didn't hit you?" Another television example comes from *The Simpsons* [19] when Bart is spanked by a former US president who says, "I'm going to do something your daddy should have done a long time ago." In the sitcom *Joey* [20], Matt LeBlanc's character gets tired of being insulted by a spoiled and bossy child star, and then he turns the child over on his knee, spanking him, while saying "You need discipline." As can be seen from these pop culture examples, spanking is often portrayed as the antidote to spoiled children. A character from the show *Game of Thrones* provides one last example. Stannis Baratheon, a potential heir to the throne, has one daughter (an only child); and his advisor, The Red Priestess, says of his daughter, "She is sullen and stubborn and sinful ... she needs the rod" [21]. The Red Priestess clearly does not mean gentle guidance.

Before examining the research on spanking, it's important to distinguish between corporal punishment and physical abuse. Spanking is usually intended to be corporal punishment, which has been defined as "the use of physical force with the intention of causing a child to experience pain but not injury for the purposes of correction or control of the child's behavior" [22]. Conversely, physical abuse is captured under the US federal definition of child abuse and neglect as "any recent act or failure to act on the part of a parent or caretaker which results in death, serious physical or emotional harm ..." [23].

Physical abuse is illegal but corporal punishment is legal in American homes. That is, American parents have the legal right to spank their children as long as it doesn't cause damage, and most instances of spanking are *not* physical abuse by definitions used in America. Spanking crosses the line to become abuse when it causes "physical or emotional harm." Spanking is more likely to cross this line when objects are used because objects can cause injury. Unfortunately, Dobson [9] recommends that spankings be done with "a switch (a small, flexible twig from a tree) or paddle ..." (p. 137). This more recent recommendation is only slightly revised from Dobson's earlier recommendation of using a belt [7]. The reason Dobson discourages spanking with the hand is that he believes, "If you're used to suddenly disciplining with the hand, your child may not know when she's about to be swatted and can develop a pattern of flinching when you make an unexpected move" [9] (p. 136). To be fair, Dobson clearly is not suggesting that parents cause injury. Rather, he's making suggestions for how to use spanking as a discipline strategy.

Typically, there are two goals to any discipline strategy. The first is to impact behavior in the short term, such as gaining immediate compliance, while the second, and perhaps most important goal, is to have a longer-lasting impact on behavior over time. In other words, parents seek ways for their children to internalize and generalize a rule (e.g., follow parent directions). The first question is: Does spanking gain immediate compliance? Research has demonstrated that spanking can improve immediate compliance and can be more effective than reasoning alone [24]. Nevertheless, attention withdrawal (e.g., ignoring the child after misbehavior) in combination with any other discipline strategy was significantly more effective than spanking alone. Three other different studies of children's compliance to time-out in a chair [25–27] also found that spanking significantly improved compliance of the child staying in time-out. However, two of these studies also compared spanking to using a room time-out as a back-up to a time-out chair. They found the room time-out strategy to be at least as effective as spanking [25] and actually sometimes more effective [26]. Therefore, it appears that although spanking does improve children's compliance in the short-term, there are other discipline strategies that are at least as effective, and sometimes even more effective.

What about the bigger goal of internalizing and generalizing that lesson? Spanking doesn't fare well in this area. Researchers have examined what is known as moral internalization, defined by Gershoff [28] as "their long term compliance, their feelings of guilt following misbehavior, and their tendencies to make reparations upon harming others" (p. 550). In a meta-analysis of outcomes related to corporal punishment, Gershoff found that spanking was actually related to lower moral internalization in 13 of the 15 existing studies on the topic.

Another consideration is the potential for negative side effects of spanking. Again, a meta-analysis of dozens of studies found that corporal punishment was significantly related to several negative outcomes in childhood, including increased aggression and antisocial behavior, poorer parent–child relationships, and poorer mental health outcomes [28]. Another noted concern was that corporal punishment was related to a much greater likelihood that the child would be a victim of physical abuse. This is perhaps one of the best arguments against corporal punishment, which is that spanking may sometimes, intentionally or unintentionally, lead to physical abuse. This outcome can be particularly likely if the initial spanking doesn't elicit immediate compliance in the child and the parent thinks that they must increase the intensity level of physical punishment to gain compliance until eventually their spanking crosses the line into abuse.

The question as to whether mild to moderate spanking (that is not abusive) is related to negative child outcomes is actually quite controversial. For example, Baumrind, Larzelere, and Cowan [29] lay out several arguments regarding the conclusions that Gershoff [28] draws in her meta-analysis. Much of the controversy is related to how corporal punishment is defined across studies. Baumrind and colleagues argue that many of the studies used in Gershoff's meta-analysis confound typical spanking on the buttocks with one's hand with much harsher physical discipline such as "beating with a stick, belt, etc." [30] (p. 133). Thus, they argue that milder forms of corporal punishment may be harmless and that the negative outcomes reported in some research studies are actually the result of harsher and abusive disciplinary tactics [29]. Moreover, the correlation between spanking and negative side effects may vary across cultures [31]. Finally, most of the research on the negative side effects of spanking is correlational, and it would be a mistake to assume that correlation equals causation.

Given all of the research on this topic, why do people continue to believe that spanking is necessary to avoid raising a spoiled child? According to Straus [22] there are several possible reasons. For example, several studies have found that spanking is so common in America that it has become accepted as the norm for disciplining children. Other reasons can be described in terms of the "Sources of Psychological Myths." For example, there's a kernel of truth to this myth, which is that if a parent "spares" all guidance and discipline then their child is more likely to be poorly behaved. We tend to remember the very permissive parents, who neither spank nor correct in any way, and assume it's the lack of spanking that causes the child's misbehavior. Spanking advocates also frequently provide a false dichotomy in which parents are described as either using spanking or using nothing. Finally, we previously described the short-term improvements in compliance related to spanking, which likely affects the parents' decision regarding the continued use of this discipline strategy.

In summary, although spanking may be an effective strategy to gain immediate compliance in some cases, it may not always be the most effective strategy, it's related to lower moral internalization in the long term, and it may have unintended negative side effects for the child. Interestingly, research on spanking has led over 30 countries to prohibit parents from spanking their children (Global Initiative to End All Corporal Punishment of Children [32]). While spanking is legal in the USA, the American Academy of Pediatrics recommends "that parents be encouraged and assisted in the development of methods other than spanking for managing undesired behavior" [33] (p. 723). Although we very much agree with this statement, we also believe that a few occasions of mild spanking will not likely cause harm to a child, and parents shouldn't be made to feel guilty for using mild spanking as an occasional discipline tactic. If parents do decide to use an occasional spanking, they should also realize that, at best, the spanking teaches children "what *not* to do," so they will also need to think about teaching the child "what *to do*," instead, by using some additional approach.

What you need to know

Behavioral parent training has emerged as a leader in the evidence-based practice of dealing with oppositional child behaviors. The book, *The Everyday Parenting Toolkit: The Kazdin Method for Easy, Step-by-Step, Lasting Change for You and Your Child* [34], describes how parents can use behavioral principles with their children. Kazdin, former president of the American Psychological Association, gives concrete advice on how to deal with specific problem scenarios such as tantrums in the supermarket, messy bedrooms, problems with homework, and many more. Our next myth further describes one alternative to spanking: time-out.

References

[1] Nelson, T. (1982). *The Holy Bible King James Version*. Nashville, TN: Thomas Nelson Publishers.
[2] Tyndale (1996). *Holy Bible, New Living Translation*. Wheaton, IL: Tyndale House Publishers Inc.
[3] Biblica (1998). *Bible: New International Reader's Version*. Grand Rapids, MI: Zondervan Publishing House.
[4] Carey, A. T. (1994). Spare the rod and spoil the child: Is this a justification for the use of corporal punishment in child rearing? *Child Abuse and Neglect*, 18, 1005–1010. doi:10.1016/0145-2134(94)90125-2.
[5] Fortune, M. M. & Hertz, J. (1982). A Commentary on Religious Issues in Family Violence. In M. M. Fortune & D. Hormann (Eds), *Family Violence: A Workshop Manual for Clergy and other Service Providers* (pp.71–78). Seattle, WA: Center for the Prevention of Sexual and Domestic Violence.

[6] Vaaler, M. L., Ellison, C. G., Horton, K. D., & Marcum, J. P. (2008). Spare the rod? Ideology, experience, and attitude toward child discipline among Presbyterian clergy. *Pastoral Psychology*, 56, 533–546. doi:10.1007/s11089-008-0129-y.

[7] Dobson, J. C. (1978). *The Strong-Willed Child: Birth Through Adolescence*. Wheaton, IL: Tyndale House.

[8] Dobson, J. C. (1970). *Dare to Discipline*. Wheaton, IL: Tyndale House Publishers.

[9] Dobson, J. C. (2004). *The New Strong-Willed Child: Birth Through Adolescence*. Wheaton, IL: Tyndale House Publishers.

[10] Scripps Howard News Service, Ohio University [Survey conducted October 7–October 24, 2006]. Americans say spanking sometimes necessary. Angus Reid Public Opinion. Retrieved from http://www.angus-reid.com/polls/6563/americans_say_spanking_sometimes_necessary/.

[11] Flynn, C. P. (1994). Regional differences in attitudes toward corporal punishment. *Journal of Marriage and the Family*, 56, 314–324. doi:10.2307/353102.

[12] Hupp, S., Stary, A., & Jewell, J. (submitted). Beliefs about myths related to child psychology, development, and parenting: Which myths need the most debunking?

[13] Straus, M. A. & Stewart, J. H. (1999). Corporal punishment by American parents: National data on prevalence, chronicity, severity, and duration, in relation to child and family characteristics. *Clinical Child and Family Psychology*, 2, 55–70. doi:10.1177/0044118x93024004006.

[14] Regalado, M., Sareen, H., Inkelas, M., et al. (2004). Parents' discipline of young children: Results from the National Survey of Early Childhood Health. *Pediatrics*, 113, 1952–1958.

[15] Straus, M. A., Sugarman, D. B., & Giles-Sims, J. (1997). Spanking by parents and subsequent antisocial behavior of children. *Archives of Pediatrics & Adolescent Medicine*, 151, 761–767. doi:10.1001/archpedi.1997.02170450011002.

[16] Zimmerman, M. (2006, January 1). On the minds of men: Corporal punishment. *Men's Health*, 21, 31.

[17] Flanagan, B., Ostrom, M., & Johnson, L. P. (Executive Producers) (2013). Adios, Mr. Still [Television series episode]. In *Moonshiners: Outlaw Cuts*. United States: Discovery Channel.

[18] Jacquemetton, A., Jacquemetton, M. (Writers), & Hunter, T. (Director) (2008). Three Sundays [Television series episode]. *Mad Men*. Los Angeles, CA: Los Angeles Center Studios.

[19] Keeler, K. (Writer) & Archer, W. (Director) (1996). Two Bad Neighbors [Television series episode]. *The Simpsons*. Los Angeles, CA: 20th Century Fox Television.

[20] Borkow, M. (Writer) & Bright, K. S. (Director) (2005). Joey and the Spanking [Television series episode]. *Joey*. Los Angeles, CA: Bright-San Productions.

[21] Martin, G. R. R. (Writer) & Graves, A. (Director) (2014). The Lion and the Rose [Television series episode]. In D. Benioff, D. B. Weiss, F. Doegler, et al. (Executive Producers), *Game of Thrones*. United States: HBO Inc.

[22] Straus, M. A. & Donnelly, D. A. (1994). *Beating the Devil Out of Them: Corporal Punishment in American Families*. New York: Lexington Books.

[23] Federal Child Abuse Prevention and Treatment Act, 42 U.S.C.A. § 5106g (2003).

[24] Chapman, M. & Zahn-Waxler, C. (1982). Young children's compliance and noncompliance to parental discipline in a natural setting. *International Journal of Behavioral Development*, 5, 81–94. doi:10.1177/016502548200500104.

[25] Day, D. E. & Roberts, M. W. (1983). An analysis of the physical punishment component of a parent training program. *Journal of Abnormal Child Psychology*, 11, 141–152. doi: 10.1007/bf00912184.

[26] Roberts, M. W. (1988). Enforcing chair timeouts with room timeouts. *Behavioral Modification*, 12, 353–370. doi:10.1177/01454455880123003.

[27] Roberts, M. W. & Powers, S. W. (1990). Adjusting chair timeout enforcement procedures for oppositional children. *Behavior Therapy*, 21, 257–271. doi: 10.1016/s0005-7894(05)80329-6.

[28] Gershoff, E. T. (2002). Corporal punishment by parents and associated child behaviors and experiences: A meta-analytic and theoretical review. *Psychological Bulletin*, 128, 539–579. doi:10.1037/0033-2909.128.4.539.

[29] Baumrind, D., Cowan, P. A., & Larzelere, R. E. (2002). Ordinary physical punishment: Is it harmful? Comment on Gershoff (2002). *Psychological Bulletin*, 128, 580–589.doi:10.1037/0033-2909.128.4.580.

[30] Engfer, A. & Schneewind, K. A. (1982). Causes and consequences of harsh parental punishment. *Child Abuse & Neglect*, 6, 129–139. doi:10.1016/0145-2134(82)90005-9.

[31] Deater-Deckard, K., Dodge, K. A., Bates, J. E., & Pettit, G. S. (1996). Physical discipline among African American and European American mothers: Links to children's externalizing behaviors. *Developmental Psychology*, 32(6), 1065–1072.

[32] Global Initiative to End All Corporal Punishment of Children (2012). States with full abolition. Retrieved from http://www.endcorporalpunishment.org/pages/frame.html [accessed August 2014].

[33] American Academy of Pediatrics (1998). Guidance for effective discipline. *Pediatrics*, 101, 723–728.

[34] Kazdin, A. E. (2013). *Everyday Parenting Toolkit: The Kazdin Method for Easy, Step-by-Step, Lasting Change for You and Your Child*. Boston: Houghton Mifflin Harcourt.

Myth #41 Brief time-outs are too weak to help decrease real behavior problems

Time-out is a commonly used discipline strategy that involves "contingent withholding of the opportunity to earn reinforcement ... as a consequence of some form of misbehavior" [1] (p. 2). Time-out emerged in the last half of the 20th century as researchers were beginning to apply the theories of behaviorism to real clinical problems. Arthur Staats, and his student

Montrose Wolf, two influential figures in the early development of applied behavior analysis, developed time-out as a disciplinary method. Although Staats was using time-out at home with his own children [2] (p. 118), Wolf was the first to apply the term "time-out from positive reinforcement" to the treatment of a child in a research study [3]. From the beginning, time-out was paired with the additional goal of making sure that the "time-in" environment was positively reinforcing. In fact, Dr. Wolf's tombstone has the inscribed words: "Time In" [4].

As popular as time-out has become, making fun of time-out is just as popular. For example, time-out is common fodder for stand-up comedians. Recently, John Wing, a semi-finalist on the show *America's Got Talent* [5], used a time-out routine in the performance that helped him advance to the third round of the talent competition:

> When I was a boy, my parents had punishment options. They could yell at me; ground me; spank me; beat me with sticks, garden implements, household utensils, sporting equipment; lock me in my room; lock me outta the house; lock me in the trunk of the car; stab me with forks. Now I'm a parent. What are my punishment options? Time-out. Whoop! Thanks Oprah, jobless billionaire; you would know all about that. The only time my father ever called "time-out" was when he was winded from beating the crap out of me.

Comedian, Bill Engvall, part of the Blue Collar Comedy Tour, also includes time-out in his routine when he says, "A time-out, let's try knock out, ma'am. We're not playing football here; spank that kid!" [6]. Many other comedians commonly include similar jokes in their routines as well. Clearly, some comedians believe that time-out is too weak to effectively decrease real behavior problems.

Comedians, however, are not the only critics of time-out. Parenting guru John Rosemond wrote, "In my experience, however, time-out is not a generally effective consequence, especially with highly defiant children" [7] (p. 202). Additionally, Gartrell [8] summarizes several other objections, suggesting that time-out: (i) confuses the child; (ii) dampens the child's spirits; (iii) fails to teach the child; (iv) inhibits the child's internal control; (v) diminishes the child's self-worth; (vi) humiliates the child; (vii) and imposes "pain and suffering" on the child (p. 10).

In our research, 41% of college students and 32% of parents agreed with the statement that "Brief 'time-outs' are too weak to help decrease real behavior problems in toddlers" [9]. In another study, about 35% of parents didn't support time-out as acceptable for a fictional child with behavior problems, and results varied by race and socio economic status [10]. For example, although 22% of African American parents in the middle-to-upper income category didn't support time-out as acceptable, this rate rose to 60% of African American parents in the lower income category. Caucasian parents were in between these two extremes with 25% of those in the middle-to-upper income category, and 35% of those in the lower income category, declining to support the use of time-out in the fictional scenario.

Even though many parents are skeptical about time-out, research shows that it's an effective method. That is, hundreds of studies have supported the use of time-out. For example, clinic-referred preschool-aged children in one study improved from being compliant with 34% of commands during baseline to being compliant with 79% of commands when time-out was used for noncompliance [11]. Another similar study demonstrated that when a time-out chair was used (with a time-out area used as a back-up for escape), 89% of the children demonstrated a high rate of compliance [12]. These behavioral improvements occurred in a short amount of time while using brief time-outs (about two minutes) when needed. Research like this has led the American Academy of Pediatrics [13] to support time-out as an effective discipline strategy.

In addition to these examples of studies focusing primarily on time-out, many studies also examine time-out as a component in a larger treatment package. As part of the American Psychological Association's goal of identifying evidence-based treatments, Eyberg, Nelson, and Turner [14] searched through studies to identify which types of treatments have solid research support for disruptive behavior in children. "Behavioral parent training" is the broad label for the approach that has the most research support, and it includes specific programs such as the Oregon Model of Parent Management Training [15], Parent-Child Interaction Therapy [16], Helping the Noncompliant Child [17], Positive Parenting Program [18], and Incredible Years [19].

Although these behavioral parent training programs vary somewhat in how they're delivered to parents, they all have many shared components. Time-out is a central component to all of these evidence-based treatments, and these programs also emphasize a focus on strengthening the time-in environment as well. Furthermore, these programs often successfully target children with substantial behavior problems including noncompliance, aggression, and other disruptive behaviors. Importantly, these programs often also show long-term gains.

Based on research findings, clinical child psychologists frequently recommend time-out as part of a treatment package, but it's quite common for distressed parents to respond to the time-out recommendation by saying something like, "I tried time-out, and it didn't work." If time-out is effective, then why are parents (and comedians) so harsh when they talk about it as a discipline strategy? For one thing, most parents actually wish they could have a few minutes to themselves with nothing to do, so forcing some "alone time" on their child just doesn't seem like a powerful discipline option. The difference is that most children don't want more alone time with nothing to do.

Although time-outs can be very effective for a lot of children, and even for children with serious disruptive behavior, they're not guaranteed to work with every child. Failed attempts at using time-out contribute to the perception that it's an ineffective strategy. Time-outs can be hard to learn and only somewhat effective at the beginning. That is, time-outs (and time-in) require consistent use over time, and once time-out has been initiated as a discipline option, "over the following two months, parents report time-out becomes significantly easier to implement and more useful in dealing with their child's strong-willed behavior" [20] (p. 130). In fact, with interventions that rely on actively ignoring some child behaviors, the behavior may actually get a little worse before it gets better (i.e., called an *extinction burst*), and parents sometimes give up on interventions before they really have a chance to work.

In terms of the "Sources of Psychological Myths," comedians may be part of the misleading media. In addition to stand-up comedy, failed time-outs are always more funny than successful time-outs in sitcoms, movies, and commercials. There could be some exaggerated kernels of truth regarding time-out's limitations. That is, time-outs don't work for everyone all of the time, and they typically require changes to the time-in environment as well. Also, the extinction burst during time-out might really include some novel inappropriate behaviors that haven't been exhibited before.

All children have behavior problems sometimes, and all parents provide discipline to their children, at least to some degree. Research consistently shows two parenting practices associated with the greatest amounts of disruptive behavior: laxness and harshness [21]. On the other hand, parents set their children up for success when they're able to provide consistent discipline without being over-reactive to behavior problems. Time-out from positive reinforcement is a form of punishment, meaning that it's designed to decrease inappropriate behavior, but it does so by removing something positive (e.g., parent attention, toys, entertainment), rather than adding something aversive like some other punishment options. Punishment based on adding aversive stimuli has greater potential for negative side effects (as described in the "spoil the rod" myth). Time-out, when used with a rich time-in environment, is one method that can help parents find a good balance of enforcing rules in a caring way.

Nevertheless, just like spanking fails to teach children "what *to do*" instead, time-out also just teaches children "what *not* to do." Thus, time-out by itself may not be effective at building new appropriate behaviors, and this is why it's typically used along with other proactive options.

What you need to know

The book, *Parenting the Strong-Willed Child* [20], includes a chapter on time-out that emphasizes the importance of consistency, choosing a boring location (e.g., in an adult-sized chair in the hallway), setting a timer for about three minutes, and avoiding talking or yelling at the child during time-out. When parents yell at children in time-out, it shouldn't be called "time-out," it should be called "time-to-shout." The chapter also clearly lays out what's involved in the time-out sequence as well as how to deal with some commonly encountered problems during time-out. Most importantly, the time-out chapter comes only after four other chapters focused on attending, rewarding, ignoring, and giving effective instructions.

References

[1] Morawska, A. & Sanders, M. (2011). Parental use of time out revisited: A useful or harmful parenting strategy?. *Journal of Child and Family Studies*, 20, 1–8. doi: 10.1007/s10826-010-9371-x.
[2] Staats, A. W. (2012). *The Marvelous Learning Animal: What Makes Human Nature Unique*. Amherst, NY: Prometheus Books.
[3] Wolf, M. M., Risely, T., & Mees, H. (1964). Application of operant conditioning procedures to the behavior problems of an autistic child. *Behavior Research and Therapy*, 1, 305–312. doi:10.1016/0005-7967(63)90045-7.
[4] Risley, T. (2005). Montrose M. Wolf (1935–2004). *Journal of Applied Behavior Analysis*, 38, 279–287.
[5] Cowell, S., Warwick, K., Raff, J., & Donnelly, S. (2013). Vegas week, night 1 [Television series episode]. In *America's Got Talent*. Los Angeles, CA: Syco Entertainment.
[6] Engvall, B. (2004). *Bill Engvall: Here's Your Sign Live*. Chatsworth, CA: Distributed by Image Entertainment.

[7] Rosemond, J. (2012). *Parent-Babble: How Parents can Recover from Fifty Years of Bad Expert Advice*. Kansas City, MO: Andrews McMeel Publishing, LLC.

[8] Gartrell, D. (2001). Replacing time-out: Part one – using guidance to build an encouraging classroom. *Young Children*, 56, 8–16.

[9] Hupp, S., Stary, A., & Jewell, J. (submitted). Beliefs about myths related to child psychology, development, and parenting: Which myths need the most debunking?

[10] Heffer, R. W. & Kelley, M. L. (1987). Mothers' acceptance of behavioral interventions for children: The influence of parent race and income. *Behavior Therapy*, 2, 153–163. doi:10.1016/s0005-7894(87)80039-4.

[11] Roberts, M. W. (1982). The effects of warned versus unwarned time-out procedures on child noncompliance. *Child & Family Behavior Therapy*, 4, 37–53. doi: 10.1300/j019v04n01_04.

[12] Roberts, M. W. & Powers, S. W. (1990). Adjusting chair timeout enforcement procedures for oppositional children. *Behavior Therapy*, 21, 257–271. doi: 10.1016/s0005-7894(05)80329-6.

[13] American Academy of Pediatrics (1998). Guidance for effective discipline. *Pediatrics*, 101, 723–728.

[14] Eyberg, S. M., Nelson, M. M., & Boggs, S. R. (2008). Evidence-based psychosocial treatments for children and adolescents with disruptive behavior. *Journal of Clinical Child and Adolescent Psychology*, 37, 215–237. doi:10.1080/15374410701820117.

[15] Patterson, G. R., Reid, J. B., Jones, R. R., & Conger, R. E. (1975). *A Social Learning Approach To Family Intervention* (Vol. 1). Eugene, OR: Castalia.

[16] Brinkmeyer, M. Y. & Eyberg, S. M. (2003). Parent-child interaction therapy for oppositional children. In A. E. Kazdin & J. R. Weisz (Eds), *Evidence-Based Psychotherapies for Children and Adolescents* (pp. 204–223). New York, NY: Guilford.

[17] McMahon, R. J. & Forehand, R. L. (2003). *Helping the Noncompliant Child* (2nd edn). New York: The Guilford Press.

[18] Sanders, M. R. (1999). Triple p – positive parenting program: Towards an empirically validated multilevel parenting and family support strategy for the prevention of behavior and emotional problems in children. *Clinical Child and Family Psychology Review*, 2, 71–90. doi:10.1037/0893-3200.22.3.506.

[19] Webster-Stratton, C. & Reid, M. (2003). The Incredible Years parents, teachers, and children training series: A multifaceted treatment approach for young children with conduct problems. In A. E. Kazdin & J. R. Weisz (Eds), *Evidence-Based Psychotherapies for Children and Adolescents* (pp. 224–240). New York, NY: The Guilford Press.

[20] Forehand, R. & Long, N. (2010). *Parenting the Strong-Willed Child: The Clinically Proven Five-Week Program for Parents of Two- to Six-Year-Olds* (3rd edn). New York, NY: McGraw-Hill.

[21] Arnold, D. S., O'Leary, S. G., Wolff, L. S., & Acker, M. M. (1993). The Parenting Scale: A measure of dysfunctional parenting in discipline situations. *Psychological Assessment*, 5, 137–144. doi:10.1037// 1040-3590.5.2.137.

Daycare damages the attachment between children and parents

During the work week, the same scenario is played out again and again. Anxious parents approach a daycare building. With an infant in their arms or a toddler by their side, they're led by the daycare staff to the appropriate room. Meant to be comforting and inviting, the modern daycare is colorful and kid-friendly – but still surreal, as many parents must leave their precious children behind. And predictably, yet understandably, many parents leave with the fear that daycare is going to interfere with the parent–child relationship.

Parents in the 1940s were warned by Benjamin Spock that "The infant whose mother can't take care of him during the daytime needs *individual care* ..." [1] (p. 485) and he also added that "The average day nursery or 'baby farm' is no good for him" (p. 485). Theories proposed by John Bowlby and Mary Ainsworth, however, really propelled the anti-daycare sentiment a few decades later. Bowlby, a British psychoanalytically trained psychiatrist, spent several years developing a comprehensive theory that could explain children's motivation to behave in certain ways, as well as how parents influence their children [2]. Some of the main tenets of his theory were that infants become attached to a parental figure, similar to how some animals (e.g., geese) "imprint" on a mother. Bowlby maintained that this attachment process is innate and evolutionarily important, as it helps the infant maintain contact with an adult caregiver who can protect and care for it [2]. The theory also goes on to explain how this parent–child attachment is especially critical in the first few years of life when both the parent and child use signaling behaviors (e.g., smiling) that are meant to elicit specific behaviors in the other (e.g., increase interaction). Thus, one can see how attachment theory could make parents worried that their infant might "imprint" on a daycare worker instead of the parent.

But how is such an attachment measured and evaluated? Mary Ainsworth, at times working directly with Bowlby, went on to develop the Strange Situation methodology, which allowed researchers to assess and classify children's attachment with their parent as either secure, anxious–resistant, or anxious–avoidant [3]. The Strange Situation can be a pretty strange experience for the child. First, the child and parent enter a room that has a few toys and chairs. Then, a stranger enters the room, and after a short time, the stranger approaches and attempts to interact with the child. The parent leaves without a word, and when the parent returns, the child's reaction is noted. This separation and reunion are repeated a second time, with additional attention given to the child's reactions [3].

In this type of research, children with a "secure" attachment style may get upset when their mother leaves, and when their mother returns they want to go to her. Conversely, children have an "insecure" attachment style if, upon their mother's re-arrival, they ignore their mother or seem to be upset with their mother. Given the importance that Attachment Theory places on the bond established between parent and child in the first few years of life, Ainsworth concluded that the daycare experience, which separated the parent and child for longer periods of time, would be damaging to their relationship [3].

Based on attachment theory, researchers used the Strange Situation to examine attachment style with 12-and 13-month-old children whose parents were in one of four groups that differed based on how much the mother worked: full-time care, high-part-time care, low-part-time care, and stay-at-home-mother [4]. The results indicated that 47% of children of parents in the full-time care group were insecurely attached, which was greater than the other groups' insecurity rates of 35% for the high-part-time care, 21% for the low-part-time care, and 25% for the stay-at-home-mother group.

Although at first glance these seem to be interesting differences, there are several important points to make. First, even this research shows that over half of the children in the full-time care group were indeed securely attached. Thus, if daycare experiences were so damaging, one would expect to see an even larger percentage of insecure attachment styles in the full-time care group. Second, this research actually demonstrated a higher percentage of insecure attachment styles for the stay-at-home-mother group than for the low-part-time care group, which is further evidence that it's not the daycare itself that is the issue. Third, this research does not provide any follow-up over time. Fourth, and most importantly, this type of research does not use an experimental design. That is, families weren't randomly assigned to their groups, so it's not possible to make a causal connection between daycare and attachment style.

Despite the inherent limitations in attachment style research like that described above, some critics used this research to bolster their very definitive views about mothers entering the workforce. One of the most outspoken critics of daycare over the last few decades has been the *physiologist* Laura Schlessinger ("Dr. Laura"). In the Introduction of her book, *Stupid Things Parents Do to Mess Up their Kids* [5], Schlessinger argues that the decision of moms to work full-time is one of several decisions that are "a *disaster* to the lives and emotional well-being of children" (p. 7). In that book and in other sources, Schlessinger has also made the following points:

The decision for a mom to work full-time "is wrong and may injure their children and society" (p. 7).

Daycare is a place "where children have to fight to claim attention, or withdraw from the pain of it all" [6] (p. 30).

Parents, preoccupied with their careers, have led to her concern that "so many children have been dying in day-care centers ..." [6] (p. 46).

It makes more sense to call daycare centers "day orphanages" because daycare staff can't care for children the same way that parents do [7].

Schlessinger's message seems to be reaching a lot of people. The belief that a child's time in daycare will cause harm to the parent–child bond continues to be widely accepted. A poll conducted in 2003 indicated that 72% of Americans agreed with the statement that "Too many children are being raised in daycare centers these days," which was actually up from 68% in 1987 [8]. In our research, 35% of college students and 39% of parents agreed with the statement that "Being in daycare interferes with the attachment between children and their parents" [9].

When examining the "rightness" of putting a child in daycare, one must also understand why parents utilize daycare in the first place. The first "day nursery" was created in Boston in 1898, but by 1937 the number of such centers had increased to 1,900 [10]. The primary reason for the increase in daycare use has been the increase in the number of women entering the labor force. For example, in 1940 only 27% of women were working, with this rate increasing to 51% in 1980 [11] and 60% in 1997 [12]. More women in the labor force didn't translate to a similar increase in two-earner households, however, as rates of divorce and single-parent households increased significantly during this time period as well [11]. Thus, working outside of the home has become increasingly essential as single mothers seek to provide for their children.

Does daycare damage the parent–child relationship? The preponderance of research says that it does not. The National Institute of Child Health and Human Development initiated a study to answer fundamental questions about a variety of possible effects that out-of-home care might have on children and parents. This large longitudinal study [13] used the Strange Situation as well as more reliable and valid measures of parent–child attachment (including observations of the child, parent questionnaire data, and telephone interviews). Results indicated that attachment between the mothers and their infants wasn't negatively affected by the amount or quality of daycare alone. On the other hand, mothers' sensitivity to their infant as well as their own psychological adjustment was related to quality of attachment. In situations where mothers' sensitivity or psychological adjustment was already problematic, more hours in daycare did magnify these existing problems, though high quality daycare helped lessen these problems [14].

Parent–child attachment was also examined throughout the first three years of life. While the results indicated that more hours in daycare and poor quality of care were found to be related to the quality of the mother–child attachment, the size of this relationship was so small that the authors concluded that the effect of daycare "is apparently not of a sufficient magnitude to disrupt the formation of a secure infant attachment" [15] (p. 245). Moreover, high quality care was found to serve as a protective factor when mothers were depressed [16]. This finding is similar to research reviewed by Vandell [17] who found that high quality preschool programs provided significant short-term and long-term benefits to children in poverty compared to similar children who didn't engage in such a program.

Therefore, research on this topic has not only dispelled the myth of daycare damage, but has actually shown that daycare can be beneficial for some mother–child interactions [13]. An important benefit of daycare is that it allows a parent in poverty to work and potentially earn a greater income. Research examining how increases in family income affected children in daycare found that for families who weren't in poverty, increases in family income over a three-year period had no effect on their children [18]. Nevertheless, for families in poverty, their increase in income over a three-year period predicted greater school readiness, language skills, and positive social behavior in their children over time.

The next question you might ask could be: Does daycare harm children in any other ways? Many parents are concerned that if their child is in daycare they will get sick more often. Research shows that children in daycare do tend to have more illnesses than children of a stay-at-home parent in the earlier years, though they may actually contract *fewer* illnesses in later years, perhaps due to an immunizing effect [19]. Research also shows that quality of daycare (e.g., lower ratios of children to adults, caregiver education, and social stimulation in daycare) is related to a number of positive outcomes, with high quality daycare predicting children's positive behaviors, lower stress levels, and greater social competence [17]. Does this mean that parents should seek "Ivy League" daycare centers? Not really, as "high quality daycare" in most of these studies simply described the daycares that met legal and professional standards for daycare centers – not the most expensive and exclusive daycare centers.

There are several reasons why this myth is widely believed. In terms of the "Sources of Psychological Myths," one contributor might be inferring causation from correlation. That is, just because some research shows that daycare is correlated with an insecure attachment style, it doesn't mean that the daycare experience *caused* that insecure attachment style, especially when that same research showed that more than half of the children in full-time daycare actually had a secure attachment style [4]. Additionally, the anti-daycare crowd contributes to this myth by providing a false dichotomy, which involves black-or-white thinking. For example, Schlessinger's critique of daycare seems to be based on the assumption that if a mother is not with her child almost all day, then she can't really be a loving parent. Although it's true that a daycare worker won't love and care for a child just like a parent will, sending a child to a daycare doesn't mean the parent stops loving or caring for their child. The same point could be made about fathers, but the anti-daycare crowd rarely seems to argue that fathers should stay home.

So to all those anxious parents in the world, we say don't fret. Human babies are not geese, and they won't "imprint" on a daycare worker instead of you. Parents shouldn't be made to feel guilty when they choose to use daycare. We're not arguing in this chapter that every child should go to a daycare center or preschool, and we greatly value all of the stay-at-home moms (and dads) in the world! It's just that we also greatly value the working moms (and dads) too.

What you need to know

For more information on how to choose the best daycare for a child, visit the Child Care Aware of America website at www.naccrra.org or the official US government website on the topic at www.childcare.gov.

References

[1] Spock, B. (1946). *The Common Sense Book of Baby and Child Care.* New York, NY: Duell, Sloan and Pearce.
[2] Bretherton, I. (1992). The origins of attachment theory: John Bowlby and Mary Ainsworth. *Developmental Psychology,* 28, 759–775. doi:10.1037// 0012-1649.28.5.759.
[3] Ainsworth, M. S. & Bell, S. M. (1970). Attachment, exploration, and separation: Illustrated by the behavior of one year olds in a strange situation. *Child Development,* 41, 49–67. doi:10.2307/1127388.

[4] Belsky, J. & Rovine, M. J. (1988). Nonmaternal care in the first year of life and the security of infant-parent attachment. *Child Development, 59*, 157–167. doi: 10.2307/1130397.

[5] Schlessinger, L. (2000). *Stupid Things Parents Do to Mess Up their Kids.* New York, NY: Harper.

[6] Schlessinger, L. (2009a). *In Praise of Stay-at-Home Moms.* New York, NY: Harper.

[7] Schlessinger, L. (2009b, February 16). So "no" to day orphanages. Retrieved from http://www.youtube.com/watch?v=Vwg3FKawIa4 [accessed September 2013].

[8] Pew Research Center (2009). [Nationwide survey conducted July 20–August 2, 2009]. The harried life of the working mother. Pew Social and Demographic Trends. Retrieved from http://www.pewsocialtrends.org/2009/10/01/the-harried-life-of-the-working-mother/ [accessed August 2014].

[9] Hupp, S., Stary, A., & Jewell, J. (submitted). Beliefs about myths related to child psychology, development, and parenting: Which myths need the most debunking?

[10] Clarke-Stewart, A. & Alhusen, V. D. (2005). *What We Know About Child Care.* Cambridge, MA: Harvard University Press.

[11] U.S. Bureau of the Census (1982). Current Population Reports, Series P-23, No.117. Trends in child care arrangements of working mothers, U.S. Government Printing Office, Washington, DC.

[12] U.S. Bureau of Labor Statistics (1998). Labor Force Statistics from the Current Population Survey. Extracted from Internet site http://146.142.4.24/cgi-bin/surveymost December, 1999. Washington, DC.

[13] NICHD Early Child Care Research Network (Ed.) (2005). *Child Care and Child Development: Results from the NICHD Study of Early Child Care and Youth Development.* New York, NY: The Guilford Press.

[14] NICHD Early Child Care Research Network (1997). The effects of infant child care on infant-mother attachment security. In The NICHD Early Child Care Research Network (Ed.), *Child Care and Child Development: Results from the NICHD Study of Early Child Care and Youth Development* (pp. 193–207). New York, NY: The Guilford Press.

[15] NICHD Early Child Care Research Network (1999). Child care and mother-child interaction in the first 3 years of life. In The NICHD Early Child Care Research Network (Ed.), *Child Care and Child Development: Results from the NICHD Study of Early Child Care and Youth Development* (pp. 231–245). New York, NY: The Guilford Press.

[16] NICHD Early Child Care Research Network (2003). Early child care and mother-child interaction from 36 months through first grade. In The NICHD Early Child Care Research Network (Ed.), *Child Care and Child Development: Results from the NICHD Study of Early Child Care and Youth Development* (pp. 246 –258). New York, NY: The Guilford Press.

[17] Vandell, D. (2004). Early child care: The known and the unknown. *Merrill Palmer Quarterly, 50*, 387–414. doi:10.1353/mpq.2004.0027.

[18] Dearing, E., McCartney, K., & Taylor, B. A. (2001). Change in family income-to-needs matters more for children with less. In The NICHD Early

Child Care Research Network (Ed.), *Child Care and Child Development: Results from the NICHD Study of Early Child Care and Youth Development* (pp. 140–150). New York, NY: The Guilford Press.

[19] NICHD Early Child Care Research Network (2001). Child care and common communicable illnesses. In The NICHD Early Child Care Research Network (Ed.), *Child Care and Child Development: Results from the NICHD Study of Early Child Care and Youth Development* (pp. 175–183). New York, NY: The Guilford Press.

Myth #43 Imaginary friends are a sign of social-emotional problems in children

You're probably familiar with the word "REDRUM" being said in a creepy voice. If not, then you might want to read Stephen King's book, *The Shining* [1], or watch Stanley Kubrick's movie adaptation [2]. If you've heard this frightening word before (and if you've seen what it chillingly stands for when read backwards with use of a mirror in the film), here's a question for you: which character in the story said, "REDRUM, REDRUM, REDRUM"? Some might guess that Jack Nicholson's character is the right answer, while others might guess it's his 5-year-old son named Danny. The correct answer is that it's actually Danny's invisible friend named Tony, a little boy living in Danny's mouth, whose talking is often represented by the movement of Danny's index finger (Figure 4).

This invisible friend plays a big role throughout the plot of *The Shining*. Early on in the story it's revealed that Danny (an only child) had a hard time making friends, and he started talking to Tony (while in a daycare)

Figure 4   In the movie *The Shining*, Danny talks to his invisible friend, and you can tell that the invisible friend is speaking by the movements of Danny's index finger.

soon after Danny's father dislocated Danny's shoulder in a drunken rage. The incident prompted his father to stop drinking, but the invisible friend stuck around. While Danny appears to like his invisible friend, Tony often frightens him by showing Danny visions such as blood pouring out of the hotel elevator and two dead sisters (played by identical twins) in the hotel hallway. It's through the invisible friend that we learn that Danny has the "shine." That is, he has the ability to see visions of the past, communicate with others telepathically, and see events yet to happen. It's also worth noting that Danny's father starts talking to invisible friends as well, such as the father of the dead sisters from Danny's visions.

Needless to say, The Shining might have contributed to some parents' anxiety when their children started talking about their own invisible friends. Other movies have piled on to the connection between invisible friends and social-emotional problems in children. In M. Night Shyamalan's The Sixth Sense [3] (the best movie ever made about a child psychologist, Bruce Willis' character begins working with a 9-year-old boy (played by Haley Joel Osment) who believes he "can see dead people." In the movie, the invisible people really are ghosts, but in real life it would be very concerning to a parent if his or her child were talking to invisible dead people. Moreover, in the movie, Hide and Seek [4], Robert De Niro plays a psychologist whose daughter (played by Dakota Fanning) appears to develop an invisible friend after the death of her mother. Once again, the invisible friend corresponds with a traumatic experience. All of these movies have surprising and quite terrifying endings, and they all put into question the social-emotional health of children with invisible friends.

Derogatory references to invisible friends can be found in television as well. In the first season of the show, The Nanny [5], 6-year-old Grace's invisible friend causes her dad to be concerned and say, "perhaps we should increase her therapy," suggesting that the invisible friend is representative of a psychological problem. In an episode of the cartoon, Arthur [6], in reaction to his littler sister's invisible friend, Arthur tells his sister that "only babies have invisible friends." Taken together, it's probably fair to say that in pop culture, invisible friends are commonly depicted as a sign of social-emotional disturbance or, at the very least, immature behavior.

Long before these movies and television shows, however, invisible friends have been concerning to parents and professionals. Klausen and Passman [7] describe some of the earlier American views of invisible friends as having supernatural origins that needed to be exorcized, and beliefs in pre-modern India included the conceptualization that invisible friends presented "spiritual connections with previous lives" (p. 351). In the mid-20th century, Benjamin Spock [8] (1946) suggested that too much time spent talking about invisible friends could be the result of an unsatisfying life and a distressed relationship with parents. Gleason, Sebanc, and Hartup [9] (2000) summarize one popular belief by saying that, "One of the most common notions concerning imaginary companions is that they may compensate for a child's poor social relationships" (p. 420). Also summarizing previous research, Trionfi and Reese [10] indicated that "early research often attributed imaginary companion play to psychopathology, personality defects, or deficiencies in social skills" (p. 1301).

Providing a psychodynamic perspective, Meyer and Tuber [11] gave the Rorschach inkblot test to 18 preschoolers with imaginary friends, and they used the results to provide support for their hypothesis that these children had "a more pronounced disowning of more powerfully conflictual feelings" (p. 165) and that the imaginary companions were used as a "means of negotiating intensely felt inner struggles" (p. 166). Overall, some professionals have also contributed to parents' worries about invisible friends.

Depictions of invisible friends in the media, in combination with the negative portrayals of invisible friends in the psychological literature, have had a lasting effect on contemporary views of children with invisible friends. Research shows that quite a few people are worried about invisible friends. In one study, 48% of fathers (whose children didn't have invisible friends) reported that they wouldn't like it if their children engaged in pretend play with invisible friends during a meal at home, and 62% of these fathers reported that they wouldn't like this type of play if they were at a restaurant [12]. In our research, 42% of college students and 32% of parents agreed with the statement that "If a child has an imaginary friend, the child is usually less sociable with real kids" [13].

The large number of people that have worries about invisible friends is concerning because most parents will probably have at least one child with an imaginary companion of some type. Researchers commonly define invisible friends as an invented person, animal, or other creature that cannot be seen. Researchers also commonly include personified objects, such as a stuffed animal that the child pretends is real, when they do research related to invisible friends. Together, invisible friends and personified objects both fit into the broader category of imaginary companions, and research shows that they're very common in childhood.

One study showed that as many as 65% of 7-year-olds had an imaginary companion at some point with about two thirds of the imaginary companions being invisible friends [14]. While other studies have shown somewhat lower percentages of imaginary companions, all studies show that they're a fairly common phenomenon. For example, Pearson et al. [15] studied 1,795 children between the ages of 5 to 12 years old and concluded that 46% of their sample had an imaginary companion at some point in their lives. Imaginary companions were once thought to be primarily limited to the preschool years; however, research has shown that 36% of 5-year-olds and 36% of 9-year-olds report having a current imaginary companion. Percentages start to decline as children become 10 years old; however, even 9% of 12-year-olds report having a current imaginary companion [15].

In addition to imaginary companions being common, research shows that they're *not* a sign of social-emotional problems and may, in fact, be correlated with some positive traits. One early study of 222 children demonstrated that children with imaginary companions did not have more behavior problems than other children [16]. A more recent study of 88 children demonstrated that those with invisible friends or personified objects had just as many reciprocal friendships as children without imaginary companions [17]. Parents of children with imaginary companions have also rated their children as more outgoing than parents of children without imaginary companions [18]. Other positive attributes of children with imaginary companions have been reported to include communication skills [18], storytelling [10], and interacting with adults [16].

Why do imaginary companions get such a bad rap? One reason may be due to the nature of early psychological research that was based more on case studies or clinical samples without comparison groups. Because it was common for children with clinical problems to have imaginary companions, clinicians were making a connection without realizing that it was just as common for children without clinical problems to have imaginary companions [19]. That is, clinicians primarily saw children with clinical problems and rarely saw children without clinical problems, so they assumed any common thread between the children they saw was part of the clinical problem. This is one major reason why comparison groups are so important.

Media portrayals, such as the invisible friend from *The Shining*, also have the potential to influence perceptions. Seeing people that aren't really there is great fodder for scary movies, because it taps into our curiosity about paranormal topics and complex mental disorders like schizophrenia.

Because invisible friends make for an interesting plot device, we're likely to see new examples in pop culture every year.

Seeing research showing positive correlates of having an imaginary companion might leave some parents wondering if they should be concerned if their child does *not* have an imaginary companion. We want to be clear that not having an imaginary companion is fine too. It's very normal for a child to never have an imaginary companion, as well. Also, children without imaginary companions might engage in other types of healthy imaginative play such as make-believe worlds or role-playing a character.

There are actually very few well-designed studies comparing the social-emotional health of children with or without imaginary companions. Most of the studies have small sample sizes and few replications. Nevertheless, research showing that about half of children (ages 5 to 12 years old) have imaginary companions, while the other half do not have imaginary companions [15], is a strong indicator that the mere presence or absence of an imaginary companion is nothing to worry about.

What you need to know

If a child is having a hard time making real friends, that doesn't mean the imaginary companion is the problem. Regardless, there are some things parents can do to help children make friends. The book, *Friends Forever: How Parents Can Help Their Kids Make and Keep Good Friends* [20], offers many suggestions for parents regarding how to help their child make and keep friends. This book is rooted in the author's research involving friendships [21], and a small sampling of the topics includes: (i) finding friends; (ii) developing interests conducive to friendships; (iii) demonstrating sportsmanlike behavior; and (iv) dealing with teasing.

References

[1] King, S. (1977). *The Shining*. Garden City, NY: Doubleday.
[2] Kubrick, S. (Producer & Director) (1980). *The Shining* [Motion picture]. United States: Warner Bros.
[3] Kennedy, K., Marshall, F., Mendel, B. (Producers), & Shyamalan, M. N. (Director) (1999). *The Sixth Sense* [Motion picture]. United States: Buena Vista Pictures.
[4] Josephson, B. (Producer) & Polson, J. (Director) (2005). *Hide and Seek* [Motion picture]. United States: 20th Century Fox.

[5] Sternin, R., Fraser, P. (Writers), & Chemel, L. S. (Director) (1993). Imaginary friend [Television series episode]. In P. Fraser & R. Sternin (Executive Producers), *The Nanny*. Culver City, CA: Sony Pictures Television.

[6] Brown, M. (Writer) & Bailey, G. (Director) (1996). D. W.'s imaginary friend/Arthur's lost library book [Television series episode]. In M. Charest & C. Greenwald (Executive Producers), *Arthur*. Burbank, CA: Cinar.

[7] Klausen, E. & Passman, R. H. (2006). Pretend companions (imaginary playmates): The emergence of a field. *Journal of Genetic Psychology*, 167, 349–364. doi: 10.3200/gntp.167.4.349-364.

[8] Spock, B. (1946). *The Common Sense Book of Baby and Child Care*. New York, NY: Duell, Sloan and Pearce.

[9] Gleason, T. R., Sebanc, A. M., & Hartup, W. W. (2000). Imaginary companionsofpreschoolchildren.*DevelopmentalPsychology*,36,419.doi:10.1037//0012-1649.36.4.419.

[10] Trionfi, G. & Reese, E. (2009). A good story: Children with imaginary companions create richer narratives. *Child Development*, 80, 1301–1313. doi: 10.1111/ j.1467-8624.2009.01333.x.

[11] Meyer, J. R. & Tuber, S. (1989). Intrapsychic and behavioral correlates of the phenomenon of imaginary companions in young children. *Psychoanalytic Psychology*, 6, 151–168. doi:10.1037/0736-9735.6.2.151.

[12] Gleason, T. R. (2005). Mothers' and fathers' attitudes regarding pretend play in the context of imaginary companions and of child gender. *Merrill-Palmer Quarterly*, 51, 412–436.

[13] Hupp, S., Stary, A., & Jewell, J. (submitted). Beliefs about myths related to child psychology, development, and parenting: Which myths need the most debunking?

[14] Taylor, M., Carlson, S. M., Maring, B. L., et al. (2004). The characteristics and correlates of fantasy in school-age children: Imaginary companions, impersonation, and social understanding. *Developmental Psychology*, 40, 1173–1187. doi: 10.1037/0012-1649.40.6.1173.

[15] Pearson, D., Rouse, H., Doswell, S., et al. (2001). Prevalence of imaginary companions in a normal child population. *Child: Care, Health and Development*, 27, 13–22. doi:10.1046/j.1365-2214.2001.00167.x.

[16] Manosevitz, M., Prentice, N. M., & Wilson, F. (1973). Individual and family correlates of imaginary companions in preschool children. *Developmental Psychology*, 8, 72–79. doi:10.1037/h0033834.

[17] Gleason, T. (2004). Imaginary companions and peer acceptance. *International Journal of Behavioral Development*, 28, 204–209. doi: 10.1080/01650250344000415.

[18] Roby, A. C. & Kidd, E. (2008). The referential communication skills of children with imaginary companions. *Developmental Science*, 11, 531–540. doi: 10.1111/ j.1467-7687.2008.00699.x.

[19] Taylor, M. (1999). *Imaginary Companions and the Children Who Create Them*. New York, NY: Oxford University Press.

[20] Frankel, F. (2010). *Friends Forever: How Parents Can Help Their Kids Make and Keep Good Friends*. San Francisco, CA: Jossey-Bass.

[21] Frankel, F. & Mintz, J. (2011). Maternal reports of play dates of clinic referred and community children. *Journal of Child and Family Studies*, 20, 623–630. doi: 10.1007/s10826-010-9437-9.

Speed busting for social environment

Myth #44 Birth order is a powerful predictor of a child's personality

The back cover of Kevin Leman's book, *The Birth Order Book* [1], states that "Birth order powerfully influences who you are." According to Leman, firstborn children are reliable, conscientious, and achievement-oriented. Middleborn children, on the other hand, are mediators and "can get away with occasional laziness and indifference" (p. 21). Finally, lastborn children are social, outgoing, and spontaneous. While you might be able to see the logical connection of these traits (e.g., the middle child needing to mediate between the oldest and the youngest), research shows either no relationship or only a mild relationship between birth order and personality [2, 3]. Lilienfeld et al. [4] characterize the research by saying that "birth order may be weakly related to a few personality traits, although it's a far cry from the powerful predictor that folk psychology would have us believe" (p. 157).

Myth #45 The most common reason for sibling fights is the rivalry for parental love

Sigmund Freud [5] argued that conflict between siblings was based largely on rivalry for parent attention. Nevertheless, when school-aged siblings were asked about the source of their conflicts, rivalry for parent attention was mentioned infrequently [6]. Some of the more commonly reported sources of conflict included sharing objects, privacy issues, and friendships.

Myth #46 Parent–child relationship disruptions can be repaired with holding therapy

During holding therapy, a parent forces the child to be held for at least an hour (though it can last several hours) so that the child has the feeling of giving up control, and "If the therapy is working, the child will resist in every way" [7] (p. 92). That is, children can become quite infuriated and aggressive while being forced to engage in a hug that lasts hours, leaving us to suggest that the primary difference between holding therapy and ultimate fighting is that the dominated person can tap out in ultimate fighting. Holding therapy is designed "to repair the postulated disruption that occurred in the formative years between the infant and primary caregiver" [8] (p. 304). In other words, holding therapists believe that negative parenting practices disrupt the attachment between the child and parent. Thus, holding therapy is designed to improve attachment by replacing negative parenting practices with positive practices such as hugging and eye contact. Often this approach is used as a treatment of attachment in children that are adopted. There's no controlled research to show that holding therapy is effective, and many children and parents have become injured during this approach [9, 10]. Jean Mercer (who has done excellent work clearing up child development misperceptions) writes more about holding therapy and attachment in her book *Understanding Attachment: Parenting, Child Care, and Emotional Development* [11].

Myth #47 Fathers use more corporal punishment than mothers

The word "spanking" often evokes the image of a father taking his son behind the toolshed, and this word also brings to mind the phrase, "Just wait until your father gets home." Nevertheless, mothers spank just as much as fathers (if not more). For example, in one study of American parents, 58% of fathers and 65% of mothers used some type of corporal punishment in the last year [12]. When considering older children (ages 9 to 12 years old), mothers' spanking rates decreased slightly to 57% while fathers' stayed the same at 58%.

Myth #48 Rewards usually decrease the desirable behavior they're intended to increase

Rewards are commonly used to increase a child's prosocial behavior. However, one popular concern about reward use is represented by this statement: "when reinforcement is withdrawn, people engage in the activity even less than they did before reinforcement was introduced" [13] (p. 10). This idea is further elaborated in the book *Punished by*

Rewards: The Trouble with Gold Stars, Incentive Plans, A's, Praise, and other Bribes [14], which asserts that rewards cause a decrease in "intrinsic motivation," resulting in a decrease in behavior when the reward is no longer present (see Reitman [15] for an excellent critique of Kohn's book). Although a reinforced behavior can decrease later for several reasons [16], this potential decrease is not enough reason to give up on rewards as part of an approach for increasing a child's behavior.

The value of rewards can be illustrated by an early case from the behavioral literature in which a preschool-aged child refused to wear his glasses [17]. The behavior analyst used tangible rewards (e.g., bites of fruit) as well as privilege rewards (e.g., taking strolls through the neighborhood) in order to gradually shape the child's behavior of simply carrying his glasses and eventually wearing his glasses. Once the child started wearing his glasses, these arbitrary rewards were faded out because a natural reinforcer (i.e., being able to see the world better) took over. That is, the rewards actually helped the child come in contact with what is intrinsically reinforcing about wearing glasses. Thus, while decreases in desirable behavior can occur following rewards, rewards quite often are followed by sustained increases in desirable behavior. This increase is quite frequently maintained once the reward is faded out.

Myth #49 Praise undermines children's ability to be successful

Peggy Drexler, a research psychologist and author, wrote an article entitled, "The Key to Raising Confident Kids? Stop Complimenting Them!" [18]. In the article she made statements such as, "praise might actually undermine success." She also stated that "research with children and families has indeed told us that praise has the opposite intended effect." Her answer: stop complimenting children. Alfie Kohn's book [14], described in the previous myth, makes similar points. Critics of praise often point to laboratory research showing that, after children experience a failure, they respond differently to different types of praise. For example, one study showed that when children are given praise about their intelligence (e.g., "you are smart") after experiencing failure, they commonly choose to then do easier problems after the praise rather than challenging themselves [19]. That is, only 34% of the children who experienced praise about their intelligence chose to do more challenging problems, which was lower than the child who received no praise (about 50%). If we stop here, you might assume that children shouldn't be praised. However, children who received praise about their effort (e.g., "you worked hard") were actually the most likely to choose to do challenging problems (92%). Thus, in this study *effort praise* was better than *no praise* and *intelligence praise*. Even the praise critics encourage the use of some praise; they just call it "encouragement" instead of "praise." For example, praise critics advise parents to use statements like, "You did a great job on your spelling quiz" [18], and, "That's a really nice story" [14] (p. 108), and we'd say those are actually just other examples of praise.

Myth #50 Parents were not permissive when I was a kid

Try to guess the decade of the following three quotes: (i) "today's parents do not provide proper leadership during years three to thirteen, when a child's need for leadership is paramount"; (ii) "Permissiveness has not just been a failure; it's been a disaster!"; and (iii) "Children brought up permissively were often allowed to do practically anything they wanted to." They may all sound like they could be recent quotes, and in fact the first quote was from Rosemond [20] in 2012 (p. 20). However, the other quotes are quite a bit older. The second quote was from Dobson [21] in 1970 (p. 14), and the third quote was from Ilg and Ames [22] in 1955 (p. 353). These quotes all illustrate that people like to complain about the new-fangled problem of permissive parenting. Nevertheless, there have always been parents with high degrees of permissiveness, and there probably always will be. Indeed, there will also always be someone there to complain about them.

References

[1] Leman, K. & Leman, K. (2009). *The Birth Order Book: Why You Are The Way You Are.* Grand Rapids, MI: Revell.

[2] Ernst, C. & Angst, J. (1983). *Birth Order: Its Influence on Personality.* Berlin & New York, NY: Springer-Verlag.

[3] Jefferson Jr, T., Herbst, J. H., & McCrae, R. R. (1998). Associations between birth order and personality traits: Evidence from self-reports and observer ratings. *Journal of Research in Personality,* 32, 498–509.

[4] Lilienfeld, S. O., Lynn, S. J., Ruscio, J., & Beyerstein, B. L. (2010). *50 Great Myths of Popular Psychology: Shattering Widespread Misconceptions about Human Behavior*. Malden, MA: Wiley-Blackwell.

[5] Freud, S., Strachey, J., & Gay, P. (1989). *Introductory Lectures on Psycho-Analysis*. New York: W. W. Norton.

[6] McGuire, S., Manke, B., Eftekhari, A., & Dunn, J. (2000). Children's perceptions of sibling conflict during middle childhood: Issues and sibling (dis)similarity. *Social Development*, 9, 173–190.

[7] Anderson, J. (1990) Holding therapy: A way of helping unattached children. In P. V. Grabe (Ed.), *Adoption Resources for Mental Health Professionals* (pp. 87–97). New Brunswick, NJ: Transaction Publishers.

[8] Myeroff, R., Mertlich, G., & Gross, J. (1999). Comparative effectiveness of holding therapy with aggressive children. *Child Psychiatry and Human Development*, 29, 303–313.

[9] Chaffin, M., Hanson, R., Saunders, B. E., et al. (2006). Report of the APSAC task force on attachment therapy, reactive attachment disorder, and attachment problems. *Child Maltreatment*, 11, 76–89.

[10] Pignotti, M. & Mercer, J. (2007). Holding therapy and dyadic developmental psychotherapy are not supported and acceptable social work interventions: A systematic research synthesis revisited. *Research on Social Work Practice*, 17, 513–519.

[11] Mercer, J. (2006). *Understanding Attachment: Parenting, Child Care, and Emotional Development*. Westport, CT: Praeger Publishers.

[12] Straus, M. A. & Stewart, J. H. (1999). Corporal punishment by American parents: National data on prevalence, chronicity, severity, and duration, in relation to child and family characteristics. *Clinical Child and Family Psychology Review*, 2, 55–70.

[13] Schwartz, B. (1990). The creation and destruction of value. *American Psychologist*, 45, 7–15.

[14] Kohn, A. (1993). *Punished by Rewards: The Trouble with Gold Stars, Incentive Plans, A's, Praise, and other Bribes*. Boston, MA: Houghton Mifflin Co.

[15] Reitman, D. (1998). Punished by misunderstanding: A critical evaluation of Kohn's punished by rewards and its implications for behavioral interventions with children. *The Behavior Analyst*, 21, 143–157.

[16] Eisenberger, R. & Cameron, J. (1996). Detrimental effects of reward: Reality or myth? *American Psychologist*, 51, 1153.

[17] Wolf, M., Risley, T., & Mees, H. (1963). Application of operant conditioning procedures to the behaviour problems of an autistic child. *Behaviour Research and Therapy*, 1, 305–312.

[18] Drexler, P. (2012). The key to raising confident kids? Stop complimenting them! Retrieved from http://www.psychologytoday.com/blog/our-gender-ourselves/201208/the-key-raising-confident-kids-stop-complimenting-them [accessed August 2014].

[19] Mueller, C. M. & Dweck, C. S. (1998). Praise for intelligence can undermine children's motivation and performance. *Journal of Personality and Social Psychology*, 75, 33.

[20] Rosemond, J. K. (2012). *Parent-Babble: How Parents can Recover from Fifty Years of Bad Expert Advice.* Kansas City, MO: Andrews McMeel Pub.

[21] Dobson, J. C. (1970). *Dare to Discipline.* Wheaton, IL: Tyndale House Publishers.

[22] Ilg, F. L. & Ames, L. B. (1955). *Child Behavior.* New York, NY: Harper.

POSTSCRIPT: CLOSING THOUGHTS

In his book, *The Demon-Haunted World: Science as a Candle in the Dark* [1], Carl Sagan argued that science can often be more fascinating than pseudoscience when he wrote that "there's so much in real science that's equally exciting, more mysterious, a greater intellectual challenge – as well as being a lot closer to the truth" (p. 4). This also holds true for the science of child development. Thus, we share here several interesting research-based findings of child development, many of which are only recent discoveries.

Truth is more surprising than fiction

1. A woman can get pregnant by two different men on the same day. That is, in some cases of fraternal twins, they actually have different fathers, and this is called *heteropaternal superfecundation*. In a study of fraternal twins whose parents were getting genetic testing due to paternity suits, heteropaternal superfecundation occurred 2.4% of the time [2].
2. Some twins can be *semi-identical*. Though very rare, it's possible for twins to be both identical and fraternal at the same time. That is, recently twins were discovered whose DNA from their mother was identical but whose DNA from their father was not identical [3]. Although the exact process of how this happens is debatable, one hypothesis suggests that somehow two sperm fertilize one egg, and then the fertilized egg splits into two zygotes [3].
3. It's possible for one fetus to grow completely inside of another fetus, and this is called *fetus in fetu*. This occurs when one embryo twin envelops the other embryo twin, and they both continue to

Great Myths of Child Development, First Edition. Stephen Hupp and Jeremy Jewell.
© 2015 John Wiley & Sons, Inc. Published 2015 by John Wiley & Sons, Inc.

grow [4]. The inner fetus doesn't have a brain, but much of the body tissue can survive by drawing from the blood supply of the host fetus. In one such case, a man carried his twin fetus until he was 36 years old (Man With Twin Living Inside Him – A Medical Mystery Classic [5]). The doctor, who thought he was going to be removing a tumor, was quite surprised with what he found instead … so was the patient!

4. Some of a fetus's cells travel to the mother's brain and stay there. It's been known for some time that cells from a fetus can stay in the mother's body, and this is called *fetomaternal microchimerism*. However, it's only recently been discovered that the cells from the fetus can travel to (and stay in) the mother's brain [6]. It's no wonder why mothers spend a lot of time with their children on their mind.

5. Advanced father's age at time of conception increases the risk of genetic mutations that may have a role in autism and other disorders. Advanced mother's age has long been associated with increased risk for genetic disorders, such as Down's Syndrome [7]. Advanced father's age is more recently being connected to disorders like autism, due to the increased risk of genetic mutations [8].

6. Fetuses can recognize their mother's voice. Using tape recordings of mothers and female strangers, fetuses respond differently to their mother's voice as compared with the stranger's voice [9]. Specifically, the heart rate of the fetus tends to increase for the mother's voice but tends to decrease for the stranger's voice.

7. Thumb-sucking begins in the womb. Fetuses have frequently been observed in the womb sucking their thumbs, and they commonly have a preferred thumb to suck [10]. Interestingly, the preferred thumb may be an early indicator of handedness. In one study, all 60 fetuses that sucked their right thumb ultimately became right-handed as children, and of the 15 fetuses that preferred their left thumb, 10 of them were left-handed as children [11].

8. Breast milk has different tastes depending on what the mother ate. Researchers have demonstrated that breast milk can vary in taste based on the food consumption of the mother [12].

9. It used to be common for boys to wear dresses and the color pink. The book, *Pink and Blue: Telling the Boys from the Girls in America* [13], describes how common it was for young boys to wear dresses about a century ago. Maglaty [14] includes a picture of President Franklin D. Roosevelt (America's longest serving president) wearing a cute dress and pretty shoes at age two-and-a-half years old. Also, pink didn't come to be considered a girl's color until around World War I [14]. Today a boy in a pink dress

would likely turn a few heads. Taken together, this all illustrates how society's representation of masculinity and femininity changes over time.

10. Five year-old children perform better than college students on some memory tests. In one study, 5-year-olds and college students were shown several pictures of animals [15]. Then, the participants in both groups were again shown several more pictures to see if they recognized the pictures (half of the new set of pictures were part of the original set of pictures). The college students did better than the children on this task until the experimenters added a twist. Experimenters then required the participants to compare each of the first set of pictures to one other picture (i.e., they had to see if each of the pictures matched a target picture in some way). With this new twist, recognition accuracy rates for the college students dropped significantly lower than the children's accuracy. This surprising finding has been replicated by another team of researchers [16]. Thus, there are some situations in which children can have a better memory than adults.

Does the field of child development consist of heroes and villains?

Mythbusting is a risky business, especially when it comes to myths about kids. Paul Offit sums it up best with the opening to his book, *Autism's False Prophets* [17]. In the first sentence of the prologue, he writes "I get a lot of hate mail" (p. xi). That is to say, some people think that Offit is considered such a villain that they're inspired to send him hate mail. On the other hand, we're hopeful that Offit also gets a lot of "like mail."

While we have disagreed with some of the statements made by famous professionals, we don't think of them as villains, and they aren't deserving of hate mail. Most professionals have their heart in the right place. In fact, a lot of these people have done quite a bit of good too. To illustrate our point, we'd like to point out some of the best things that have come from some of the folks discussed in this book.

Sigmund Freud. We admit that we've really beaten up on Freud in our book. Admittedly, he wrote a lot of things that either aren't supported by research or are otherwise untestable. But Freud also did a lot of good for the world. Although his specific methods are mostly discredited, he really popularized the idea that people could get better through therapy. For that, we'd like to say "thank you" to Freud.

Alfred Adler. We didn't agree with what Adler had to say about single-tons. Nevertheless, we do like a lot about Adler. He was the first major figure in Freud's circle to break away from Freud. Because of this, he was basically one of the first well-known skeptics in psychology. Additionally, Adler suggested that children benefit when parents are able to strike a balance in parenting. He argued parents should be tender without being overly indulgent [18]. Diana Baumrind [19] encouraged a similar style of parenting many years later. She called this style of parenting *authoritative*, and it continues to be encouraged today.

Benjamin Spock. In this book we've used a few quotes from Spock to show how he propagated some myths. In a sense it's really not that fair to Spock (or any of the previously-mentioned advice-givers, for that matter), because he didn't have access to all of the research that has been conducted since his time. Today we have evidence that some of his statements were inaccurate; however, much of what Spock had to say about caring for children's development was likely very helpful to parents.

William Sears. We've criticized Sears a few times for some of his statements related to attachment parenting. Like Spock, however, much of his advice about caring for an infant's physical health is helpful. Furthermore, as we mentioned in an earlier chapter, he's also done a lot of good in his general promotion of breastfeeding.

John B. Watson. In this book, we haven't yet criticized anything that Watson had to say. He's the founder of behaviorism, a theoretical approach that has shaped our understanding of human behavior. Watson also was a skeptic of Freud's philosophy and argued for the importance of the science of psychology. In fact, most of the evidence-based treatments described in this book have a strong behavioral influence. However, we include Watson here to make the point that everyone makes mistakes. Watson is known for giving parents the advice to rarely, if ever, hug or kiss their children [20]. Nevertheless, he would allow for one kiss on the forehead at bedtime and a handshake in the morning. Thus, even the notable Watson gave some bad advice.

We took the time to give some praise to the above influential figures to illustrate that the field of child development doesn't consist of some professionals who are villains and others that are heroes. Most of the advice-givers are well-intentioned, and have a lot of useful information to share. Unfortunately, everybody is fallible, and even the most conscientious professional will say the wrong thing from time to time. That being said, we've probably inadvertently made a misleading statement or two in our book. In the Introduction we asked you to look for our mistakes and to let us know when we made them. It's one thing to be skeptical about a claim, but it's another thing entirely to call it a myth. Skepticism involves doubt until evidence can be provided, but evidence is rarely absolute. New evidence is always on the horizon. We provided evidence for why we called several claims myths. At the same time, we are aware that it's possible that new information will come in that will force us to rethink something we've said. You should feel free to seek out current research and continue to look for future research that supports something that we called a myth. New technology (such as Google Scholar) has put academic research in the hands of the whole world like never before. We hope you'll agree that shattering myths of child development is an important job. If you walk away with one idea from this book, let it be this: you know more myths than you think you do, but you'll always have science to move you in the right direction.

Taking action: One Million Gently-Used Kid Books Project

Some of the myths in our book (e.g., numbers 16, 22) are related to the promotion of literacy in children. Working on *Great Myths of Child Development* has inspired us to take action, and we developed the One Million Gently-Used Kid Books Project. For this project, faculty, teachers, staff, students, and other members of our community have started donating gently-used books for infants, toddlers, and preschool-aged children. So far we have collected over 5000 books, and we have been giving them to youngsters in the East St. Louis Head Start program. Each book goes home with a note that says this:

Your child chose this gift from several options, and we hope you can enjoy it together!

Read every day with your child (starting from birth).
- this is the recommendation of the American Academy of Pediatrics

Read as part of the bedtime routine.
- this is a great way to help make sure that daily reading happens

Ask questions about letters and words while reading.
- this increases how quickly children learn to read

Examples: *"Can you show me where to start reading on this page?"*
"What do you think the animal is saying here?"
"What letter is this?"
"Can you find a really long word on this page?"

The examples on the note were taken directly from a research study showing that asking questions about letters and words while reading is an effective way to promote literacy development [21]. We hope that you can also use tips like this to help promote the reading skills of the children in your lives.

You may also consider donating books to local Head Start programs or other similar programs that serve kids in your area. In our experience, children love getting these books during center-wide giveaways and as rewards for accomplishments. You can learn more about what we are doing with this project by visiting www.stephenhupp.com.

Assignment: Investigate Child Development Questions for Yourself

We had a lot of fun doing the research for this book, and we didn't want to leave you out of the fun! Below, we have provided a short list of questions. Several of the questions could be answered "yes," several could be answered "no," and a few might be more complicated. We hope this could be fun research for any reader (but assigning one question per student can be great homework for a child development course).

Beginnings

Do identical twins run in families?
Can a fetus taste food that the mother ate from the amniotic fluid?
Is a "silent birth" better for the baby during delivery?
Does eating the placenta (i.e., placentophagy) help decrease post-partum depression?
Do newborns have tears?
Are there commercially available devices that can reliably test for alcohol in breast milk?
Can a man lactate?

Growth, Body, & Mind

Does neurofeedback help children with ADHD pay attention better in their classrooms?
Does sitting too close to the TV hurt a child's eyesight?
After eating, is it safest to wait 30 minutes before swimming?
Is childhood obesity influenced by genes?
Do colored overlays (i.e., the Irlen method) help children with reading disorders?

Is direct instruction an effective way to teach academic skills to children?

Can social narratives (i.e., Social Stories©) help children with autism learn new skills?

Emotions & Behavior

Is thumb-sucking an early sign of psychological problems?

Does pediatric bipolar disorder have different criteria than adult bipolar disorder?

Are humans the only beings that can recognize themselves in a mirror?

Do 1-year-olds use social referencing to influence how they feel?

Can 2-year-olds experience complex emotions (e.g., pride, embarrassment)?

Do kids have worse behavior these days than in previous generations?

Are token economies effective at decreasing behavior problems?

Social Environment

Does rebirthing therapy help improve attachment?

Can children who've been adopted develop a secure attachment with their new parents?

Do boys get spanked more than girls?

Are there currently school districts in which school personnel can spank children?

Are children with chronic illnesses more likely to be physically abused?

If a child is sexually abused, is that child very likely to grow up to abuse others?

Do teachers spend more time with girls than boys in their classroom?

A note to instructors

If you're teaching a child psychology course and would like to have students research the questions from "Assignment: Investigate Child Development Questions for Yourself," you could write about this assignment in your syllabus like this: "On the first day of class, everyone will randomly draw one question out of a hat. Students will then research the questions and try to determine if the answer is 'yes' or 'no.' Throughout the semester, students will provide presentations (about 5–7 minutes in length) on each topic. The structure of the presentation is up to the student, but most of the following components should usually be covered: (i) definitions and descriptions; (ii) experts promoting the idea; (iii) pop culture references; (iv) opinion polls; (v) research on the topic; and (vi) a clear statement about whether research shows the answer is 'yes' or a 'no' (if the research is mixed, you should still state which way you are leaning)." For larger classes, this can work as a group assignment as well.

References

[1] Sagan, C. (1996). *The Demon-Haunted World: Science as a Candle in the Dark*. New York, NY: Random House.

[2] Wenk, R. E., Houtz, T., Brooks, M., & Chiafari, F. A. (1992). How frequent is heteropaternal superfecundation? *Acta Geneticae Medicae et Gemellologiae*, 41, 43.

[3] Souter, V. L., Parisi, M. A., Nyholt, D. R., et al. (2007). A case of true hermaphroditism reveals an unusual mechanism of twinning. *Human Genetics*, 121(2), 179–185. doi:10.1007/s00439-006-0279-x.

[4] Ghazle, H. & Dolbow, K. (2009). Fetus in fetu. *Journal of Diagnostic Medical Sonography*, 25, 272–276. doi:10.1177/8756479309344099.

[5] Man With Twin Living Inside Him – A Medical Mystery Classic (2006, August 23). Retrieved from http://abcnews.go.com.

[6] Chan, W. F., Gurnot, C., Montine, T. J., et al. (2012). Male microchimerism in the human female brain. *PLoS One*, 7, e45592.

[7] Loane, M., Morris, J. K., Addor, M. C., et al. (2012). Twenty-year trends in the prevalence of Down syndrome and other trisomies in Europe: Impact of maternal age and prenatal screening. *European Journal of Human Genetics*, 21(1), 27–33.

[8] Kong, A., Frigge, M. L., Masson, G., et al. (2012). Rate of de novo mutations and the importance of father's age to disease risk. *Nature*, 488(7412), 471–475. doi:10.1038/nature11396.

[9] Kisilevsky, B. S., Hains, S. M., Lee, K., et al. (2003). Effects of experience on fetal voice recognition. *Psychological Science*, 14, 220–224.

[10] Hepper, P. G., Shahidullah, S., & White, R. (1991). Handedness in the human fetus. *Neuropsychologia*, 29, 1107–1111.

[11] Hepper, P. G., Wells, D. L., & Lynch, C. (2005). Prenatal thumb sucking is related to postnatal handedness. *Neuropsychologia*, 43, 313–315.

[12] Hausner, H., Bredie, W. L., Mølgaard, C., Petersen, M. A., & Møller, P. (2008). Differential transfer of dietary flavour compounds into human breast milk. *Physiology & Behavior*, 95(1), 118–124.

[13] Paoletti, J. B. (2012). *Pink and Blue: Telling the Boys from the Girls in America*. Bloomington, IN: Indiana University Press.

[14] Maglaty, J. (2011). When did girls start wearing pink? Retrieved from http://www.smithsonianmag.com/arts-culture/When-Did-Girls-Start-Wearing-Pink.html [accessed August 2014].

[15] Sloutsky, V. M. & Fisher, A. V. (2004). When development and learning decrease memory evidence against category-based induction in children. *Psychological Science*, 15, 553–558.

[16] Wilburn, C. & Feeney, A. (2008). Do development and learning really decrease memory? On similarity and category-based induction in adults and children. *Cognition*, 106, 1451–1464.

[17] Offit, P. A. (2008). *Autism's False Prophets: Bad Science, Risky Medicine, and the Search for a Cure*. New York, NY: Columbia University Press.

[18] Adler, A. (1927). *Understanding Human Nature*. Garden City, NY: Garden City Pub. Co.

[19] Baumrind, D. (1966). Effects of authoritative parental control on child behavior. *Child Development*, 37, 887–907.

[20] Watson, J. B. & Watson, R. A. R. (1928). *Psychological Care of Infant and Child*. New York, NY: W.W. Norton.

[21] Justice, L. M., Kaderavek, J. N., Fan, X., et al. (2009). Accelerating pre-schoolers' early literacy development through classroom-based teacher–child storybook reading and explicit print referencing. *Language, Speech, and Hearing Services in Schools*, 40(1), 67–85.

INDEX

Great Myths of Child Development, First Edition. Stephen Hupp and Jeremy Jewell.
© 2015 John Wiley & Sons, Inc. Published 2015 by John Wiley & Sons, Inc.